D1545919

Lucan and the Sublime

This is the first comprehensive study of the sublime in Lucan. Drawing upon renewed literary-critical interest in the tradition of philosophical aesthetics, Henry Day argues that the category of the sublime offers a means of moving beyond readings of Lucan's *Bellum civile* in terms of the poem's political commitment or, alternatively, nihilism. Demonstrating in dialogue with theorists from Burke and Kant to Freud, Lyotard and Ankersmit the continuing vitality of Longinus' foundational treatise *On the Sublime*, Day charts Lucan's complex and instructive exploration of the relationship between sublimity and ethical discourses of freedom and oppression. Through the *Bellum civile*'s cataclysmic vision of civil war and metapoetic accounts of its own genesis, through its heated linguistic texture and proclaimed effects upon future readers, and, most powerfully of all, through its representation of its twin protagonists Caesar and Pompey, Lucan's great epic emerges as a central text in the history of the sublime.

HENRY DAY has taught at the universities of Oxford and Cambridge and at Birkbeck, University of London, and has worked as a consultant on classical subjects for the *London Review of Books* and BBC television. He was called to the Bar of England and Wales in 2011 by Lincoln's Inn and is now pursuing a career as a barrister.

CAMBRIDGE CLASSICAL STUDIES

General editors
R. L. HUNTER, R. G. OSBORNE, M. MILLETT,
D. N. SEDLEY, G. C. HORROCKS, S. P. OAKLEY,
W. M. BEARD

LUCAN AND THE SUBLIME

Power, Representation and Aesthetic Experience

HENRY J. M. DAY

CAMBRIDGE
UNIVERSITY PRESS

CAMBRIDGE UNIVERSITY PRESS
Cambridge, New York, Melbourne, Madrid, Cape Town,
Singapore, São Paulo, Delhi, Mexico City

Cambridge University Press
The Edinburgh Building, Cambridge CB2 8RU, UK

Published in the United States of America by Cambridge University Press, New York

www.cambridge.org
Information on this title: www.cambridge.org/9781107020603

© Faculty of Classics, University of Cambridge 2013

This publication is in copyright. Subject to statutory exception
and to the provisions of relevant collective licensing agreements,
no reproduction of any part may take place without the written
permission of Cambridge University Press.

First published 2013

Printed and bound in the United Kingdom by the MPG Books Group

A catalogue record for this publication is available from the British Library

Library of Congress Cataloguing in Publication data
Day, Henry J. M., 1981–
Lucan and the sublime : power, representation and aesthetic experience / Henry J. M. Day.
p.   cm. – (Cambridge classical studies)
ISBN 978-1-107-02060-3 (hardback)
1. Lucan, 39–65 – Criticism and interpretation.   2. Sublime, The, in literature.   I. Title.
PA6480.D39   2012
873'.01 – dc23   2012015309

ISBN 978-1-107-02060-3 Hardback

Cambridge University Press has no responsibility for the persistence or
accuracy of URLs for external or third-party internet websites referred to
in this publication and does not guarantee that any content on such
websites is, or will remain, accurate or appropriate.

For Frederick – our new arrival – and for all my family

CONTENTS

ACKNOWLEDGEMENTS

This book is a revised version of my doctoral dissertation, undertaken at Trinity College, Cambridge, between 2005 and 2009. I would like to thank my supervisors, William Fitzgerald and Emily Gowers, for their encouragement and for ensuring, despite my best efforts, that the project stayed on track. To Emily I owe a special debt for putting me up (and up with me) as I approached my submission deadline. I am immensely grateful to my examiners, Philip Hardie and Charles Martindale, for the time they took to read the dissertation so painstakingly, for their instructive criticism and for their post-viva advice and guidance. As detailed in my footnotes, their work marks this book throughout. Stephen Oakley and Richard Hunter recommended the dissertation for publication in the Cambridge Classical Studies series and offered valuable suggestions for its improvement; my thanks to them both and to all the CCS editors. Thanks also to Michael Sharp, Jo Breeze, Josephine Lane and Liz Hanlon at Cambridge University Press for shepherding the manuscript through the publication process with such care and patience, to Iveta Adams, my eagle-eyed copyeditor, for saving me from numerous errors of fact and infelicities of style, and to Siobhan Chomse for compiling the indexes so diligently and swiftly. Needless to say, all faults that remain are my own.

Professor Hardie and Professor Hunter gave time and expertise to help me organise and secure funding for a conference on 'The Classical Sublime' at Cambridge in March 2008. I am indebted to them for ensuring the success of the event and to all who attended and contributed to discussion, especially to those who delivered papers: Patrick Cheney, Andrew Laird, Charles Martindale, James Porter, Alessandro Schiesaro, Philip Shaw and Michael Silk. Particular thanks are due to Professor Schiesaro for sending me a copy of his book *The Passions in Play* and to Professor Cheney and Professor Porter for kindly allowing me to read draft chapters of their respective studies of Marlowe and ancient aesthetics. The insights afforded by Professor Porter's groundbreaking work first suggested to me how to go about reading Lucan in terms of the sublime, while correspondence with Professor Cheney helped give shape to my ideas. Drafts of parts of Chapter 3 and Chapter 4 were presented at conferences in Princeton and Swansea; my thanks to the organisers and audiences of both for making me think harder.

I was sustained in my research by the resources and generosity of several institutions. The Arts and Humanities Research Council provided the financial support that made my project possible in the first place. Supplementary funding was gratefully received from the Cambridge Classics Faculty, Trinity College Cambridge and the Deutscher Akademischer Austausch Dienst. This assistance enabled me to spend time researching away from Cambridge and in so doing I accumulated further debts. In particular, I would like to acknowledge the help provided by the staff of the Institute of Classical Studies and the British Library in London; the Institut für Griechische und Lateinische Philologie at Ludwig-Maximilians-Universität in Munich; and the Philologische Bibliothek at the Freie Universität in Berlin.

I am fortunate to have benefited over the years from a number of stellar Classics teachers, first as a pupil at Downside School and then as an undergraduate and postgraduate student at Merton College, Oxford. I would like to thank especially Austin Bennett, Martin Fisher, Dom. David Foster, John Eidinow, Nicholas Richardson and Matthew Leigh. The learning, dedication and intellectual enthusiasm of each have been a continuing source of inspiration.

Thanks and much more go lastly to my wife Verena, to my parents Alice and Nigel and to my sister Eleanor, all of whom have in different ways lived with the writing of this book. Words fail. Without their unstinting love and support I would never have reached the finish line.

I have used Housman's edition of Lucan and have for the most part adopted the translations of S. H. Braund. Unless otherwise stated, quotations and translations of Lucretius and Longinus are taken from the respective Loeb editions of W. H. D. Rouse (revised by M. F. Smith) and W. H. Fyfe (revised by D. Russell). Translations of other texts are identified where appropriate in the footnotes and bibliography. Abbreviations of ancient authors and texts mostly follow the conventions of the *Oxford Latin Dictionary* for Latin authors and of Liddell and Scott's *Greek-English Lexicon* for Greek.

INTRODUCTION

The sublime is a nameless and mercurial event...Scholars have only begun to graze the surface of its history, which remains to be written and is truly inexhaustible.[1]

Published in 1674 as a preface to the poem's second edition, Andrew Marvell's 'On Mr. Milton's *Paradise Lost*' attempts to give voice to his experience of reading Milton's epic of the biblical Fall. Marvell expresses initial reservations, casting doubt in turn upon the integrity of Milton's motivation, his ability to achieve his artistic aim, and the effects of the epic on other writers. But these fears suddenly subside and Marvell begs pardon:

> That majesty which through thy work doth reign
> Draws the devout, deterring the profane.
> And things divine thou treatest of in such state
> As them preserves, and thee, inviolate.
> At once delight and horror on us seize,   35
> Thou singest with so much gravity and ease;
> And above human flight dost soar aloft
> With plume so strong, so equal, and so soft.
> The bird named from that Paradise you sing
> So never flags, but always keeps on wing.   40
>   'On Mr. Milton's *Paradise Lost*' 31–40

For Marvell, Milton's poem is a thing of amazement. Moreover, as David Sedley has shown, this amazement is intimately bound up with Marvell's earlier uncertainties.[2] It seems beyond belief that within his 'slender book' Milton could really accomplish his 'vast design' (2), encompassing 'Heaven, hell, earth, chaos, all' (5). The startling ambition of the project renders its success at best hypothetical ('if a work so infinite he spanned', 17),

---

[1] Porter (forthcoming).   [2] Sedley (2005) 125–33.

suspending the blind poet precariously over the void of failure. Yet, in a flash, Marvell's anxieties transmute into the realisation that Milton truly has scaled the poetic heights at which he aimed, indeed that, surmounting them, he 'soar[s] aloft'. 'Where couldst thou words of such a compass find? / Whence furnish such a vast expense of mind?' (41–2), Marvell asks, the rhetorical questions at once replaying the reservations of the poem's first thirty lines and redirecting them: he no longer doubts Milton's powers but instead confesses himself unable to comprehend their source. Previously fearful that with his epic Milton would 'ruin . . . The sacred truths' (7–8), 'The world o'erwhelming to revenge his sight' (10), Marvell now acknowledges that Milton has preserved 'inviolate' the 'things divine' (33–4), the prophetic power of his verse a God-given recompense for his loss of sight (43–4). Similarly, the movement of Marvell's poem suggests, where at first Marvell's doubts rendered him metaphorically blind, *Paradise Lost* has now so overwhelmed his vision that, paradoxically, he is able to recognise, if not to explain, its true 'majesty' (31). And this majesty, as Marvell declares in his final couplet, is the sublime. Flying beyond the known frontiers of artistic achievement, Milton's epic exceeds all bounds of thought and expectation, dispensing (unlike Marvell's own lines) even with the conventions of poetic form: 'Thy verse created like thy theme sublime, / In number, weight, and measure, needs not rhyme' (53–4). Thus Marvell identifies *Paradise Lost* with the aesthetic category for which the poem would within a hundred years have become a byword.[3]

This is a book about the Roman poet Lucan and about the workings of the sublime in his epic on the collapse of the Roman Republic, *Bellum civile*, written some sixteen hundred years before *Paradise Lost*. I begin, however, with Marvell's encomium as a uniquely powerful expression of the experience of the sublime, and as a model for the kind of response that poetry of the sublime can engender. In particular, 'On Mr. Milton's *Paradise Lost*' prompts several observations about sublimity – and about certain conceptual confusions or elisions to which the sublime often gives

[3] E.g. Burke (1990) 55, 57, 73–4, 159; see Moore (1990) and the bibliography in Sedley (2005) 171, n. 1.

rise – that should be kept firmly in mind during any discussion of the concept and that I want briefly to emphasise here at the outset.

First, Marvell's poem reminds us that, contrary perhaps to common popular usage, 'sublimity' means more than mere 'greatness' or 'excellence' and cannot simply be understood as a synonym for such terms. It is, rather, a distinct and peculiar form of ineffability, a greatness to be sure but one that, because beyond ordinary comprehension, is also paradoxically rooted in the intangible and shadowed by a sense of erasure. As 'On Mr. Milton's *Paradise Lost*' reveals, it is the connection between the majesty of Milton's poem, defying all understanding, and his initial misgivings about the epic's success that enables Marvell to realise its sublimity. It will be one of this book's tasks to tease out further this strange dynamic.

Marvell's poem also demonstrates that sublimity functions not only as an objective attribute of things but also as a particular kind of experience, inspired by an encounter between the sublime object and the perceiving subject. It is Milton's poem that Marvell labels sublime but the 'delight and horror' inspired by this sublimity are experienced by Marvell himself. In fact, the situation is more complicated than this, for alongside his readers, anticipating and reflecting their experience, Milton also experiences sublimity, 'soar[ing] aloft' 'above human flight' in his poetic response to 'things divine'. We are thus presented with a movement of transference as the sublimity of Milton's theme inspires him with sublimity, which is in turn expressed in his poem and then transports Marvell into the sublime. Accordingly, we need to exercise care when analysing the sublime to identify its precise location, while at the same time remaining alive to the difficulties of fixing sublimity within either subject or object.

Taken as an object of experience, Milton's poem is itself for Marvell something sublime. But *Paradise Lost* also represents subjective experiences of the sublime within its own narrative: in Book 1, for instance, we see Satan, 'thunderstruck and astonished',[4] cast out of heaven and rolling in the fiery chaos of hell, but then he rallies, rousing his fallen legions; in Book 6, Michael

---

[4] Milton (2007) 1.56.

and the angels, momentarily confounded by Satan's war engines, swiftly regain the initiative, endangering heaven itself as they hurl uprooted mountains at the suddenly terrified rebels. Such instances contribute to the perception of *Paradise Lost* as a sublime object, while also modelling both the sublimity that Marvell attributes to Milton's experience as a poet and the sublimity of Marvell's own readerly response. For analytical purposes, however, it helps to distinguish the sublimity of a work of art from that work's representations of sublimity. As we will see, the latter may be configured in ways that do not straightforwardly account for the sublimity of the work itself. (Indeed, although the *Bellum Civile* is not such a case, it is worth bearing in mind that sublime experience may plausibly be represented within a work of art without that work itself attaining, or even aspiring to, sublimity.)

Retrospective: modern experiences of the sublime

While in large part the history of the sublime indeed remains to be written, its development in the three hundred or so years since the appearance of *Paradise Lost* has been well charted[5] and, before we can turn our attention to Lucan, requires some introduction. Marvell experienced the sublime as a response to a work of verbal art but sublimity, we will see, has been felt to arise in relation to a wide range of objects and as a consequence of a variety of situations. A comprehensive account of these many instantiations is not feasible here. It is possible, however, and helpful, to highlight some examples.

Sublimity attained what is usually considered its greatest cultural prominence (in Western Europe, at least) in the long eighteenth century. During this period sublimity came to be understood in particular as a property and consequence of huge or powerful phenomena in the natural world: storms, earthquakes, volcanoes, great waterfalls, and especially mountains. The discovery of and attraction to the sublimity of the earth's splendours and terrors constitutes a substantial shift from earlier sensibilities – Marvell

---

[5] See, for example, the useful overviews provided by Kirwan (2005) and Shaw (2006).

regarded mountains, which with their 'hook-shoulder'd height /
The Earth deform and Heaven fright', as an 'excrescence ill
design'd'[6] – but was a development that proved long-lasting. In
his *Sacred Theory of the Earth*, written between 1680 and 1689,
Thomas Burnet gives an early example of the new vogue: observ-
ing that 'the greatest Objects of Nature are ... the most pleasing
to behold', he lists 'the Mountains of the Earth' as a source of
inspiration next only to 'the Great Concave of the Heavens, and
those boundless Regions where the Stars inhabit':

There is something august and stately in the Air of these things, that inspires
the Mind with great Thoughts and Passions; we do naturally, upon such Occasions, think of God and his Greatness: And whatsoever hath but the Shadow
and Appearance of the INFINITE, as all Things have that are too big for our
Comprehension, they fill and overbear the Mind with their Excess, and cast it
into a pleasing kind of Stupor and Admiration.[7]

Throughout the following hundred years, Burnet's raptures were
to be re-enacted repeatedly, with or without religious colouring, in
the writings of John Dennis, Joseph Addison, Shaftesbury, John
Baillie and the host of other eighteenth-century authors attracted
by the sublime.[8]

The idea that the natural world formed a fit, indeed primary,
trigger for experiences of sublimity reached an apogee in the poetry
of the Romantics; their rhapsodies' far-reaching influence ensures
that sublimity continues to strike us today as an entirely 'natural'
response to nature in its enormity. Wordsworth's account of his
crossing of the Alps in Book 6 of *The Prelude* (1805) is a *locus
classicus*.[9] Amid the peaks, the poet feels his 'Imagination' 'lifting
up itself' (525); it grows into a 'Power' that 'In all the might of
its endowments, came / Athwart me' (527–9) and he finds himself
'lost as in a cloud' (529), his physical and artistic progress 'halted'
(530). But, turning suddenly, he manages to contain this incipient
threat: 'And now recovering, to my Soul I say / 'I recognise thy

[6] 'Upon the Hill and Grove at Bill-borow' 11–13, cited by Shaw (2006) 29.
[7] Cited by Shaw (2006) 29. On the emerging sensibility behind Burnet's observations, see
further Nicolson (1959); Macfarlane (2004) 22–31, 72–7.
[8] For a selection of these writings, see Ashfield and de Bolla (1996).
[9] Cited by Shaw (2006) 101.

glory' (531–2). Instead of overwhelming the poet, the power of his imagination unites his consciousness with the infinite: 'in such visitings / Of awful promise, when the light of sense / Goes out in flashes that have shewn to us / The invisible world, doth Greatness make abode' (533–6).[10] Self-loss transmutes into the sublime.

We find the same dynamic expressed more simply in Wordsworth's 'Lines Composed a Few Miles above Tintern Abbey' (1798):

> And I have felt
> A presence that disturbs me with the joy
> Of elevated thoughts; a sense sublime   95
> Of something far more deeply interfused,
> Whose dwelling is the light of setting suns,
> And the round ocean, and the living air,
> And the blue sky, and in the mind of man:
> A motion and a spirit, that impels   100
> All thinking things, all objects of all thought,
> And rolls through all things.
> Wordsworth, 'Lines Composed a
> Few Miles above Tintern Abbey' 93–102[11]

As Marvell is struck by 'delight and horror' on reading *Paradise Lost*, so Wordsworth finds himself strangely 'disturb[ed]' with 'joy' at nature's magnificence, uplifted as he feels the 'motion' and 'spirit' through which his consciousness is joined with 'all things', his lines' repeated connectives offering a verbal representation of this unifying thread.[12]

For all its prominence, however, Wordsworth's 'egotistical sublime', as Keats called it, was not the only form of sublimity constructed by the Romantics, nor was nature's grandeur sublimity's only impetus during this period. The ruined monument, for instance, exerts a powerful attraction for Wordsworth's contemporaries; our reading of such sites in terms of the elegiac conjunction of loss and splendour, the latter paradoxically arising out of the former, owes much to works such as Shelley's 'Ozymandias' or

---

[10] See further Weiskel (1976) 204 on 'the positive and negative poles of the Romantic sublime'.
[11] Cited by Kirwan (2005) 125.
[12] So Shaw (2006) 9. See further Wlecke (1973/2010).

Keats' 'Ode on a Grecian Urn'. 'On seeing the Elgin Marbles' (1817) sees Keats discovering in the fragments of the classical past a mirror for his own reflections upon mortality:

> My spirit is too weak – mortality
> Weighs heavily on me like unwilling sleep,
> And each imagined pinnacle and steep
> Of godlike hardship tells me I must die
> Like a sick eagle looking at the sky.
> Yet 'tis a gentle luxury to weep
> That I have not the cloudy winds to keep
> Fresh for the opening of the morning's eye.
> Such dim-conceived glories of the brain
> Bring round the heart an undescribable feud;
> So do these wonders a most dizzy pain,
> That mingles Grecian grandeur with the rude
> Wasting of old time – with a billowy main –
> A sun – a shadow of a magnitude.[13]

Encountering an impasse evocative of that experienced by Wordsworth amid the Alps in *The Prelude* ('each imagined pinnacle and steep / Of godlike hardship tells me I must die', 3–4), the poet likens himself to 'a sick eagle looking at the sky' (5), the very antithesis of Marvell's image of Miltonic flight. Yet the ensuing thought that he has 'not the cloudy winds to keep / Fresh for the opening of the morning's eye' (7–8) becomes for the poet a source of 'dim-conceived' glory, alike to that 'most dizzy pain' induced by the Marbles, 'That mingles Grecian grandeur with the rude / Wasting of old time – with a billowy main – / A sun – a shadow of a magnitude'. The Marbles thus become for Keats a source of sublimity, their mingled majesty and decay inducing in him a strange sense of exaltation even as they reflect his life's transience.[14]

While the eighteenth and nineteenth centuries saw artistic engagements with the sublime at their most widespread (alongside the Romantic poets, we might think for instance in painting of Turner, John Martin and Caspar David Friedrich, in music of Wagner and Beethoven, in fiction of Horace Walpole and Anne Radcliffe)[15] the twentieth century witnessed a dramatic shift in

---

[13] Cited by Shaw (2006) 2–3.
[14] On Keats and the sublime, see further Ende (1976).   [15] See Kirwan (2005) 126–8.

the concept's status, as the two world wars, the Holocaust and the obliteration of Hiroshima by the first atomic bomb undermined faith in the redemptive potential of the divine, the natural world or one's own humanity and at the same time terrifyingly reinstantiated the sublime as a function of traumatic world historical events.[16] The destruction of the World Trade Center in New York at the beginning of the twenty-first century reminded us that man's capacity for spectacular violence persists, while technology's onward march and the increasingly connected and mediated character of life in the internet's global village, where the virtual and the real become indistinguishable and we never seem more than a mouse-click away from all the information, goods and inhabitants that the world contains, provide cues for further new manifestations of the sublime.[17]

Hollywood and the 'blockbuster' movie offer one location in which responses to this modern sublime may be found, wherein the threat of war, terrorism or environmental catastrophe is staged as escapist entertainment, enhanced by the visual thrills of CGI and 3D, and thereby contained. Rather differently, critics often point to the work of Daniel Libeskind, the architect who designed Berlin's Jewish Museum (opened in 2001) and who has also been involved in the plans for the reconstruction of the World Trade Center site in New York, for its focus upon the obstacles to representation posed by the events of recent history; in the case of the Jewish Museum, these obstacles – the permanent wounds caused by the Nazi genocide – appear literally as dead-end spaces and cut-up corridors.[18] The sublime here comes to signify not communion with the infinite but a sense of radical alienation, of a trauma so overwhelming that it defies comprehension.

One of the most searching explorations of the sublime and its relations to the history of the last few decades is to be found in Don DeLillo's magisterial novel *Underworld* (1997). Its epic plot winds back and forth through the second half of America's 20th century, a fragmented, apocalyptic katabasis that takes the reader from the

---

[16] See e.g. Ray (2005).   [17] See e.g. Nye (1994); Mosco (2004).
[18] Shaw (2006) 7. For a detailed discussion of the sublime dimensions of Libeskind's Jewish Museum, and comparison with Peter Eisenman's Holocaust Memorial, see Ball (2008) 73–86.

Cuban Missile Crisis and the Soviet Union's atomic weapons tests in Kazakhstan to the millennial world of cyberspace, in which human desire seems to demand 'a method of production that will custom-cater to cultural and personal needs, not to cold war ideologies of massive uniformity' yet in which, simultaneously,

the force of converging markets produces an instantaneous capital that shoots across horizons at the speed of light, making for a certain furtive sameness, a planing away of particulars that affects everything from architecture to leisure time to the way people eat and sleep and dream.[19]

With its sinuous, vaulting prose and global-historical concerns, the novel's own dominant affect might well be said to be that of the sublime, but sublimity's conditions of possibility, and the range of meanings that sublimity might bear, also emerge as one of DeLillo's recurrent concerns. The explosion of the Space Shuttle *Challenger* on 28 January 1986, for instance, prompts one character, a high-school science teacher, to speculate upon the disaster's unsettling melding of human tragedy and aesthetic grandeur:

Space burial. He thought of the contrails on that blue day out over the ocean . . . – how the boosters sailed apart and hung the terrible letter Y in the still air. The vapor stayed intact for some time, the astronauts fallen to sea but also still up there, graved in frozen smoke, and he lay awake in the night and saw that deep Atlantic sky and thought this death was soaring and clean, an exalted thing, a passing of the troubled body into vapor and flame, out above the world, monogrammed, the Y of dying young.

He wasn't sure people wanted to see this. Willing to see the systems failure and the human suffering. But the beauty, the high faith of space, how could such qualities be linked to death? Seven men and women. Their beauty and ours, revealed in a failed mission as we haven't seen it in a hundred triumphs. Apotheosis. Yes they were god-statured, transformed in those swanny streaks into the only sort of gods he cared to acknowledge, poetic and fleeting.[20]

There are reflections here of the Keatsian feeling for immortality amid material destruction. Beneath this impulse, however, lies an awareness of the difficulty of attuning oneself to such a mode of perception. Can such terrible events give rise to the sublime, we wonder, and, if so, how?

[19] DeLillo (1997) 785–6.   [20] DeLillo (1997) 227.

The question recurs at the very end of the novel. A young homeless girl is murdered in the Bronx and, in the nights following her death, her face is seen to appear on a billboard advertisement, a Turin Shroud for the consumer age, shining forth through the poster paper under the headlights of a passing train. Ecstatic crowds gather to witness this strange event, this miracle, growing bigger each night, seeking salvation, redemption, stirred by 'the hope that grows when things surpass their limits',[21] until one day the advertisement is taken down, replaced by a white sheet bearing a telephone number and the words 'Space Available', and the girl's face abruptly vanishes. But, as the public hysteria subsides, a thought continues to nag:

> ... what do you remember, finally, when everyone has gone home and the streets are empty of devotion and hope, swept by the river wind? Is the memory thin and bitter and does it shame you with its fundamental untruth – all nuance and wishful silhouette? Or does the power of transcendence linger, the sense of an event that violates natural forces, something holy that throbs on the hot horizon, the vision you crave because you need a sign to stand against your doubt?[22]

Can sublimity today still be sustained? Can it be understood as anything more than a cultural construct, 'a sign' to stand against our 'doubt'? Can it bear even this much weight, or must it stand simply as an index of moral or epistemological bankruptcy, a 'wishful silhouette'? We seem here to have moved a long way from sublimity as experienced by Burnet or Wordsworth. If previously the sublime operated for most as a fundamentally positive affect, working to affirm human selfhood in the light of the divine, to post-modern, disenchanted eyes it appears at best as a marker of the insecurity of our place in the world, as the mere trace of the implosion of humanity's claims to greatness.

Yet we should also remember that this sense of uncertainty, disruption and loss has always been present within the sublime. 'Doubt' is precisely the attitude upon which Marvell's realisation of the Miltonic sublime is built, while the impasse encountered by Wordsworth in the Alps provokes in the poet a dramatic crisis of identity. If in one sense contemporary articulations of the sublime such as DeLillo's or Libeskind's appear deconstructive, working

[21] DeLillo (1997) 818. [22] DeLillo (1997) 824.

to expose the sublime's inner inconsistencies and instabilities, in another they simply place renewed emphasis upon those more troubling aspects of the sublime that have always been integral to its operation but that we may previously have ignored. Sublimity forever hovers on the edge of an abyss: its very grandiosity threatens persistently to obliterate not only our sense of self but, still more radically, its own ability to cohere.

Aims and objectives

The Lucanian sublime

The few preceding examples can give only a cursory indication of humanity's encounters with and expressions of the sublime since the eighteenth century. This book aims to add another chapter to the story. Marvell's 'On Mr. Milton's *Paradise Lost*' was published in the same year as Nicolas Boileau-Despréaux's landmark translation into French of the *Peri hupsous*, the ancient Greek treatise on the sublime attributed to 'Longinus'.[23] Boileau's translation played a pivotal role in Longinus' popularisation during the eighteenth century but even before Boileau sublimity was in the air in Europe: following Francesco Robortello's *editio princeps* of Longinus in 1554, translations and commentaries had appeared in a variety of languages, including Latin and Italian.[24] Moving several centuries further back, I want to pick up the narrative in the first century AD with the *Bellum civile*, Lucan's epic account of the civil war of 49–45 BC between Julius Caesar and Pompey that brought the Roman Republic to an end and inaugurated the Caesars' dictatorial rule over the Roman Empire. Lucan's poem enables us to understand the sublime not merely as a preoccupation of eighteenth-century aesthetics or as a post-Romantic response to the technological forces looming over our existence today, but as a vital and complex means of engaging with questions of power and its representation whose roots go back to Graeco-Roman antiquity;

[23] In referring to specific sections of the treatise I use throughout the conventional Latin abbreviation *De sub*. On the uncertainties of the author's name and identity, see Russell (1964) xxii–xxx; Heath (1999).
[24] Russell (1964) xliii–xliv; Sedley (2005) 9–10.

as such, I argue, it is a poem that deserves to be accounted one of the major texts in the history of the concept.

My initial reasons for framing Lucan in terms of the sublime are intertextual, and relate both to the literary environment in which Lucan was writing and to his later reception. One tantalising consideration is the possible dating of the *Peri hupsous*. Lucan was forced by the emperor Nero to commit suicide in 65 AD at the age of 25 and so may be presumed to have been working on the *Bellum civile* in the early sixties AD. Although the date of Longinus' treatise remains uncertain, scholars now tend to place it in the late first century AD.[25] Their arguments focus on the lament for lost freedom at *De sub.* 44, echoed in different ways by Seneca the Elder, Petronius, Tacitus and Quintilian,[26] and interpreted as a reference to Rome's shift from Republic to Principate. The *Bellum civile* is similarly shot through with a bitter sense of nostalgia for the Republic. It is hence tempting to regard the two texts as approximately contemporaneous. While the impossibility of identifying a definitive date for the *Peri hupsous* prevents us from positing any line of direct influence, I hope to show that there is significant value in reading Longinus and Lucan in tandem. As Alessandro Schiesaro has observed with regard to Seneca's tragedy *Thyestes*, probably written around the mid-first century AD, 'there is little to be gained in exploiting *On the Sublime* as a "source" for Seneca's conception of tragedy, and not just because its elusive chronology would make such a strategy risky, at best. But it is surely fruitful to turn to this work in search of a contemporary analysis of the sublime.'[27]

The potential contemporaneity of Lucan and Longinus, however, is not the only reason to attempt a reading of the *Bellum*

---

[25] See Russell (1981a) 55, (1995) 146–7; Porter (2001) 274; Whitmarsh (2001) 57; Hunter (2009) 128. Crosset and Arieti (1975) actually propose a date during the age of Nero. While a few critics, depending on the identification of the author with the chief minister of the Palmyrene Queen Zenobia and Plotinus' pupil Cassius Longinus, date the treatise as late as the third century AD (e.g. Luck 1967; Williams 1978: 17–25; Heath 1999), it has also been argued that it should be dated much earlier, to the reign of Tiberius (Selb 1957; Schrijvers 2006: 97) or even that of Augustus (Goold 1961; cf. Conte 1996: 43 n. 8).

[26] Sen. *Con.* 1.praef.6–7, 3.praef.12–13; Petr. 1–4; Tac. *Dial.* 13.4; Quint. *Inst.* 5.12.23, 6.praef.3.

[27] Schiesaro (2003) 128.

civile in terms of the sublime. Critics such as David Norbrook and Patrick Cheney have demonstrated both the influence exerted by Lucan over English authors of the later sixteenth and seventeenth centuries and the various investments of these authors in the sublime: Marlowe, for instance, in his early translation of Lucan's first book and throughout his subsequent plays, exploits the *Bellum civile* in pursuit of a personal politics of the sublime,[28] while Lucan's poem constitutes a, if not the, major intertext for *Paradise Lost*.[29] The association drawn by these poets between Lucan and the sublime is instructive; their insights encourage further investigation. In what ways, precisely, does the *Bellum civile* engage with the sublime? How might we think of the *Bellum civile* as itself a work of sublimity?

This book aims to provide some answers to such questions. Attending carefully to the different sites within which the sublime may operate, and the different objects by which sublimity may be provoked, I attempt to offer what one might call an anatomy of the Lucanian sublime. In generic terms, the totalising, panoptic aspirations of epic exhibit affinities with the sublime's suprahuman impulses. More specifically, the epoch-defining civil war that is the *Bellum civile*'s theme constitutes for Lucan an event of such historical magnitude and devastating effect that it can only be approached in terms of the sublime. The visceral, heated language in which Lucan recounts this event relates closely to many of Longinus' ideas about linguistic sublimity and to more recent theorists' emphasis upon the presentation of the unpresentable. Lucan's narrator frames his imaginative experience of his theme in terms of the sublime, an experience that he tells future generations they too will share upon reading the poem. Most significantly of all, the *Bellum civile*'s two main protagonists, Caesar and Pompey, are each consistently presented both as experiencing subjects of sublimity and as objects that themselves inspire sublimity in others.

In the pages that follow I explore each of these several aspects of the Lucanian sublime and examine the ways in which they interact. The *Bellum civile* reveals itself as a work fascinated by and profoundly implicated in the operations of the sublime, exhibiting

[28] Cheney (2009) 6–21, 42–9.   [29] Norbrook (1999) 442–66.

a far-reaching engagement with the concept that repays detailed investigation.[30] Indeed, anticipating many of those manifestations of sublimity traced above, Lucan's poem emerges as a crucial link in a chain that binds the aesthetics of the 'classical' and the 'modern' in perhaps surprising ways.

Longinus and his successors

Following Boileau's translation of Longinus, and in tandem with the growing taste for the sublime and its artistic expression during the eighteenth century, theorisations of the concept's sources, mechanics and effects proliferated, culminating with the famous analyses of Edmund Burke and Immanuel Kant. Another critical high-water mark was reached in the latter half of the twentieth century, as Burke's and Kant's insights were read afresh and developed in striking, frequently provocative directions by post-modern theorists such as Jacques Derrida, Jean-François Lyotard and Slavoj Žižek. In the wake of these approaches, Longinus' treatise, with its overt focus on the effects of language, is often today dismissed as a narrow analysis of literary style, concerned merely with rhetorical tropes and devices, and with little contribution to make to an understanding of the concept's broader affective and philosophical dimensions.[31]

In an attempt to correct this tendency, and mirroring my attempt to locate Lucan alongside other works of the sublime, this book's second objective is to re-establish Longinus' position within the sublime's theoretical history. The *Peri hupsous* is the first text in the Western tradition to explore the sublime in detail and can be seen to foreshadow many of the conclusions of later theorists.

[30] To be sure, the sublime is not the *Bellum civile*'s only mode. Its black humour is also vital; see e.g. Johnson (1987) 19–33. Quint (1993) 140 sees the episodes of the Adriatic storm in Book 5 and the Libyan snakes in Book 9 as two of the *Bellum civile*'s 'sublime – and, to be truthful, often sublimely ridiculous – highlights'. The easy slide from the sublime to the ridiculous is noted by Longinus (*De sub.* 3.1) and by Burke (1990) 12, 59, 79. Exploration of this slippage is beyond the scope of the present study; for some general pointers, see e.g. Phillips (1990) xii, Žižek (2000) or the films of Werner Herzog (inter alia, *Aguirre, der Zorn Gottes* (1972) and *Fitzcarraldo* (1982)).
[31] Guerlac (1990) 1. See e.g. Kirwan (2005) vii: 'The Longinian sublime was largely a matter of the power of rhetoric, and those who dealt exclusively with this power in terms of art tended to end by identifying sublimity simply with excellence.'

Although not all of the sublime's more recent constructions are of concern to the present study, I aim to show how the most important can be connected more closely with the *Peri hupsous* than is commonly assumed to be the case. My means of doing so is twofold. I endeavour first (in Chapter 1) to highlight particular correspondences through direct comparison of the sublime's different historical formulations. This analysis is then developed through my subsequent reading of Lucan. The *Bellum civile* responds powerfully to Longinian modes of sublimity but also allows us to identify forms familiar from sublimity's other theorists. The recognition of these different modes alongside each other is illuminating and offers one way in which we can move towards an improved understanding of the place of the Longinian sublime within the overall history of the concept's theorisation.

Politics, ethics and the sublime

One common thread running through both theoretical and artistic explorations of the sublime concerns its ideological dimensions: sublimity, as experienced and as theorised, recurrently brushes up against discourses of both freedom and oppression. A further objective of this book is to examine afresh, through the insights afforded by the *Bellum civile*, these politico-ethical ramifications.

On the one hand, as has already been hinted at, sublimity has long been associated with ideas of liberty, of expanded capabilities, of personal and social enlargement. Longinus asserts that 'the true sublime naturally elevates us' (φύσει γάρ πως ὑπὸ τἀληθοῦς ὕψους ἐπαίρεταί τε ἡμῶν ἡ ψυχή, *De sub.* 7.2). Kant likewise observes that sublime objects 'elevate the strength of our soul above its usual level'.[32] Similarly, the experience of crossing the Alps prompts Wordsworth to exclaim in *The Prelude*: 'Our destiny, our nature, and our home, / Is with infinitude, and only there' (6.539–40). More recently, theorists such as Lyotard have claimed the sublime as a crucial site of social liberation, an aesthetic spur to a progressive politics: Lyotard sees the sublime as powerfully transformative, an affect that forces us to 'bear witness' to 'the

---

[32] Kant (2003) 144.

unpresentable', liberating us from the cultural 'slackening', the insidious reification of the status quo, that he argues the contemporary capitalist system promotes.[33] The sublime, on Lyotard's view, thus comes to acquire a place at the heart of post-modern culture: it is concerned, as Tsang Lap-Chuen puts it, with 'our creative tendency to go beyond ourselves, to go beyond tradition and convention, to radically redefine ourselves'.[34]

Yet, against this alignment with liberation and the free play of our mental faculties, the sublime has also been understood as a function of, and protreptic towards, tyranny, violent aggression and totalitarianism. Burke is especially drawn to this aspect of sublimity, emphasising that 'terror is in all cases whatsoever, either more openly or latently the ruling principle of the sublime'.[35] This sublime terror is for Burke invariably the consequence of a painful encounter with 'a power in some way superior' to us.[36] We are dealing here not with a liberating experience but on the contrary with one that demands submission. Nor is Burke the only theorist to mark this tendency. Its tremors are felt from the concept's very beginnings. Longinus explains how, for instance, visualisation (φαντασία) in oratory 'not only convinces the audience but positively masters [or enslaves] them' (οὐ πείθει τὸν ἀκροατὴν μόνον ἀλλὰ καὶ δουλοῦται, De sub. 15.9). By the same token, it is the overwhelming violence of Demosthenes' rhetoric that establishes him as one of Longinus' heroes (De sub. 12.4). Significantly, however, like Burke, Longinus does not point up this facet of sublimity in order to condemn it. It is simply accepted as part of the sublime's compulsive attraction.

By contrast, recent commentators have found this tyrannical, even sadistic, side to the sublime acutely troubling. Gene Ray, for example, framing the sublime in terms of our response to the explosion of the first atomic bomb, warns of how it can produce 'a kind of intoxication' resulting in 'moral blinding and paralysis'.[37] Dominick LaCapra gives a similar account of the sublime's

[33] Lyotard (1984) 82. [34] Tsang (1998) xv. [35] Burke (1990) 54.
[36] Burke (1990) 60. [37] Ray (2005) 97.

16

function within Nazism's genocidal fantasies.[38] Far from being an experience that enables self-betterment, sublimity here becomes synonymous with mass murder.

The sublime's ethical status, then, is deeply confusing, assimilable to positions at opposite ends of the moral spectrum. I want to ask, however, whether we need, or indeed are able, to identify the sublime completely with a single ethical perspective. This is, undoubtedly, the easier option, both intellectually and morally. Liberty *or* submission: the sublime, depending upon our ideological leanings, prompts one or the other. An alternative approach is simply to remove such considerations. James Kirwan, for instance, attacks Kant's co-opting of the sublime for ethical purposes (and indeed ethical approaches to aesthetics in general), maintaining that, prior to Kant, 'aesthetics... had yet to learn the benefits to self-esteem of confusing fleeting imaginative dispositions with that realm of praxis that does properly belong to ethics'.[39] As we have seen, however, an awareness of the ethical dimensions of the sublime is present as early as the *Peri hupsous* – for Longinus, the sublime is 'the echo of a noble mind' (ὕψος μεγαλοφροσύνης ἀπήχημα, *De sub.* 9.2) but is achieved through overwhelming violence – and it is to this Longinian insight, namely that diametrically opposite ethical strands are bound into the sublime, that I want to return, arguing for this very ambivalence as a defining feature of the concept. The two faces of sublimity cannot be separated; the one necessarily implies the other.

Lucan's *Bellum civile* offers an artistic exploration of this ambivalence, all the more valuable for its rarity. Not only does the poem claim sublimity as its primary aesthetic mode, it also foregrounds the sublime's ethical instabilities, configuring sublimity in terms of Caesarism, violence and political absolutism, as much as through its attitude towards Pompey and the Republican cause, its championing of lost liberty. The *Bellum civile*, in other words, stages a conflict that goes to the very heart of sublime experience.

---

[38] LaCapra (1994) 13–15, 62–3, 91–6, 105–9, 148–9.
[39] Kirwan (2005) 51. Kirwan asserts this view repeatedly: ibid. 26, 32, 39, 156, 165.

A turn towards the aesthetic

Recent decades have seen the development across the humanities of a strong current of scholarly interest in the concept of the sublime. In particular, the sublime has gained recognition as an aesthetic appropriate to 'that excess of signifiers and significa-tion . . . linked to problems in the interpretation and reception of texts'.[40] As Suzanne Guerlac observes, 'many of the issues with which the thinking of French deconstruction has been concerned – questions of representation, force, limitation and iteration, for example – are at stake independently in the intertextual field of the sublime'.[41] This interest has prompted both philosophical investi-gations of the sublime as a concept and analysis of its representa-tions across a broad range of modern artistic works and genres.[42]

Classicists have duly begun to follow suit. The operations of the sublime at points in the *Iliad*,[43] Pausanias,[44] Lucretius,[45] Catullus,[46] the *Aeneid*,[47] Horace,[48] Ovid's *Metamorphoses*,[49] Seneca's *Thyestes*,[50] Petronius,[51] Pliny,[52] Statius' *Thebaid*[53] and Silius Italicus' *Punica*[54] have all received analysis. However, these studies largely avoid theoretical discussion of the sublime or extended reference to the concept's complex history; what the sub-lime actually is and how it works – its sources, logic and effects – are questions rarely examined in detail (Porter's work is a notable exception). Moreover, there is currently no full-scale analysis of the *Bellum civile* as a text of the sublime, despite the complex

---

[40] Crowther (2004) i. Cf. Sedley (2005) 1–7.

[41] Guerlac (1990) 12. Cf. Shaw (2006) 11. See for example the essays in Silverman and Aylesworth (1990) and Librett (1993).

[42] To cite a handful of examples that have informed my thinking: Weiskel (1976), Ferguson (1992) and Brooks (1995) on the Romantics; Arensberg (1986) on twentieth-century American literature; Bernstein (1991) on the Victorian novel; Mishra (1994) on the Gothic novel; Norbrook (1999) on the poetry and prose of the English civil war; Ram (2003) on imperial Russian poetry; Sedley (2005) on Montaigne and Milton; Ray (2005) on post-WWII visual art; Gilby (2006) on Boileau, Corneille and Pascal; Cheney (2009) on Marlowe.

[43] Ford (1992) 72–9; Porter (2010) 476–9.   [44] Porter (2001).

[45] Conte (1994); Most (2003); Porter (2007).   [46] Miller (2004) 31–59.

[47] Conte (2007); Hardie (2009a) and (2009b).   [48] Hardie (2009c).

[49] Barchiesi (2009).   [50] Schiesaro (2003) 128–32; cf. Michel (1969).

[51] Conte (1996) viii, 7–9, 37–72 and *passim*; Hardie (2009c) 225–8.

[52] Armisen-Marchetti (1990); Hutchinson (2011).   [53] Leigh (2006).

[54] Schrijvers (2006).

ways in which it exploits this aesthetic.[55] This book is thus positioned alongside these studies but seeks also to widen the scope of their enquiries, bringing a clearer lens to bear on the nature of the sublime itself.

Against this background I would like to note Charles Martindale's recent plea in *Latin Poetry and the Judgement of Taste* (2005) for an 'aesthetic turn' in Classical studies and to explain briefly my enthusiasm for and reservations about his arguments. His position displays striking affinities with that of Frank Ankersmit, whose book *Sublime Historical Experience* (2005) provides a theoretical basis for much of my fourth chapter. Emerging from the thickets of post-modern textualism, both critics have come to view aesthetic approaches to their objects of study (respectively, classical Latin texts and historical events) as offering a more thoroughgoing anti-foundationalism than textualism itself allows. As a means of situating Martindale's work, and hence also my own approach, I here consider the two critics alongside each other.

First, two alternative stories regarding Derrida's famous dictum, 'There is no outside-the-text' ('il n'y a pas d'hors-texte'). As Duncan Kennedy has observed,

any reading, any act of interpretation of a text ... is analysable in terms of on the one hand a hermeneutics, which seeks out an originary meaning for a text, and on the other the appropriation of the text by, and its accommodation to, the matrix of practices and beliefs out of which the reading is produced ... But however much an approach succeeds in marginalising one term at the expense of the other, the other always remains operative within it, however occluded, and renders the reading available for recuperation for and in the very terms occluded.[56]

On this view, Derridean textuality is simply a given. It governs both 'hermeneutic' and 'appropriative' modes of criticism and, indeed, if pushed hard enough, collapses the differences between the two. More than this, textuality should be seen as an enabling force. It ensures that there is always more to say, that no single 'right'

---

[55] There are passing references to the sublimity of the *Bellum civile* in Johnson (1987) 12–13; Quint (1993) 140; Sklenár (2003) 152; Martindale (2005) 230–2; Porter (2007) 176 and (2010) 516. Leigh (1997) 11–14 and D'Alessandro Behr (2007) 1–2, 165 briefly cite the *Peri hupsous* for its interest in ἐνάργεια and emotional intensity. Alston and Spentzou (2011) 56–9 identify Caesar's sublimity but their understanding of its effects is faulty.

[56] Kennedy (1993) 10–11.

answer ever exists. Criticism, like its objects, can always be deconstructed.

But we could also frame this critical status quo more critically. Rather than emphasising how textuality mediates between 'hermeneutic' and 'appropriative' reading strategies, we might consider the ways in which textualism can itself be deconstructed. On the one hand, if all is text, if all is merely construction, from where can analysis of any text, of the business of construction, begin? The critic is hamstrung. Instead of enjoying the liberation promised by the ceaseless movement of the sign, he finds himself struggling within the coils of a never-ending relativism. Yet, at the same time, the Derridean paradigm unwittingly reinforces the universalist impulse it claims to have ousted in its triumph over objectivism. 'Text' becomes the new epistemological 'truth' to which all else can be reduced. 'Language', in Richard Rorty's phrase, 'goes all the way down'. Such is the paradox of all textualising methodologies: in their thoroughgoing anti-foundationalism, they manage both to disable their own means of analysis and to usher in a covert, back-door absolutism long thought vanquished.[57]

In highlighting rather than harmonising textualism's internal contradictions, this latter view might encourage us to look for possible alternative modes of criticism. In particular, I want to draw attention to the specific interpretive aims from which these contradictions arise. Whether we formulate our reading in terms of hermeneutics or appropriation, we fixate upon the question of what a text *means*: interpretive anxiety motivates those of us shoring up our absolutist sandcastles as well as those who have already surrendered to the cross-currents of the relativist tide. Is there a way out of this bind?

In *Redeeming the Text* (1993), Martindale emphasised, against the concept of a 'reified text-in-itself, its meaning placed beyond contingency',[58] the way in which *'meaning is always realised at the point of reception'*.[59] In dialogue with Hans-Georg Gadamer, Martindale sought to remind us that *'we read from within a tradition, or a discourse, or a set of reading practices, or we do not read at all'*.[60] *Latin Poetry and the Judgement of Taste* takes this

---

[57] Cf. Roth (1995) 4–8. [58] Martindale (1993) 4.
[59] Martindale (1993) 3. [60] Martindale (1993) 73.

reception-oriented reading practice a stage further, championing the aesthetic experience of the text over the now-dominant practice of cultural criticism and its associated rhetoric of truth:[61] where textualism points out that all statements are already interpretations, and that all interpretations are necessarily indeterminate, aesthetic criticism fully embraces indeterminacy, sidelining the objectives of interpretation altogether.[62] 'My own "aesthetic turn"', Martindale thus writes, 'might . . . be seen as a further move in my war against the determination of classicists to ground their discipline in "history" – I would like to see "history" giving place to "reception", and historical to aesthetic criticism.'[63] Experiential analysis, with its non-hermeneutic aims, emerges in Martindale's essay as textualism's ultimate radicalisation.

Ankersmit's thinking has developed along remarkably similar lines. His research in the 1980s and 1990s, exemplified by studies such as *The Reality Effect in the Writing of History* (1989) and *History and Tropology* (1994), was strongly influenced by post-modern linguistic theory. A disciple of Hayden White, Ankersmit was interested in the ways in which history is constituted as narrative, as story. Like Martindale, however, Ankersmit has recently moved beyond this textualist approach,[64] calling instead for 'a resuscitation of the notion of experience' in historical writing.[65] Gadamer is again, as for Martindale, Ankersmit's main 'discussion partner'. But Ankersmit stresses how Gadamerian hermeneutics, though edging towards an idea of experience divorced from questions of truth, remains at heart a system wedded to the transcendentalist concerns of epistemology, a system tied

[61] Martindale (2005) 2, 11–12 especially singles out the studies of Too (1998) and Habinek (1998). Cf. Laird (2006) 22–3: 'Notions of value, the aesthetic and the sublime . . . which were so important from the 17th century onwards, and which had some equivalents in ancient literary criticism, have all but vanished from contemporary literary theory – moreover, they have been discarded without ever having been decisively discredited.' See also Armstrong (2000) for a critique of the academic suspicion surrounding the category of the aesthetic.
[62] Martindale (2005) 5: 'such criticism is not primarily concerned with offering "new" readings'.
[63] Martindale (2005) 29.
[64] Ankersmit (2005) 7. For a related critique of White, see Roth (1995) 139–41.
[65] Ankersmit (2005) 241–62. See Jay (2005) 255–60 for a helpful overview of Ankersmit's approach to experience, historically contextualised in relation to Dewey's seminal study *Art as Experience* (1934/1989).

up, to adopt Nietzsche's phrase, within 'the prisonhouse of language'. 'For Gadamer,' writes Ankersmit, 'there is nothing outside interpretation-histories or outside the language of interpretation within which these histories are encapsulated... What is now left to us is only language, only the historian's language – this is the world within which we move and there is nothing outside it.'[66] Instead of opening up a space for the experience of the text, for the aesthetic, Gadamer's anti-foundationalist notion of *Wirkungsgeschichte*, 'effective history', thus points paradoxically towards 'the realisation of interpretative Truth'.[67] By contrast, Ankersmit exhorts us to abandon the transcendentalist apparatus of hermeneutics – Gadamerian, Derridean or otherwise: 'Let us... wave goodbye to hermeneutics, deconstructivism, semiotics, tropology, and so on and see, next, in what way the notion of experience can take their place.'[68] Yet Ankersmit is the first to admit that this position can only be reached by passing through the concept of textuality. It is a position attainable 'only in a thoroughly historicised world, only after the past itself and the historical subject have lost their contours and have been reduced to being mere moments in a Gadamerian effective history',[69] because only then do we become fully aware of the indeterminacy of both the subject (that is, ourselves) and the object of enquiry (that is, our texts) and of the relationship between the two.[70] Faced with these multiplying uncertainties, the notion of experience rises to the fore and, as it does so, those of truth and knowledge slip into the background.

We can think of this conceptual development, this circumscription of truth, literally – as a diagram showing truth enclosed by two circles. The first circle in Ankersmit's schema is associated with representation. As we have seen, textualism's infinite regress

[66] Ankersmit (2005) 79.   [67] Ankersmit (2005) 199.
[68] Ankersmit (2005) 107.   [69] Ankersmit (2005) 277.
[70] Cf. Martindale (1993) 31–2: 'The text can be read, in the author's "absence", "non-presence", because meaning is constituted, not within consciousness, but within textuality... Reading would then be, not simply a matter of "decoding" meanings, but rather *an encounter*. As with people, so with books, both the subjectivist and the objectivist reveal a desire to dominate, the one by imposing *his* (supposedly subjective) meaning, the other by imposing *the* ("true") meaning.' It is a short step from this deconstruction of subject and object to Martindale's subsequent championing of aesthetic, experiential criticism.

reminds us that the relationship between representation and that which is represented cannot ultimately be articulated in terms of 'truth'. The gap, as it were, between representation and represented can never be completely elided. 'Nevertheless,' Ankersmit emphasises, 'we can meaningfully ask for the adequacy of historical representations of the past – and the issue of the criteria for the adequacy of historical representation undoubtedly still has a strong reminiscence of what is at stake in the discussion of (historical) truth.' But things are different if we consider the second circle, circumscribing both truth and the concept of representation. This circle belongs to experience and here 'even the issue of adequacy will have lost its relevance. Adequacy still presupposes the distinction between world, past, and object on the one hand, and text, historical writing and representation on the other.'[71] But in a fully textualised world this distinction breaks down and, along with it, the concept of adequacy. Experience then supplants epistemology, aesthetics takes the place of hermeneutics.

It is important to emphasise, however, that even as this focus on experience takes us beyond the framework of hermeneutic theory, it is also *dependent* upon – a product of – this theory's insights. Aesthetics emerges not as a refusal but as an *extension* of textualism. And this has two important consequences. In the first place, it should be noted that aesthetic analysis does not invalidate the hermeneutic search for meaning and truth; it simply has different aims. 'What our analysis of Gadamer has made clear', reflects Ankersmit, ' . . . is an awareness of the limitations of the discourse of truth and that the movement toward experience . . . is a movement *away* from truth (although not *against* it).'[72] In turning to aesthetics, we are not denying the validity of hermeneutic enquiry but simply seeking a different, an alternative, means of engaging with our objects of study, our texts. *Pace* Martindale, it is not a case of instating aesthetic 'over' cultural criticism but of training attention on the experiential *as well as* the hermeneutic.

This observation points in turn towards the co-implication of these alternative categories: each can be analysed in the terms of the other. Accordingly, and this is the second consequence of

---

[71] Ankersmit (2005) 239.   [72] Ibid.

the intellectual trajectory I have been trying to plot, the experiential and the aesthetic should not be thought to operate in a realm outside the grasp of context and constructivism. On the contrary, experiences can be regarded as functions of our own and of our culture's cognitive frameworks, aesthetics can be analysed for their ideological content. Indeed, the identification and delineation of the aesthetic contours of any historical or, for that matter, contemporary text will require sensitivity to the different, contextually determined, ways in which these contours might manifest themselves.

Martindale's arguments only cursorily acknowledge this co-implication. His desire to get away from the concerns of history and politics directs him towards Kant's judgement of taste. Kant argues that a pure judgement of taste is 'disinterested' (*uninteressiert*), that it is wholly uninstrumental, unaffected by external criteria of purpose or value. 'It is', Martindale observes, 'partly because a pure judgement of taste is disinterested that its maker readily assumes its universality. If I have removed the effects of needs and wants that are purely personal to myself, there seems no reason why someone else should disagree with me.'[73] In response to Pierre Bourdieu's criticism that this Kantian judgement is merely 'the universalisation of the dispositions associated with a particular social and economic condition',[74] Martindale concedes the pure judgement's rarity but denies that this renders the aesthetic invalid as a category. Difficulty does not equate with impossibility:

The fact (if fact it is) that some, even the great majority, of supposedly aesthetic judgements are occluded judgements of other kinds leaves the theory unaffected; Kant's point that there is a kind of knowledge which is neither rational nor empirical remains unrefuted. In effect Bourdieu wholly elides interest and judgement, so that nothing is left after the interest has been subtracted.[75]

Bourdieu's assertion of ideology's total primacy is extreme but, as Martindale himself admits, it is *in practice* just as difficult to claim total autonomy for the aesthetic. He goes on to argue that, contrary to its critics, the aesthetic can be claimed by radicals as well as conservatives but this observation in itself implies that the

---

[73] Martindale (2005) 22.
[74] Bourdieu (1984) 493, cited by Martindale (2005) 23.   [75] Martindale (2005) 23.

aesthetic is, in practice, rarely without an ideological dimension.[76] The argument that the aesthetic should not be subsumed beneath a 'means-end' rationality is important and timely; there is no reason the political should always be the privileged, dominating factor, the aesthetic its 'demonised Other'.[77] This does not mean, however, that the political can be done away with entirely. I would like to add more weight to Martindale's concession that 'we get different readings, clearly, depending on whether we foreground the political or the aesthetic'.[78] As Barthes observes:

There are those who want a text (an art, a painting) without a shadow, without the 'dominant ideology'; but this is to want a text without fecundity, without productivity, a sterile text ... The text needs its shadow: this shadow is *a bit* of ideology, *a bit* of representation, *a bit* of subject: ghosts, pockets, traces, necessary clouds: subversion must produce its own chiaroscuro.[79]

Martindale cites Barthes' words in a footnote; they require greater prominence.

As Ankersmit sees himself offering a new 'research programme',[80] so Martindale presents his work as 'a protreptic towards a new aesthetic criticism':[81] 'My aim [is] to encourage my fellow Latinists and others in the humanities to take an interest in the modern tradition of Western aesthetics as it applies to literature.'[82] Where Martindale, however, explicitly refrains

[76] Martindale (2005) 25: 'it is not true that the aesthetic is *inherently* a conservative discourse ... Pure beauty is not instrumentalist, but it might be transformative, and is thus at least compatible with "progressive" politics. There is a sense in which a utopia is created whenever a judgement of taste is made.' Cf. Armstrong (2000) 2 on the 'democratic and radical potential' of the aesthetic. See further Eagleton (1990) 2–9, who emphasises the aesthetic's historical role 'at the heart of the middle class's struggle for political hegemony' (p. 3). On claims for the 'counterhegemonic' capacities of the category of experience, see Ireland (2004) xiv.
[77] Martindale (2005) 24.
[78] Martindale (2005) 136. Cf. ibid. 26: '[Today's] politicising critics try, in Manichean vein, to force us to make a choice between politics and aesthetics ... [but] critics and theorists down the centuries have supposed that "art" could be appreciated according to both categories.'
[79] Barthes (1990) 32, cited by Martindale (2005) 122 n. 49.
[80] Ankersmit (2005) 13.   [81] Martindale (2005) 5.
[82] Martindale (2005) 2; cf. Scarry (1999) 30, 48, cited by Martindale (2005) 30: 'What is beautiful prompts the mind to move chronologically back in the search for precedents and parallels, to move forward into new acts of creation, to move conceptually over, to bring things into relation ... The material world constrains us, often with great beneficence, to see each person and thing in its time and place, its historical context. But mental life

from stipulating how one might go about 'doing' experiential criticism,[83] Ankersmit sets his sights on mapping a particular kind of experience – that of the sublime, specifically as it relates to our experience of the past. It is this latter model of experiential, aesthetic criticism that the present study adopts:[84] rather than attempting the disinterested Kantian judgement, I aim to explore the particular aesthetic concept of the sublime. The task will be to examine the ways in which the sublime is manifested in Lucan's *Bellum civile* and, moreover, to investigate this sublimity's different shades of 'interest', its appropriation by and for different kinds of 'truth'. This project will refrain from the aims of hermeneutics – I am not attempting to reinterpret what the *Bellum civile* 'means' – but will, nonetheless, remain responsive to the claims of ideology, the different ways in which the text's 'meanings' might emerge from its aesthetics.

It is in fact the 'interestedness' of the sublime that leads Martindale largely to exclude the category from his essay:

In the period after the Second World War, and later among postmodernists, there was a definite preference for [Kant's] 'Analytic of the Sublime', largely because of the way that the sublime exceeds the human capacity to encompass it. However, the Kantian sublime is in a sense a sub-category of the beautiful... Moreover in his account of the sublime Kant draws back, at least to a degree, from the more radical implications of his account of beauty, by associating the sublime more closely with morality... Many self-styled 'progressives' today continue to prefer the category of the sublime, which is more easily recuperable for existing discourses. This book by contrast deliberately stresses the beautiful, partly on the basis that it has the potential to be the more 'radical' category.[85]

The oppositions that Martindale constructs are not as clear-cut as he suggests. Kant is more overtly interested in the ethical dimensions of the sublime than the beautiful, but this does not mean

---

doesn't so constrain us. It is porous, open to the air and light, swings forward while swaying back, scatters its stripes in all directions, and delights to find itself beached beside something invented only that morning or instead standing beside an altar from three millennia ago.'

[83] Martindale (2005) 181: 'it is not possible to say in advance what form [aesthetic] criticism might take'.

[84] I also align my methodology with the experiential approach to ancient aesthetics proposed by Porter (2010): see esp. pp. 4–7, 36–7, 49, 174–5. Like Ankersmit, Porter draws inspiration from Dewey's notion of aesthetic experience.

[85] Martindale (2005) 12–13 n. 14.

that the beautiful as it is commonly identified (rather than in its ideal manifestations) is free from considerations of ideology. Conversely, not all theorists of the sublime have argued for its moral implications; its eighteenth-century proponents kept the two firmly separate, and Kirwan takes Kant to task precisely for appropriating the sublime in the name of ethics. I am not sympathetic to Kirwan's view, but my point here is simply a theoretical one, that both the sublime and the beautiful can be, and have been, variously associated with and distinguished from the ethical; contrary to Martindale's suggestion, there is no inherent difference between the two categories on this score.

If, however, as I am arguing, both the sublime and the beautiful, indeed any aesthetic category, always displays an ideological dimension, the nature of this dimension requires examination. Martindale assumes 'progressive' potential on the part of the sublime, while claiming that the disinterestedness of the beautiful is in fact more radical. Ankersmit, on the other hand, proposes a model of sublimity strongly conservative in its historical impulses: the 'experience of the past' that he describes is marked by the desire to return to the way things were. By contrast, I want to emphasise that the sublime cannot be located exclusively at either end of the ideological spectrum. Its persistent overstepping of such bounds is one of its defining characteristics.

The structure of the book

My analysis develops as follows. Chapter I sets out what may be termed the sublime's 'sources' (what gives rise to the experience of the sublime?), 'logic' (how does the sublime work?) and 'effects' (for present purposes, what are the ethico-political ramifications of the sublime?). I consider first the different models of the sublime that have been formulated by the concept's major theorists – Longinus, Burke and Kant – as well as the under-appreciated contribution of Lucretius, one of Lucan's sublime forebears. I do not endeavour to construct a conventional history or genealogy (Boileau and Žižek, for instance, I mention only briefly); the turns and doublings of sublimity's evolution would render such an

27

exercise precarious at best. Rather, positioning these different writers synchronically as well as diachronically, I attempt to discern what common ground exists between them. Reading Longinus through his fellow sublimicists, and vice versa, I argue in particular for the idea that sublime experience, however formulated, hinges upon a transference of power from object to subject. This view of the sublime as a concept fundamentally implicated in questions of power also brings to the fore the issues of freedom and its curtailment upon which subsequent chapters focus.

Working with this model, Chapter 2 considers how the *Bellum civile* responds linguistically to the challenge of the sublime, represents the claims to sublime experience made by the Lucanian narrator and projects these same claims onto its readers. In particular, I suggest, Longinus' conception of sublime utterance offers an aesthetic commensurate with the spectacular and unspeakable nature of the violence that characterises Lucan's poem. This violence informs both Lucan's 'positive' Pompeian and 'negative' Caesarian sublimes, and underpins my argument for the sublime's politico-ethical duality. Chapter 3 centres on the version of sublimity offered by Lucan's Caesar as he sweeps all obstacles before him on his march to power; Chapter 4, pegged to the figures of Pompey and the narrator, aims to show how Lucan also exploits the sublime as a means of negotiating a relationship with Rome's traumatic past – of recuperating an idealised Republic even after, indeed because of, the actual Republic's destruction.

Through consideration of these competing sublimes I suggest that sublimity provides Lucan with a means for thinking both Empire and Republic and that careful examination of this aesthetic offers insights into the epic that go beyond the standard engagement/nihilism dichotomy around which Lucanian criticism tends to polarise.[86] The book thus aims to construct a cumulative response to its several overarching objectives, arguing both for the importance of Longinus' place within the history of the sublime and for sublimity – Longinian, Kantian or otherwise – as

---

[86] The divergent strands of Lucanian criticism are well sketched by Bartsch (1997) 5–7. As Braund (2010) demonstrates, the decade that has elapsed since the publication of Bartsch's book has seen Lucanian studies proceed apace but without any real shift in scholars' basic lines of enquiry.

a concept that does not simply engender or arise from states of freedom or subjection but that persistently confounds any straightforward opposition between the two. It is in enabling these insights that Lucan's particular contribution to this concept's history lies.

CHAPTER I

THE EXPERIENCE OF THE SUBLIME

Sources and theories

What is the sublime? I briefly canvassed some possible answers in the Introduction. It is now time to give this perplexing question our full attention. Definitions have proved notoriously elusive but we may make a start by reminding ourselves that the sublime has regularly been regarded as a particular kind of subjective *experience*.[1] More specifically, the sublime may be said to name any experience in which we encounter an object that exceeds our everyday categories of comprehension. In the words of Philip Shaw, in his recent survey of the concept, 'whenever experience slips out of conventional understanding, whenever the power of an object or event is such that words fail and points of comparison disappear, *then* we resort to the feeling of the sublime. As such, the sublime marks the limits of reason and expression together with a sense of what might lie beyond these limits.'[2] Or as James Porter puts it, echoing Žižek's analysis but with reference to Longinus, the sublime is any confrontation with 'a positive, material object elevated to the status of [an] impossible Thing',[3] an object that, 'simultaneously fascinating and fearful, both invites and resists integration into symbolic frameworks of understanding'.[4]

Longinus

What sorts of object have been thought to occupy the place of this 'impossible Thing'? The *Peri hupsous*, a work of literary criticism and our first extant discussion of the concept, focuses upon the

---

[1] Ankersmit (2005) 317–68 and *passim*; Kirwan (2005) 160–5; Gilby (2006) 1; Shaw (2006) 2; Cheney (2009) 12, 224 n. 40.

[2] Shaw (2006) 2.   [3] See Žižek (1989) 71.

[4] Porter (2001) 65. Cf. Porter (2007) 254.

power of language to provoke sublime experience. For Longinus, the sublime constitutes 'a consummate excellence and distinction in language' (ἀκρότης καὶ ἐξοχή τις λόγων ἐστὶ τὰ ὕψη) by which the greatest poets and prose writers have won immortal fame (1.3). There is, as he asserts at the very beginning of the treatise, an 'art' to such sublimity, and this art can be taught; it is, we are told, of particular value to 'public speakers' (ἀνδράσι, πολιτικοῖς 1.2.) Accordingly, Longinus sets out what he considers the 'five most productive sources of the sublime' (πέντε... πηγαί... αἱ τῆς ὑψηγορίας γονιμώταται), namely, 'the power of grand conceptions' (τὸ περὶ τὰς νοήσεις ἀδρεπήβολον), 'the inspiration of vehement emotion' (τὸ σφοδρὸν καὶ ἐνθουσιαστικὸν πάθος), 'the proper construction of figures' (ἥ τε ποιὰ τῶν σχημάτων πλάσις), 'nobility of language' (ἡ γενναία φράσις) and, finally, 'dignified and elevated word-arrangement' (ἡ ἐν ἀξιώματι καὶ διάρσει σύνθεσις) (8.1). While the discussion of emotion is missing from our text, probably as a consequence of lacunae following 9.4 and 44.12, Longinus goes on to treat each of the other sources, exemplifying his claims with frequent quotations from Homer, Plato and Demosthenes, his favourite authors, as well as (among many others) Aeschylus, Sophocles, Euripides, Herodotus and Xenophon; striking examples are also adduced from Sappho and Genesis. Throughout, Longinus seeks to tie his definition of sublimity to qualities of moral grandeur and nobility: the achievement of sublimity requires true greatness of soul, he maintains, and will inspire such greatness in turn.

The *Peri hupsous* thus emerges as a 'how to' rhetorical manual; constructed around examples from the literary greats, it aims to identify and teach the particular devices and techniques necessary for linguistic excellence, while also fostering the student's personal integrity and moral development. In this, the treatise appears in keeping with much ancient literary criticism, tending as the genre did to focus upon the concerns of 'the scholar, the moralist and the teacher of rhetoric'.[5] Chief among the educational

---

[5] Russell (1981a) 1; see further ibid. 2–17 and *passim*. Cf. Hunter (2009) 1–6; Ford (2002) likewise begins from the premise that the ancients' view of poetry was 'essentially rhetorical' (p. 2). Porter (2010) offers a valuable alternative to such approaches. On the

objectives of the latter was the stylistic differentiation of texts according to various defined rhetorical 'characters' (χαρακτῆρες) or *genera dicendi*; such analysis served as a basis of instruction for aspiring authors and orators.[6] The treatise's declared intent aside, however, it is worth stopping to ask whether ὕψος, as expounded in the *Peri hupsous*, can in fact be numbered among these 'characters'. Adopting an overtly rhetoricising reading, many of the *Peri hupsous*' modern interpreters have, either explicitly or implicitly, sought to answer this question in the affirmative.[7] Is this an adequate response?

Longinus was by no means the first to apply the term ὕψος, literally 'height' or, by extension, 'the top', to speech or written words. The first known usage in ancient literature occurs in the *Odyssey*, where on four occasions Penelope's suitor Antinous describes Odysseus' son Telemachus as ὑψαγόρης.[8] As Donald Russell points out, the term denotes not so much Telemachus' style of speech as his noble character, a moral association that persists in Longinus and indeed throughout sublimity's history. As terms of literary criticism, ὕψος and its cognates in fact remain uncommon until the later first century BC. Related literary-critical

connections and discrepancies between ancient and modern literary criticism, see further
Laird (2006) 1–9; Feeney (1995/2006).
6 Demetrius (*On Style*, 36–7) names four normative χαρακτῆρες: the 'grand' (μεγαλοπρεπής), 'forceful' (δεινός), 'elegant' (γλαφυρός) and 'plain' (ἰσχνός). Quintilian identifies three *genera dicendi*: the 'grand' (*grande*), the 'simple' (*subtile*) and the 'elegant'
(*medium, floridum*) (*Inst.* 12.10.58); cf. *Ad Herennium* 4.8.11; Cic. *Brutus* 40, *De oratore*
3.177, 199, 210–12, *Orator* 20, 100; see also Horace's satirical treatment at *Ep.* 2.1.55–
9. The division between styles can be traced back as far as the ἀγών in Aristophanes'
Frogs between Aeschylus and Euripides, perhaps even to the Homeric contrast between
Menelaus' clear, swift words and the tempestuous speech of Odysseus (*Il.* 3.214): see
Russell (1995) 153, Hunter (2009) 128–34. In addition to the doctrine of styles there
existed a doctrine of virtues (ἀρεταί), developed from Aristotle's theory of diction and
divided by Theophrastus in his lost work *On Style* into four types: correctness, lucidity,
propriety and ornamentation (of which last grandeur formed a sub-category); see e.g.
Cic. *Orator* 79. The relation between the two doctrines is intricate: see further Goold
(1961); Russell (1981a) 129–47; Innes (1985) 647 and (1995b) 324–32.
7 See e.g. Wehrli (1946); Michel (1976); Conte (1996) 43–44; Walker (2000) 118–19;
Hunter (2009) 128–41, 149–60.
8 Russell (1964) xxx: *Od.* 1.385, 2.85, 2.303, 17.406. My remarks here are indebted to
Russell (1964) and (1965), which, despite reluctance to admit any relationship between
Longinus and later theorists of the sublime, remain the best all-round introductions to
the *Peri hupsous*.

32

terms, however, did exist, most notably μέγας ('great') and associated words; although a relative latecomer to the ancient critical scene, ὕψος may thus be regarded as giving 'a fresh nuance to existing theories', not as constituting an entirely new concept.[9] In particular, of the several established 'characters' of writing and speaking, Longinian ὕψος displays certain resemblances to that variously known as the 'high' or 'grand' manner (μεγαλοπρεπής, *grande*).

One of the most detailed extant discussions of the grand style is contained in the treatise *On Style*, attributed to 'Demetrius' and variously thought to have been written sometime between the second century BC and the first century AD.[10] Focusing on the style's constitutive elements of 'thought, diction and composition' (διανοίᾳ, λέξει, τῷ συγκεῖσθαι προσφόρως, *On Style* 38), Demetrius echoes Longinus both in his choice of examples, typically drawn from descriptions of the earth and heavens, mighty natural phenomena and great battles (75–76), with particular emphasis on the Homeric epics, and occasionally in his linguistic prescriptions, most notably in his recommendation of the expressive powers of metaphor (78–90, cf. *De sub.* 31–2) and of figures such as anaphora and asyndeton (59–62, cf. *De sub.* 19–21). Demetrius' discussion (*On Style* 99–102) of the impressive, even terrifying, impact of allegory's potential for semantic obscurity (πᾶν γὰρ τὸ ὑπονοούμενον φοβερώτερον, καὶ ἄλλος εἰκάζει ἄλλο τι, 100) also bears some relation to Longinus' enthusiasm for the 'terrible', τὸ φοβερόν (*De sub.* 9.7, 10.6, 22.4, 34.4), while both writers are united in their criticism of 'frigidity' (τὸ ψυχρὸν), defined by Demetrius (quoting Theophrastus) as 'that which exceeds its appropriate form of expression' (τὸ ὑπερβάλλον τὴν οἰκείαν ἀπαγγελίαν, 114), as being the very opposite of great writing (114–27, cf. *De sub.* 4).

Yet there are also crucial differences between Longinian ὕψος and Demetrius' account of the grand style. Where Demetrius, for instance, considers hyperbole as without exception 'the most frigid of all devices' (μάλιστα δὲ ἡ ὑπερβολὴ ψυχρότατον πάντων, 124), Longinus, although conceding that the trope can easily be overdone, extols the power of the hyperbole that, uttered in

---

[9] Russell (1964) xxxii.   [10] See Innes (1995b) 312–21.

circumstances of heightened emotion, is able to conceal the fact of its own existence (*De sub.* 38). Where Demetrius criticises the Homeric phrase, 'all around the mighty heaven trumpeted' (ἀμφὶ δ'ἐσάλπιγξεν μέγας οὐρανός, *Il.* 21.388; *On Style* 83), Longinus deems these same words 'marvellous' (ὑπερφυᾶ, *De sub.* 9.6).

And there are more general considerations too that prevent any straightforward mapping of ὕψος onto the grand style. Strong emotion, identified by Longinus as vital for the generation of sublimity (*De sub.* 8.1), is nowhere mentioned by Demetrius. So too, although the entirety of Demetrius' treatise, and indeed the ancient doctrine of rhetorical styles in general, can be seen to be predicated upon the principle of imitation of 'the classics', the particular emphasis given to imitation, μίμησις, by Longinus, and his use of metaphors of inspiration and possession to describe this process (*De sub.* 13.2–14), are unique.[11] Instead of something inert, in Longinus' hands imitation becomes an active means of engagement with one's literary forebears, a mutually empowering process in which the imitated text bestows vitality upon the imitator while at the same time gaining a fresh life of its own. Again, there are no parallels in Demetrius for Longinus' interest in visualisation (φαντασία, *De sub.* 15), another form of verbal immediacy 'where, inspired by strong emotion, you seem to see what you describe and bring it vividly before the eyes of your audience' (ὅταν ἃ λέγεις ὑπ' ἐνθουσιασμοῦ καὶ πάθους βλέπειν δοκῇς καὶ ὑπ' ὄψιν τιθῇς τοῖς ἀκούουσιν, *De sub.* 15.1). Indeed, most of the figures discussed by Longinus (rhetorical questions, hyperbaton, use of the historic present, the second person, direct speech and periphrasis, *De sub.* 18, 22–9) bear no determinate relation to the grand style at all.

One is prompted to conclude that, although the *Peri hupsous* makes use of concepts and vocabulary taken from ancient stylistic theory, the endeavour to assimilate sublimity with the rhetorical *genus grande* or indeed with any of the other ancient stylistic classifications can only lead to frustration. As Russell has well observed, the sublime emerges in Longinus' text as 'a special effect, not a special style', one that can be created by a wide variety of devices, which might otherwise be considered opposite

[11] Russell (1965) xii.

in their stylistic associations, and that can be discerned across a range of authors, genres and subjects.[12]

Any attempt to read the *Peri hupsous* as a straightforward manual of rhetorical style must also reckon with the difficulties and innovations presented by its exposition of its theme. Despite initial assurances, Longinus does not offer a systematic explanation of how to achieve sublimity in writing but instead proceeds by means of association, it can seem at times haphazardly, one quotation suggesting another, the underlying conceptual thread left unstated; by the same token (lacunae aside) a topic of discussion is often raised then left behind, only to resurface subsequently (as Longinus himself says happens at the level of the individual sentence in Demosthenes' speeches, *De sub.* 22.4).[13] The question of the relation between art, τέχνη, and nature, φύσις, first addressed at *De sub.* 2.1–3, is never fully resolved;[14] how, after all, can the sublime – a 'je ne sais quoi' to which Longinus' tissue of quotations insistently and, for all the treatise's careful distinctions, almost mutely points, the avowedly mimetic source of which is variously and paradoxically identified as a form of innate genius and of inspiration (e.g. 9.1–2, 13.2–4) – properly be taught? Longinus himself states that sublimity is not a matter of simple adherence to rules (33–4): 'the greatest natures are least immaculate' (αἱ ὑπερμεγέθεις φύσεις ἥκιστα καθαραί) while 'perfect precision runs the risk of triviality' (τὸ γὰρ ἐν παντὶ ἀκριβὲς κίνδυνος μικρότη-τος) (33.2). Notwithstanding the traditionally functional purposes of ancient criticism, the student who attempts to use the *Peri hupsous* as a guide for imbuing his own writing with sublimity is thus unlikely to get very far; it is notable that, as Russell points out, during the Renaissance Longinus' 'difficulty and the fact that he gives few practical rules of a teachable kind debarred him from any great educational influence'.[15]

---

[12] Russell (1964) xxxvii, citing Boileau's declaration that 'par sublime, Longin n'entend pas ce que les Orateurs appelent le stile sublime'; cf. Nancy (1993b) 52 ('there is no sublime style'). See also Russell (1965) xiii, (1981a) 55–6, 139, 146–7.

[13] *De sub.* 43.1–5, for instance, deals with diction rather than, as advertised at *De sub.* 39, word arrangement; cf. the non-summary of the previous sections at *De sub.* 15.12. See Russell (1981a) 55–6.

[14] Walsh (1988) 253; Deguy (1993) 14–17; Whitmarsh (2001) 62–3.

[15] Russell (1964) xliii.

Most damagingly, a restrictively rhetorical approach to Longinus also blinds us to some of his most penetrating insights. Philippe Lacoue-Labarthe puts the point provocatively: the *Peri hupsous* is to be read 'not as a work of rhetoric or poetics, that is... of "criticism" (which it *also*, of course, incontestably is), but rather as a philosophical work, or at least as illegible without the presupposition of a precise philosophical intent beneath each of its fundamental statements, an intent which moreover has nothing to do with the occasional recall of this or that ancient banality from stoicism or anywhere else'.[16] Lacoue-Labarthe proceeds to examine the sublime as 'the original oxymoron', as that which in Kant, in Hegel and 'ever since Longinus' presents the fact 'that there is the nonpresentable'.[17] It is sometimes objected that such attempts to read Longinus 'philosophically' are anachronistic: it is claimed that the treatise's modern title, *On the Sublime*, is misleading; it made its first appearance with the initial translations of Longinus in the sixteenth century, most notably Boileau's *Traité du Sublime*, and denotes a concept alien to the classical world.[18] To so object is to substitute questions of terminology for analysis of the treatise's actual concerns. How are we to translate terms such as ὕψος or *sublimis*? Did the ancients have a word for our modern 'sublime'? These are valid questions. Their answers, however, do not depend upon the chronology of literary history. Even if the ancients had no word that conveyed exactly what we mean by 'sublime', this does not mean that they lacked a comparable concept.[19] To adduce 'the sublime' as something stable and unproblematically defined is, in any event, to claim too much; our task is not to force the *Peri hupsous* into conformity with misleadingly reified modern categories but to place Longinus and the sublime's later theorists

---

[16] Lacoue-Labarthe (1993) 96–7. The desire to privilege particular theorisations of the sublime can cut the other way too: see Nicolson (1959) 30 on critical views of the 'natural sublime' of the eighteenth century as 'a degraded form of Longinianism'. For the Stoics' views on rhetoric and poetry, and their relation to Longinus' treatise, see Russell (1981a) 41–2, 135–7, 144.

[17] Lacoue-Labarthe (1993) 86, 74; for brief but salutary comments upon the importance of Longinus' role within the sublime tradition, see further ibid. 72–3, 84 and esp. 98–106.

[18] Kellner (2005) 245, cf. Russell (1965) xvi; Kirwan (2005) 159; Thomas (2007) 219.

[19] Contra Russell (1965) xvii, who explains his use of the term 'sublimity' to translate ὕψος as a direct attempt to 'diminish some of the associations which "the sublime" has had since the later eighteenth century'.

into (hopefully illuminating) dialogue. As I aim to show, Longinus' concerns (and Lucan's) do reveal important connections with those of these later theorists; moreover, as their texts often explicitly demonstrate, these theorists themselves clearly had Longinus in mind. We should not be constrained by misplaced anxieties of discipline or genre into artificially divorcing our reading of the *Peri hupsous* from this rich and fertile tradition.[20]

For the moment, I want briefly to introduce two ways of thinking about Longinus' treatise beyond the purely rhetorical; we will subsequently consider each in further detail as part of our analysis of Lucan. Russell, we saw above, describes the Longinian sublime as a 'special effect, not a special style'. But what, precisely, is this effect? In one sense, we might say, it simply denotes whatever makes a piece of writing great. Such an effect will of course emerge as the result of a reader's individual and culturally conditioned tastes; thus Russell argues that for Longinus ὕψος functions as a combined product of his admiration for Plato's literary style and ideas and for the apothegms and epigrammatic flourishes of Rome's rhetorical schools; Longinus' attempt to reconcile these differing literary preferences is reflected in his own style of writing, defined on the one hand by 'lavish metaphor and immense richness', on the other by 'a marked fondness for *graves sententiae* of a Tacitean ring'.[21]

But Longinian ὕψος need not be understood simply as a defence of a particular literary taste. It denotes something at once more specific and of more universal application. Longinus declares that the effect of a sublime text is 'not to persuade the audience but rather to transport them out of themselves' (οὐ γὰρ εἰς πειθὼ τοὺς ἀκροωμένους ἀλλ' εἰς ἔκστασιν ἄγει τὰ ὑπερφυᾶ, 1.4):[22] 'the true sublime naturally elevates us: uplifted with a sense of proud exaltation, we are filled with joy and pride, as if we had ourselves produced the very thing we heard' (φύσει γάρ πως ὑπὸ τἀληθοῦς ὕψους

---

[20] Cf. *New Literary History* 16, no. 2 (1985) and *Aevum Antiquum* 3 (2003), two essay collections that take an exemplarily panoptic view of the sublime and its history.

[21] Russell (1964) xxxix–xl.

[22] Cf. *De sub.* 15.9, 39.1, 44.1: the impact of the sublime goes beyond mere persuasion; it is a matter of τὸ θαυμάσιον, ἔκστασις, ἔκπληξις; see Innes (1995a) 323. For the distinction between words that move and words that persuade, cf. Cic. *Orator* 69.

ἐπαίρεταί τε ἡμῶν ἡ ψυχὴ καὶ γαῦρόν τι παράστημα λαμβά-
νουσα πληροῦται χαρᾶς καὶ μεγαλαυχίας, ὡς αὐτὴ γεννήσασα
ὅπερ ἤκουσεν, 7.2).[23] These statements are central to Longinus'
text. They gesture towards the sublime as a phenomenon that rises
above the sum of the treatise's specific linguistic prescriptions to
denote a particular experience of language, one in which the intensity of communication between author and reader leads practically
to a fusion of the two. 'The sublime,' as Emma Gilby puts it, 'is
the result of an author coming into cognitive contact with a reader
who can identify with that author via discourse.'[24] It is for their
ability to model and promote this contact that Longinus is especially interested in, and groups together, the processes of μίμησις
and φαντασία (De sub. 13.2–15). And it is within this contact that
the tension between τέχνη and φύσις is resolved: figures of speech
such as Demosthenes' oath upon the Battle of Marathon (Dem.
De corona 208; De sub. 16.2–4, 17.2) so touch the hearer that,
swept along by their power, their art becomes for him nature – his
own, 'second', nature, its artful difference hidden from himself; it
is here that the sublimity of figurality, of speech itself, lies.[25]

This 'textual' sublimity can also be considered as part of a
much broader sensibility, a structure of feeling not confined solely
to the relationship between reader and author. One of Longinus'
most striking examples of the sublime is taken from Sappho's love
poem Φαίνεταί μοι.[26] In it the speaker, gazing longingly on her

[23] In his essay 'A new refutation of time', Borges (2000) 259 takes Longinus' 'as if' a step
further: 'Do not the fervent readers who surrender themselves to Shakespeare become,
literally, Shakespeare?'; cf. Borges' fable 'Pierre Menard, author of the Quixote', in
which the protagonist sets out to write Cervantes' novel ((2000) 62–71).

[24] Gilby (2006) 25. Cf. Innes (1985) 646 on the Longinian sublime as 'perhaps the first
truly affective theory of literature'. See also Guerlac (1990) 3 on the 'proud flight' of
sublime identification effected by the thunderbolt of Longinian utterance: 'the listener
is displaced to the position of speaker, raised to the status of master, as the force of
enunciation continues to operate inscribed in memory. This paradoxical moment is
presented by the text as being both the effect and the origin of the sublime, which
engenders itself through "impregnating" the soul of the listener.'

[25] Cf. Deguy (1993) 17–18, 22–4.

[26] Russell (1964) xvi notes that, under the spell of the treatise's typical focus on grand and
heroic subjects, English critics have often attacked Longinus for including Sappho's
poem as an example of sublimity: see for example Hugh Blair's Lecture on Rhetoric
(1783). The tendency continues today: Hunter (2009) 134 maintains that the inclusion
of Sappho fr. 31 'in the general context of a discussion of ὕψος, is in fact much more
suprising than is often acknowledged'. Notwithstanding Demetrius' identification of

beloved, feels her body dissolve so that she thinks herself 'very near to death':

φαίνεταί μοι κῆνος ἴσος θέοισιν
ἔμμεν' ὤνηρ, ὄττις ἐνάντιός τοι
ἰζάνει καὶ πλάσιον ἆδυ φωνείσας ὐπακούει
καὶ γελαίσας ἰμερόεν, τό μ' ἦ μὰν
καρδίαν ἐν στήθεσιν ἐπτόαισεν.
ὠς γὰρ <ἐς> σ' ἴδω βρόχε' ὠς με φώνας οὐδὲν ἔτ' εἴκει·
ἀλλὰ κὰμ μὲν γλῶσσα ἔαγε· λέπτον δ'
αὔτικα χρῷ πῦρ ὐποδεδρόμακεν
ὀππάτεσσι δ' οὐδὲν ὄρημμ', ἐπιρόμβεισι δ' ἄκουαι·
ἀ δέ μ' ἴδρως κακχέεται, τρόμος δὲ
παῖσαν ἄγρει, χλωροτέρα δὲ ποίας
ἔμμι· τεθνάκην δ' ὀλίγω 'πιδεύης φαίνομ' <ἐμαυτᾷ>·
ἀλλὰ πᾶν τόλματον, ἐπεὶ ...

I think him God's peer that sits near you face to
    face, and listens to your sweet speech and
    lovely laughter.
It's this that makes my heart flutter in my breast. If
    I see you but for a little, my voice comes no
    more and my tongue is broken.
At once a delicate flame runs through my limbs; I
    see nothing with my eyes, and my ears thunder.
The sweat pours down: shivers grip me all over. I
    am grown paler than grass, and seem to
    myself to be very near to death.
But all must be endured, since ...

Sappho fr. 31 Voigt (*De sub.* 10.2)

Here the quotation breaks off and Longinus observes: 'Is it not wonderful how she *summons* at the same time soul, body, hearing, tongue, sight, skin, all as though *they had wandered off apart from herself*?' (οὐ θαυμάζεις, ὡς, ὐπ<ὸ τὸ> αὐτὸ τὴν ψυχὴν τὸ σῶμα τὰς ἀκοὰς τὴν γλῶσσαν τὰς ὄψεις τὴν χρόαν, πάνθ' ὡς ἀλλότρια διοιχόμενα ἐπιζητεῖ, 10.3, my italics). For Longinus, the appeal of the poem stems from its complex interplay of loss and recuperation: restitution and wholeness (in this case artistic,

Sappho as an exponent of the elegant style (*On Style* 127, 132, 140–1, 146, 148, 162, 166), my argument is that the sublime, correctly understood, cannot be conceived as a property only of particular categories of subject or genre. While it may display certain common associations, sublimity can emerge in any context.

39

Segal (1959);

that is to say, the poem itself) is achieved as a result of traumatic rupture, as a function of near-death, of self-objectification and dissociation.[27] At one level, Sappho's poem can be read as a metaphor for the intense processes of writing and reading that Longinus is attempting to describe; indeed, her technique of 'selection (violent fragmentation) and combination, of estrangement and rearrangement'[28] parallels Longinus' own compositional practice, his decontextualisation and reconstitution of literary fragments. But this practice, and Longinus' interest in texts' power to move, is also reflective of, and by implication suggests, a deeper, underlying concern: the continuing presence of the past and the expression of how this presence is experienced.[29]

Aside from his citation of Genesis 1:3–9 ('εἶπεν ὁ θεός', φησί· τί; 'γενέσθω φῶς, καὶ ἐγένετο· γενέσθω γῆ, καὶ ἐγένετο' "'God said," – what? "Let there be light, and there was light, Let there be earth, and there was earth"', *De sub.* 9.9), all Longinus' examples of sublime writing are drawn from authors from Greece's lost classical past;[30] indeed, he directs our attention to the fact when he explicitly identifies 'zealous imitation of the great prose writers and poets of the past' (τῶν ἔμπροσθεν μεγάλων συγγραφέων καὶ

---

[27] Guerlac (1985) 281. One of the striking features of this example is its apparently feminine subject-position. For all the sublime's traditionally masculine appeal, its co-implication with the feminine persists: see the discussion in Chapter 2 of the Longinian Pythia (*De sub.* 13.2) and of the Lucanian figures of the Bacchic *matrona* (Luc. 1.674–95), Phemonoe (5.64–236) and Erictho (6.430–830). On Sappho fr. 31 and the sublime, see further eg. DeJean (1989) 84–7; Warren (1989) 204; Freeman (1995) 13–26. On the female sublime more broadly, see Battersby (1989); Yaeger (1989); Maxwell (2001); Shaw (2006) 56–63, 105–11.

[28] Porter (forthcoming).

[29] See Porter (2001) and (forthcoming); cf. Porter (2010) 512–21. See also Segal (1959); Too (1998) 196–217; Whitmarsh (2001) 57–71. Porter (2001) identifies Longinus' orientation towards the past through comparison with Pausanias and Dio Chrysostom, also Greeks living under imperial Roman rule: all three writers, in their self-consciously staged uncertainties of identity and negotiations with a lost and longed-for past, are typical of what scholars have identified as the Second Sophistic. On this period/movement and its cultural imaginary, see further e.g. Goldhill (2001); Whitmarsh (2011) 8, 9–10 expresses scepticism about the validity of the term. Porter develops his observations about the *Peri hupsous'* retrospective gaze into a valuable discussion of the emergence, structure and role of classicism in antiquity in Porter (2006a) and (2006b): the 'Longinian sublime captures the intensity . . . of the experience of classicism itself' (2006b: 347).

[30] But note West (1995) 338–42, who, by way of explanation for Longinus' apparently anomalous quotation from Genesis, argues that the preceding Homeric examples at *De sub.* 9.4–9 all derive from Near Eastern poetic tradition.

ποιητῶν μίμησίς τε καὶ ζήλωσις, 13.2) as a route to sublimity. Yet it is precisely in the achievement of sublimity that this past is brought to life once again: Longinus declares that 'emulation will bring those great characters before our eyes' (προσπίπτοντα γὰρ ἡμῖν κατὰ ζῆλον ἐκεῖνα τὰ πρόσωπα, *De sub.* 14.1, cf. the discussion of the effects of φαντασία at *De sub.* 7.3, 15.1–12); the would-be writer is advised to ask himself, 'How would Homer or Demosthenes, had either been *present*, have listened to this passage of mine?' (πῶς ἂν τόδε τι ὑπ᾽ ἐμοῦ λεγόμενον παρὼν Ὅμηρος ἤκουσεν ἢ Δημοσθένης, 14.2, my italics). And no sooner has he raised this question than Longinus thinks of another, 'even more stimulating': 'If I write this, how would all posterity receive it?' (πῶς ἂν ἐμοῦ ταῦτα γράψαντος ὁ μετ᾽ ἐμὲ πᾶς ἀκούσειεν αἰών; 14.3). At the same time as it reaches into the past, the sublime stretches out to encompass the future. 'Immortal fame' (εὐκλείαις τὸν αἰῶνα, 1.3) is its lasting gift.[31] As Tim Whitmarsh observes: 'Just as sublime style flits between order and chaos, so it probes the barriers of time and culture. At the same time as he recognises a substantive difference between the ancients and "us" (ἡμεῖς, 14.1), "Longinus" presents sublime writing as an effacement of that difference, a form of communion with the greats.'[32]

But more than this, for Longinus knows that the sublimity of the past is not simply a matter of the felt juxtaposition of difference and communion. Rather, it is from the very awareness of difference that the sense of communion arises. Porter makes the point eloquently: 'sublimity nearly obliterates the present with a kind of violence, through an "invincible power and force" (δυναστείαν καὶ βίαν ἄμαχον, 1.4)'; it is thus 'linked to the near-death – the "beautiful death" – of posthumousness'.[33] Sappho's poem, in its representation of violent loss and paradoxical presence, offers a powerful image for such experience: like the *Peri hupsous* itself, it is governed by 'an aesthetics not of perfect wholes but of rup-tured wholes'; as it anatomises 'the blissfulness of an alienated identity',[34] it reminds us that for Longinus, as he looks towards

---

[31] Cf. *De sub.* 4.7, 9.3, 36.2, 44.1, 44.9.
[32] Whitmarsh (2001) 66, cf. Too (1998) 213.
[33] Porter (forthcoming). Cf. Deguy (1993) 9–10.   [34] Porter (2001) 90.

the Greece that was, 'sublimity is effective *only* as a deracinated moment, in a violent, numbing decontextualisation that leaves a reader breathless and disoriented'.[35] We will return to this idea, and to Longinus' articulation of it, in Chapter 4.

Lucretius

Written sometime during the first half of the first century BC, Lucretius' great didactic poem upon 'the nature of things', expounding the scientific views of the Greek philosopher Epicurus (341–270 BC), does not provide any direct theorisation of the sublime and is not commonly included in discussions of the concept. As classicists have recently observed, however, Lucretius' physicalist speculations upon atomism and the wonders of the universe, and his aim of freeing mankind from superstition and the fear of death, promoting in their place joy and mental tranquillity, are clearly conducive to sublime experience. Indeed, the poem offers a valuable classical counterpart both to Longinus' text-based approach to the sublime and to subsequent analyses of sublimity.[36] As we will see in Chapter 3, Lucretius (via Virgil) also forms a crucial building block in Lucan's construction of the sublime. His contribution to the history of the concept consequently requires a brief sketch.

As Gian Biagio Conte points out, both Longinus and Lucretius place considerable emphasis on the role of vision in their respective treatments of words and things. Longinus extols the virtues of φαντασία (*De sub.* 15.1) because of the way in which, effectively deployed, it allows both speaker and listener (or writer and reader) to see what is being described. Likewise in the *De rerum natura*, 'the sensualistic materialism of Lucretius' thought coincides with the language of a poetry of evident and concretely perceptible images'.[37] However, where in Longinus φαντασία works to effect a connection between (present) reader and (past) text, in Lucretius true vision emerges as a result of atomistic enlightenment:

---

[35] Porter (forthcoming).

[36] See Conte (1994); Most (2003); Porter (2007) and (forthcoming). Cf. Else (1930).

[37] Conte (1994) 17. See also De Lacy (1964/2007) and Hardie (2009b) 153–79 on Lucretius' 'distant views'; cf. Martindale (2005) 189–90, 197.

latest alteque videndum
et longe cunctas in partis dispiciendum,
ut reminiscaris summam rerum esse profundam
et videas caelum summai totius unum   650
quam sit parvula pars et quam multesima constet,
nec tota pars, homo terrai quota totius unus.

[You] must cast your view wide and deep,
and survey all quarters far abroad,
that you may remember how profound is the sum of things,
and see how very small a part, how infinitesimal a fraction
of the whole universe is one sky –
not so large a part as one man is of the whole earth.

Lucr. 6.647–52[38]

The atomist's prism, wherein all matter in the universe is shown to consist of an infinite number of minute, unchangeable, indestructible, indivisible particles, moving through infinite void, prompts a dramatic readjustment to our customary ways of seeing. It places the heavens in a radically new perspective – as it does volcanoes, earthquakes, the raging ocean, mountains, thunderstorms, lightning and all the other mighty natural phenomena that, in anticipation of many eighteenth-century dissections of the sublime, Lucretius discusses. Lucretius' atomic world, as it unsettles conventional conceptions of scale and frames of reference, overwhelms the human subject. Yet, in this very moment of devastation, as the subject grasps the immensity of the new knowledge he has attained, he finds himself uplifted, exalted by the power of his own mental faculties. The atomic initiate is thus enabled to follow in the footsteps of Epicurus:

humana ante oculos foede cum vita iaceret
in terris oppressa gravi sub religione,
quae caput a caeli regionibus ostendebat
horribili super aspectu mortalibus instans,   65
primum Graius homo mortalis tollere contra
est oculos ausus primusque obsistere contra;
quem neque fama deum nec fulmina nec minitanti
murmure compressit caelum, sed eo magis acrem
inritat animi virtutem, effringere ut arta   70

---

[38] Cf. Lucr. 6.674–9, 4.414–19.

naturae primus portarum claustra cupiret.
ergo vivida vis animi pervicit et extra
processit longe flammantia moenia mundi
atque omne immensum peragravit mente animoque,
unde refert nobis victor quid possit oriri,   75
quid nequeat, finita potestas denique cuique
quanam sit ratione atque alte terminus haerens.
quare religio pedibus subiecta vicissim
obteritur, nos exaequat victoria caelo.

When man's life lay for all to see foully grovelling
upon the ground, crushed beneath the weight of Superstition,
which displayed her head from the regions of heaven,
lowering over mortals with horrible aspect,
a man of Greece [Epicurus] was the first that dared to uplift mortal
eyes against her, the first to make stand against her;
for neither fables of the gods could quell him, nor thunderbolts
nor heaven with menacing roar, but all the more
they goaded the eager courage of his soul, so that
he should desire, first of all men, to shatter the confining bars of nature's
      gates.
Therefore the lively power of his mind prevailed, and forth
he marched far beyond the flaming walls of the world,
as he traversed the immeasurable universe in thought and imagination;
whence victorious he returns bearing his prize, the knowledge what can
      come into being,
what can not, in a word, how each thing has its powers limited
and its deep-set boundary mark.
Therefore Superstition is now in her turn cast down and trampled
underfoot, while we by the victory are exalted high as heaven.

                                                    Lucr. 1.62–79[39]

This programmatic account of Epicurus' achievement is mirrored
in the proem to Book 3, but this time it describes the progress of
Lucretius himself and, by implication, that of his reader. Addressing Epicurus, the poet declares:

---

[39] *Pace* Lucretius' designation of Epicurus as *primus* (1.66–67, 71), Porter (2010) 158–
67 demonstrates that the theme of matter's sublimity originated with the Presocratic philosophers, most notably Xenophanes and Empedocles. The *De rerum natura*
remains, however, the ancients' fullest extant exploration of the idea. On the relation between Lucretius and the Presocratics, see further Tatum (1984/2007); Sedley
(1998/2007).

nam simul ac ratio tua coepit vociferari
naturam rerum, divina mente coortam,   15
diffugiunt animi terrores, moenia mundi
discedunt, totum video per inane geri res.
apparet divum numen sedesque quietae
quas neque concutiunt venti nec nubila nimbis
aspergunt neque nix acri concreta pruina   20
cana cadens violat semperque innubilus aether
integit, et large diffuso lumine ridet:
omnia suppeditat porro natura neque ulla
res animi pacem delibat tempore in ullo.
at contra nusquam apparent Acherusia templa,   25
nec tellus obstat quin omnia dispiciantur,
sub pedibus quaecumque infra per inane geruntur.
his ibi me rebus quaedam divina voluptas
percipit atque horror, quod sic natura tua vi
tam manifesta patens ex omni parte retecta est.   30

For as soon as your reasoning begins to proclaim
the nature of things revealed by your divine mind,
away flee the mind's terrors, the walls of the world
open out, I see action going on throughout the whole void:
before me appear the gods in their majesty, and their peaceful abodes,
which no winds ever shake nor clouds besprinkle with rain,
which no snow congealed by the bitter frost
mars with its white fall, but the air ever cloudless
encompasses them and laughs with its light spread wide abroad.
There moreover nature supplies everything, and nothing
at any time impairs their peace of mind.
But contrariwise nowhere appear the regions of Acheron;
yet the earth is no hindrance to all being clearly seen,
whatsoever goes on below under our feet throughout the void.
Thereupon from all these things a sort of divine delight
gets hold upon me and a shuddering, because nature thus by your power
has been so manifestly laid open and uncovered in every part.
                                                   Lucr. 3.14–30[40]

Identified by Lucretius as a product of atomism rather than literature, the flight beyond the *moenia mundi* (Lucr. 1.73, 3.16, cf. 1.1102–10, 2.1045) is also the guiding aspiration of the *Peri hupsous*: we have, says Longinus, 'an unconquerable passion for whatever is great and more divine than ourselves. Thus the whole

---

[40] Cf. Lucr. 2.1047, 1.968–82.

THE EXPERIENCE OF THE SUBLIME

universe is not enough to satisfy the speculative intelligence of human thought; our ideas often pass beyond the limits that confine us. Look at life from all sides and see how in all things the extraordinary, the great, the beautiful stand supreme, and you will soon realise what we were born for' (ἄμαχον ἔρωτα... παντὸς ἀεὶ τοῦ μεγάλου καὶ ὡς πρὸς ἡμᾶς δαιμονιωτέρου. διόπερ τῇ θεωρίᾳ καὶ διανοίᾳ τῆς ἀνθρωπίνης ἐπιβολῆς οὐδ' ὁ σύμπας κόσμος ἀρκεῖ, ἀλλὰ καὶ τοὺς τοῦ περιέχοντος πολλάκις ὅρους ἐκβαίνουσιν αἱ ἐπίνοιαι. καὶ εἴ τις περιβλέψαιτο ἐν κύκλῳ τὸν βίον, ὅσῳ πλέον ἔχει τὸ περιττὸν ἐν πᾶσι καὶ μέγα καὶ καλόν, ταχέως εἴσεται πρὸς ἃ γεγόναμεν, *De sub.* 35.2–3).[41]

Moreover, as Porter has demonstrated, Lucretius' means of launching himself upon this flight is structurally very similar to that of Longinus. In both cases, sublimity is paradoxically grounded in an experience of collapse and fragmentation. For Lucretius, the capacity of upheavals in nature to sunder the world's fabric (*vis / exagitata foras erumpitur et simul altam / diffindens terram magnum concinnat hiatum*, 6.582–4) mirrors the process through which Epicurus broke open nature's gates (1.70–1) and so attained sublimity. More than this, it is upon the very prospect of void presented by such upheavals (cf. how in an earthquake the earth 'torn asunder may open abroad her own gaping maw, and in confusion seek to gorge it with her own ruins', *distracta suum late dispandat hiatum / idque suis confusa velit complere ruinis*, 6.599–600, and how the final apocalypse 'stands open and awaits with vast and hideous maw', *patet immani et vasto respectat hiatu*, 5.375) that the sublimity of Lucretius (and of his addressee) is predicated:[42] as he surveys all that goes on in the void (*inane*, 3.17, 27) beneath his feet, he is seized by a magnificent thrill, a 'divine delight... and shuddering' (*divina voluptas /... atque horror*, 3.28–9). In Porter's words:

---

[41] Echoing Marvell's praise for *Paradise Lost*, Thomas Gray in *The Progress of Poesy* 3.2 (1754) redeploys Lucretius' image of Epicurus marching beyond the walls of the world to describe Milton's achievement of sublimity: 'He, that rode sublime / Upon the seraph-wings of Ecstasy, / The secrets of th' Abyss to spy. He pass'd the flaming bounds of Place and Time'; see Rouse (1992) ad Lucr. 1.73.
[42] Cf. Porter (2007) 171.

Lucretius' philosophical vision typically tends to evacuate the reality one intu-
itively knows and understands, even as it seeks to anchor this reality in the
reassuring bedrock of physics (atoms and void). This gives us the true *maiestas*,
the majesty or sublimity, of nature... Sublimity results from the sheer exhilaration that a glimpse of scientific truth affords. But it also draws its power from the
fundamental discrepancy between such an insight into the nature of things and
one's customary perspectives. The stark contrast of atoms and void presages this
discrepancy in the very foundations of nature.[43]

In this sense, 'by virtue of estranging and then rearranging reality, or at least our view of it, atomism performs a gesture on
the self and the world very like Sappho's'.[44] Like the Longinian,
the Lucretian sublime displays a vertiginous ability to induce
a kind of mental jack-knifing in the perceiving subject, as this
subject simultaneously buckles and swells under the violence
of the sublime experience, at once emptied out and filled to
overflowing.

There is also, however, an aspect of this Lucretian sensibility
that would seem on superficial inspection to militate against the
sublime. Lucretius himself tells his reader that, if he can achieve
true understanding of Epicurus' discoveries, he will 'cease wonder-
ing at many things' (*mirari multa relinquas*, 6.654): the atomistic
view of reality works not to magnify but to deflate the grandeur of
natural phenomena. In comparing an earthquake with the shaking
of houses as a waggon passes (6.543–51), Lucretius relativises the
earthquake's power; he puts its awesomeness 'in perspective'. But
Lucretius' point is that it is not in the earthquake that sublimity
lies. Rather, it is the perceiving subject's mental ability to 'rise
above' such phenomena that is truly sublime – and this elevation is dependent upon the dramatic contrast between the earthquake and the trembling house. Lucretius, in other words, does
not deflate the sublimity he has constructed,[45] but rather uses such
deflationary tactics to direct us from the 'false' sublime of natural
phenomena to the true sublime of our own rational faculties: atomism replaces terrified incomprehension with an elevating sense of

---

[43] Porter (2007) 169.   [44] Porter (forthcoming).
[45] Contra Conte (1994) 152; Hardie (2009c) 186–7.

wonder inspired by true understanding.[46] The injunction *nil mirari* should not simply be taken at face value. Its object requires careful consideration.

Burke

Traces of both Longinus and Lucretius are visible in the first of the modern era's two most influential studies of sublimity. Among the numerous English texts of the eighteenth century that in the wake of Boileau's translation of Longinus attempted to analyse the sublime,[47] Burke's treatise of 1757, *A Philosophical Enquiry into the Origin of our Ideas of the Sublime and Beautiful*, stands out on account of its thoroughness and clarity of argument as well as its occasional eccentricity (it includes, for instance, a section on 'smell and taste').[48] Burke theorises sublimity in terms of an overwhelming encounter with forces or objects beyond one's control. In the first stage of this encounter the mind opens up to and is overcome by the object; this in turn leads to 'an intensification of self-presence and a corresponding re-assertion of the power of the subject over the object'.[49] 'Terror' plays a crucial role within this schema:

Whatever is fitted in any sort to excite the ideas of pain, and danger, that is to say, whatever is in any sort terrible, or is conversant about terrible objects, or operates in a manner analogous to terror, is a source of the *sublime*; that is, it is productive of the strongest emotion which the mind is capable of feeling.[50]

[46] Cf. DeLillo (1997) 735–6: of Einstein's E = mc2, a science teacher exclaims to his class: 'How small is the atom? I will tell you. If people were the size of atoms... the population of the earth would fit on the head of a pin... Never mind the energy packed in the atom. What about the energy contained in this equation? This is the real power. How the mind operates. How the mind identifies, analyzes and represents. What beauty and power. What marvels of imagination does it require to reduce the complex forces of nature, all those unseeable magical actions inside the atom – to express all this with a bing and a bang on a blackboard. The atom.'

[47] On Boileau's translation and its impact, see further Brody (1958); Cronk (2003); Gilby (2006), esp. 1–14, 58–66, 118–31, 132–42.

[48] Helpful explorations of the Burkeian sublime include Eagleton (1990) 54–6; Phillips (1990); Furniss (1993); Gibbons (2003); Shaw (2006) 48–71. For other English treatments of the sublime in the eighteenth century, see Monk (1935/1960); Ashfield and de Bolla (1996); Kirwan (2005) 1–52; Shaw (2006) 27–47.

[49] Ashfield and de Bolla (1996) 128.   [50] Burke (1990) 36.

If that were all, however, the experience of the sublime would remain indistinguishable from that of being terrified, and Burke goes on to emphasise the importance of the feeling of 'delight' (a term he uses to signify the sensation of 'the removal or moderation of pain', a pleasure, in other words, 'which cannot exist without a relation... to pain').[51] Such delight arises 'when we have an idea of pain and danger, without being actually in such circumstances', and is thus linked to those 'passions which belong to self-preservation'. 'Whatever excites this delight,' concludes Burke, 'I call *sublime*.'[52] He proceeds to discuss the sources of this unique combination of pain and pleasure, including 'obscurity', superior power, the 'privations' of '*Vacuity, Darkness, Solitude* and *Silence*', 'vastness', 'infinity', 'difficulty', intense light, darkness, 'excessive loudness' and 'suddenness'.

The emphasis Burke places on terror is a distinguishing feature of his analysis. The broad structure underlying his conception of sublime experience, however, is not only consonant with other contemporary theorisations of sublimity[53] but is also closely related to the models of sublimity advanced by Longinus and Lucretius: the experience engendered by Burke's objects of threat and terror is one of exaltation which, however, can only be achieved through a moment of apparent loss or weakness. Moreover, Longinus can be seen to anticipate Burke's emphasis on terror when he approvingly cites Demosthenes' speeches (*De sub.* 22.4) and Homer's descriptions of the Battle of the Gods (*De sub.* 9.6) and of sailors caught in a storm (*De sub.* 10.5) for their exemplification of τὸ φοβερόν (*De sub.* 9.7, 10.6), while denigrating the orations of Hyperides because no one 'feels frightened' (φοβεῖται) while reading them (*De sub.* 34.4, cf. how the speech of Boreas (from Aeschylus' *Orithyia?*) sinks 'from the terrible to the ridiculous', ἐκ τοῦ φοβεροῦ... πρὸς τὸ εὐκαταφρόνητον, *De sub.* 3.1).[54]

The fearsome power, at once overbearing and elevating, that is evidenced in Longinus' examples exerts a peculiar attraction. But

---

[51] Burke (1990) 33.   [52] Burke (1990) 47.

[53] See Ashfield and de Bolla (1996) 128–30; Shaw (2006) 27–71.

[54] See Russell (1979) 14; Hunter (2009) 141–2.

we should also note Longinus' warning that fear, unalloyed, is a mean emotion, 'devoid of sublimity' (*De sub.* 8.2).[55] So for Burke it is not simple terror that engenders the sublime but 'delight', for the experience of which the source of danger must be at a remove from us. Lucretius displays a similar awareness, emphasising the distance that must exist between subject and object in order for sublimity to arise: 'Pleasant it is also to behold great encounters of warfare arrayed over the plains, with no part of yours in the peril' (*suave etiam belli certamina magna tueri / per campos instructa tua sine parte pericli*, Lucr. 2.5–6); occupancy of the Epicurean *templa serena* presupposes a detached view of the world, the ability to look down upon the turmoil of existence, godlike, from afar (*despicere unde queas alios passimque videre / errare*, Lucr. 2.9–10).

Burke also shares Longinus' emphasis on language as a source of sublimity. 'We find by experience that eloquence and poetry are as capable, nay indeed much more capable of making deep and lively impressions than any other arts, and even than nature itself in very many cases.' He explains: besides words' power to convey 'the passions of others' and to represent things 'which can seldom occur in reality', both of which can prove highly affecting, it is 'by words [that] we have it in our power to make such *combinations* as we cannot possibly do otherwise. By this power of combining we are able, by the addition of well-chosen circumstances, to give a new life and force to the simple object.'[56] Burke's insight has much in common with recent poststructuralist readings of the sublime as a function of 'discourse'[57] but it also looks back to Longinus' founding association of the sublime and language,[58] suggesting that sublimity, in so far as it is a product of our own ideas and perceptions, should always ultimately be deemed a construct, a textual effect.[59]

---

[55] Innes (1995a) 331.   [56] Burke (1990) 158.
[57] See in particular de Bolla (1989); cf. Derrida (1987) 119–47.
[58] Cf. Ashfield and de Bolla (1996) 10–11, 128–30.
[59] Shaw (2006) 52: 'it is language that enables us to select and combine ideas, so as to render even the most unprepossessing object sublime'; cf. ibid. 11, 37, 47, 95. Lyotard (1991) 84–5, 100 brilliantly turns Burke's logocentrism to serve the cause of abstract painting.

Underscoring these affinities are several direct references in the *Enquiry* to key passages from both Lucretius and Longinus. Lucretius' account at the start of his poem of Epicurus' victory over *Religio* (Lucr. 1.62–67) is (mis)quoted towards the end of the *Enquiry* as a powerful instance of sublimity: 'The terrible picture which Lucretius has drawn of religion, in order to display the magnanimity of his philosophical hero in opposing her, is thought to be designed with great boldness and spirit.'[60] Significantly, however, Burke's interest is not so much in the sublimity of Epicurus' achievement per se as in the sublime (Longinian) effect of Lucretius' language: the quotation is part of a discussion of how 'words may affect without raising images'.[61] Burke also (mis)quotes from the parallel account of Epicurean flight at the start of *De rerum natura* 3. While acknowledging the poetic power of Lucretius' words, Burke's emphasis this time is on atomism itself, specifically its characteristic affect of *divina voluptas atque horror* (Lucr. 3.28–30): when Lucretius 'supposes the whole mechanism of nature laid open by the master of his philosophy, his transport on this magnificent view which he has represented in the colours of such bold and lively poetry, is overcast with a shade of secret dread and horror'.[62] Lucretius' *divina voluptas atque horror*, in its conjunction of fear and pleasure, in fact precisely describes the quality of Burke's own sublime: 'a sort of delightful horror, a sort of tranquillity tinged with terror', labelled by Burke in its highest degree 'astonishment'.[63] And earlier in the *Enquiry* it is by reference to Longinus that Burke explains this same 'transport': the sublime 'swelling' of one's own powers and sense of self 'is never more perceived, nor operates with more force, than when without danger we are conversant with terrible objects, the mind always claiming to itself some part of the dignity and importance of the things which it contemplates. Hence proceeds what Longinus has observed of that glorying and sense of inward greatness, that always fills the reader of such passages in poets and orators as are sublime.'[64]

[60] Burke (1990) 157.   [61] Burke (1990) 153.   [62] Burke (1990) 63.
[63] Burke (1990) 123.   [64] Burke (1990) 46–7.

In the Preface to the first edition of the *Enquiry*, Burke refers to the *Peri hupsous* as that 'incomparable discourse'[65] but, as Burke himself demonstrates, common ground can be discerned between Longinus and other theorists of the sublime. Burke's citation of Longinus alongside Lucretius helps us not only to identify the *Enquiry*'s own intellectual genesis but also to gain a stronger sense of the relation between the two classical writers' patterns of thought. As we read the *Enquiry*, any straightforward division between the Longinian and the Lucretian sublimes, between the sublimity that language has the capacity to generate and that which we may feel in the face of natural phenomena, becomes increasingly difficult to sustain.

Kant

Alongside that of Burke, Kant's *Critique of the Power of Judgement* (1790, revised 1793) provides the eighteenth century's other foundational analysis of the sublime, one that has overshadowed all subsequent attempts to theorise the concept.[66] Ashfield and de Bolla argue against the critical tendency to read Kant in concert with eighteenth-century British writers on the sublime, emphasising the difference between their respective attitudes towards the ethical status of sublimity.[67] As we will see when we consider the political uses to which the sublime has been put, this distinction is important. At the structural level, however, there remain significant resemblances between the Kantian schema and that of Burke (and of Burke's immediate British predecessors such as Addison, Hutcheson and Baillie),[68] and it is consequently instructive to consider the two theorists in conjunction.

For Kant, 'that is sublime which even to be able to think of demonstrates a faculty of the mind that surpasses every measure of

---

[65] Burke (1990) 1.

[66] The bibliography on the Kantian sublime is vast and it is beyond the scope of the present study to offer more than the briefest overview, necessarily simplified, of Kant's theory, or to examine its relation to his *Critique of Pure Reason* (1781, revised 1787) and *Critique of Practical Reason* (1788). See further, by way of introduction, Cohen and Guyer (1982); Crowther (1989); Zammito (1992); Guyer (1993); Librett (1993); Cheetham (2001); Shaw (2006) 72–89.

[67] Ashfield and de Bolla (1996) 2–3. Cf. Kirwan (2005) 37–66.

[68] See Kirwan (2005) 8–11.

the senses'.[69] He divides the sublime into two types: the mathematically sublime and the dynamically sublime. The former describes our experience of any object of 'absolutely great' magnitude[70] the contemplation of which confronts us with 'the inadequacy of even the greatest effort of our imagination',[71] but which, simultaneously, and precisely because of this imaginative inadequacy, awakens our awareness of reason's 'supersensible' capacity to comprehend the phenomenon, thus generating a sense of our own 'superiority' over external nature.[72] Kant gives the universe as an example of this kind of object, but emphasises the subjective nature of such sublimity: what appears 'absolutely great' to one person will not necessarily appear so to another; 'it is', he writes, 'the disposition of the mind resulting from a certain representation occupying the reflective judgment, but not the object, which is to be called sublime'.[73]

We encounter the same movement between inadequacy and superiority, or in Burkeian terms between pain and pleasure, in the dynamically sublime. Here we are confronted with an object that, because of its irresistibly lethal power over us, is a source of fear. Yet, Kant proposes, 'as long as we find ourselves in safety . . . we gladly call these objects sublime because they elevate the strength of our soul above its usual level, and allow us to discover within ourselves a capacity for resistance of quite another kind, which gives us the courage to measure ourselves against the apparent all-powerfulness of nature'.[74] The objects selected by Kant as appropriate sources of this experience also reveal affinities with Burke's 'terror' sublime: 'threatening cliffs, thunder clouds towering up into the heavens, bringing with them flashes of lightning . . . volcanoes with their all-destroying violence, hurricanes with the devastation they leave behind, the boundless ocean set into a rage'.[75] And, again, Kant stresses the subjectivity and elevating results of the experience: 'sublimity is not contained in anything in nature, but only in our mind, insofar as we can become conscious of being superior to nature within us and thus also to nature outside us'.[76]

---

[69] Kant (2003) 134.   [70] Kant (2003) 131.   [71] Kant (2003) 138.
[72] Kant (2003) 145.   [73] Kant (2003) 134. Cf. ibid. 129, 139, 147.
[74] Kant (2003) 144–5.   [75] Kant (2003) 144.   [76] Kant (2003) 147.

Sianne Ngai well encapsulates the paradoxical nature of the affect thus generated by Kant's sublime:

Although the sublime encounter with the infinitely vast or powerful object . . . is at the outset negative, involving a failure of the imagination that threatens the mind's sense of its own capabilities (as in the case of the mathematical sublime) or precipitates a sense of physical inferiority to nature that induces fear and pain in the observer (as in the case of the dynamical sublime), both encounters end by reversing these initial challenges to the self's autonomy, culminating in 'inspiriting satisfaction' rather than unpleasure.[77]

An initial experience of shock gives way to one of elevated tranquillity, as the subject achieves an ennobling distance from the overwhelming object of experience: the sense of subjective inadequacy simultaneously awakens an awareness of the superior faculty of reason, 'capable of grasping the totality or infinity that the imagination could not in the form of a noumenal or supersensible idea, and also of revealing the self's final superiority to nature, inasmuch as its rational faculty is revealed as lying outside nature and in fact encompassing it'.[78]

Beyond its correspondences with the Burkeian dichotomy of pain and pleasure, this model of the sublime also emerges in close contact with that of Lucretius. Porter posits a direct link: 'the parallels with Lucretius, echoes indeed, ought to be plain – so plain, in fact, that one has to suspect a certain awareness on Kant's part that he is working in a Lucretian, or at the very least atomistic, tradition'.[79] 'In both authors, the sublime emerges whenever the mind comes into bruising contact with nature', an encounter that transcends fear in order to produce, paradoxically, an awareness within the human subject of his own triumphant powers of ratiocination.[80] For Lucretius, as for Kant, the true sublime lies not so much in lightning itself (for example) as in our own ability 'to understand the true nature of the fiery thunderbolt, and to see by what power it plays its part' (*igniferi naturam fulminis ipsam / perspicere et qua vi faciat rem quamque videre*, Lucr. 6.379–80); 'sublimity is not contained in anything in nature, but only in

---

[77] Ngai (2005) 265–6. [78] Ngai (2005) 266. See also Lyotard (1991) 84–5, 98–9.
[79] Porter (2007) 180. Cf. Conte (1994) 16–34, whose view of the Lucretian sublime is based on the Kantian model.
[80] Porter (2007) 178.

our mind'.[81] Lucretius' Epicurean experiences this sublimity as a paradoxical combination of *divina voluptas atque horror*, an affect that, as we have seen, lies also at the heart of Burke's *Enquiry*. Kant uses precisely the same vocabulary:

> The astonishment bordering on terror, the horror and the awesome shudder, which grip the spectator in viewing mountain ranges towering to the heavens, deep ravines and the raging torrents in them, deeply shadowed wastelands inducing melancholy reflection, etc., is, in view of the safety in which he knows himself to be, not actual fear, but only an attempt to involve ourselves in it by means of the imagination, in order to feel the power of that very faculty, to combine the movement of the mind thereby aroused with its calmness, and so to be superior to nature within us, and thus also that outside us, insofar as it can have an influence on our feeling of well-being.[82]

For all its subsequent influence, the Kantian sublime remains deeply indebted to its predecessors.

Freud and the sublime turn: the logic of the sublime

Longinus, Lucretius, Burke and Kant each formulate the sublime differently and in response to varying objects, both textual and natural. Yet significant resemblances, both structural and thematic, can also be discerned between their theorisations. In particular, I want to draw attention to the unique experience of subjectivity that emerges from each, a paradoxical dynamic of rupture and recuperation in which the self is at once lost and exalted: as Porter puts it, the sublime promotes 'an actual destitution of subjective identity in order to allow a subject to regain his or her self in an altered way';[83] more simply, in Russell's paraphrase of *De sub.* I.4 (εἰς ἔκστασιν ἄγει τὰ ὑπερφυᾶ), 'whatever knocks the reader out is "sublime"'.[84] This dynamic is accorded particular importance within psychoanalytic approaches to the sublime. Freud's twin ideas of the Oedipal agon and the uncanny can be read as stories of subjectivity parallel to the experience of the sublime and, hence, provide a helpful means of bringing the sublime's underlying structure into focus. As Shaw observes: 'Just as, in Burke, the

---

[81] Kant (2003) 147.   [82] Kant (2003) 152.
[83] Porter (forthcoming).   [84] Russell (1965) xiii.

sublime is presented as a struggle between father and son ... so in Kant the conflict between reason and imagination ends with the establishment of a pact: the mind identifies with a higher authority, the faculty of reason, so that it may be delivered from its temptation to fade into sensual or numerical excess.'[85] It is the *Peri hupsous*, however, that has spurred the most important theorisations of sublimity as a Freudian struggle and to which I now again turn.

The seminal text is Neil Hertz's 1978 article, 'A Reading of Longinus', in which he identifies at the heart of sublime experience a transference of power: 'the movement of disintegration and figurative reconstitution' that constitutes 'the sublime turn'.[86] Sappho's Φαίνεταί μοι (discussed at *De sub.* 10.3) for instance, achieves its organic unity and energy through the spiritual dismemberment and near-death of the poem's subject: 'It is clear that Longinus admires the poem because when it becomes "like a living creature" and "finds its voice", it speaks of a moment of self-estrangement[,] in language that captures the *dis*organised quality of the experience.'[87] 'Sappho-as-victimised-body' becomes 'Sappho-as-poetic-force'.[88] Longinus' next example of true sublimity is taken from the *Iliad* and evidences a similar 'turn', focused on the particle ὑπέκ (*De sub.* 10.5):

ἐν δ' ἔπεσ', ὡς ὅτε κῦμα θοῇ ἐν νηῒ πέσῃσι
λάβρον ὑπαὶ νεφέων ἀνεμοτρεφές, ἡ δέ τε πᾶσα   625
ἄχνῃ ὑπεκρύφθη, ἀνέμοιο δὲ δεινὸς ἀήτης
ἱστίῳ ἐμβρέμεται, τρομέουσι δέ τε φρένα ναῦται
δειδιότες· τυτθὸν γὰρ ὑπὲκ θανάτοιο φέρονται.

He [Hector] fell on the host as a wave of the sea on a hurrying vessel,
rising up under the clouds, a boisterous son of the storm-wind.
The good ship is lost in the shroud of the foam, and the breath of the tempest
terribly roars in the sails; and in their heart tremble the sailors,
by the breadth of a hand swept out from under the jaws of destruction.

Hom. *Il.* 15.624–8

---

85 Shaw (2006) 85. On the Oedipal dimensions of the Burkeian sublime, see Paulson (1983) 68–70. Weiskel (1976) 93–4 analyses how the sublime of Kant and the Romantic poets 'recapitulates and thereby re-establishes the Oedipus complex'; cf. Eagleton (1990) 91–2; Haywood (2006) 34–5.
86 Hertz (1978/1985) 14.   87 Hertz (1978/1985) 5.   88 Hertz (1978/1985) 7.

56

As in the simile Homer's sailors 'turn away' from annihilation, from being 'under death' to being 'out-from-under death', so in the same movement the threatening might of the storm is transferred to Homer's poetry: 'by forcing into an abnormal union prepositions not usually compounded [Homer] has tortured his language into conformity with the impending disaster, magnificently figured the disaster by the compression of his language, and almost stamped on the diction the precise form of the danger: "swept out from under the jaws of destruction"' (καὶ μὴν τὰς προθέσεις ἀσυνθέτους οὔσας συναναγκάσας παρὰ φύσιν καὶ εἰς ἀλλήλας συμβιασάμενος τῷ μὲν συνεμπίπτοντι πάθει τὸ ἔπος ὁμοίως ἐβασάνισεν, τῇ δὲ τοῦ ἔπους συνθλίψει τὸ πάθος ἄκρως ἀπεπλάσατο καὶ μόνον οὐκ ἐνετύπωσεν τῇ λέξει τοῦ κινδύνου τὸ ἰδίωμα 'ὑπὲκ θανά-τοιο φέρονται', De sub. 10.6).[89] In each case, we are presented with a scenario that maps onto an Oedipal struggle between the ego and a threatening exterior force: the poetic description of the escape from near-death figures the poetic ego's own mastery over his subject matter, over the artistic 'death' of failed communication.[90]

In a 1982 article, 'Freud and the Sublime: A Catastrophe Theory of Creativity', Harold Bloom reinforced Hertz's psychoanalytic model, locating the sublime at the heart of Freud's thinking. Bloom reads Freud's essay on 'The Uncanny' (das Unheimliche)[91] as an exploration of the Longinian statement that, within the sublime, 'we are filled with joy and pride, as if we had ourselves produced the very thing we heard' (De sub. 7.2).[92] The uncanny object, like the object of the sublime, initiates a kind of mirror-reflex in us as perceiving subjects: it triggers the weird awareness that, although suddenly presented and external to us, this object denotes a familiar part of ourselves; it is new to us yet, oddly, also something we have already heard. In the terms of Bloom's theory of the 'anxiety of

---

[89] Hertz (1978/1985) 8 compares Wordsworth's dictum that the poet is 'weak, as is a breaking wave'. Cf. Hunter (2009) 134: 'The blast of storm winds corresponds . . . to the blasts of "sublimity" through which the great poet is inspired and with which he "blasts away" the senses of his hearers and readers.'

[90] Cf. Deguy (1993) 9–10.   [91] Freud (2003) 121–62.

[92] My attention was also drawn to the connections between the sublime and Freud's uncanny by Alessandro Schiesaro's paper, 'The Sublime in Motion', during the conference on 'The Classical Sublime' held at Cambridge, 14–15 March 2008.

influence', the Freudian uncanny, like the sublime, thus becomes a way of describing the experience of the Oedipal ephebe poet who (re)creates, or 'misreads', the authoritative, potentially over-whelming, utterance of his father-predecessor:[93] this utterance, Oedipally assimilated and reconstituted by the ephebe, becomes 'uncanny', or sublime, by virtue of its unstable, shifting status, both extrinsic and belonging to the successor-poet, prior to and co-existent with him, at once 'heard' and self-produced.

Freud's delineation of the psychological underpinnings of the sublime led Bloom to label the essay on 'The Uncanny' as 'the only major contribution that the 20th century has made to the aesthetic of the Sublime'.[94] That Freud does not actually mention the sub-lime in his essay is fuel for Bloom's argument. As one of Freud's repressed concerns in 'The Uncanny', the concept of the sublime, and the writers who engaged with it prior to Freud, inspire precisely that sublime anxiety of influence that 'The Uncanny' delineates. Accordingly, reference to the concept and its pre-Freudian pro-ponents is quietly avoided, yet on reading Freud's essay we are left with the strange sensation that we have encountered its ideas before. Appropriating, reworking and hence disavowing earlier theorists' engagements with the sublime, Freud's text thus mani-fests itself as an example of the sublime critical-artistic experience it is at pains (not) to discuss.[95]

The psychoanalytic account of the power-transfer at the centre of the sublime's structure accounts well for the sublime's unruli-ness and instability as a concept, its refusal to inhere in fixed objects, its 'intersubjectivity'.[96] Pope famously praised Longinus as 'himself that great Sublime he draws',[97] gesturing towards that

---

[93] Bloom (1982/1994) 173–4: 'reading is . . . a miswriting just as writing is a misreading. As literary history lengthens, all poetry necessarily becomes verse-criticism, just as all criticism becomes prose-poetry'; cf. Bloom (1973).

[94] Bloom (1982/1994) 182. Bloom also describes Freud as 'the last great theorist of that [i.e. sublime] mode' (ibid. 182). See further Arensberg (1986) 6–8.

[95] Not everyone has given assent to Bloom's 'misreading' of Freud's uncanny. Varsamopoulou (2002) 245, for instance, concludes that the uncanny 'can only ever be a mere parallel to the sublime'.

[96] Too (1998) 189–91, 199.

[97] Pope, 'An Essay on Criticism' (1711) 680. The *sententia* was also expressed by Boileau, but originally derives from a letter written by Stephanus de Castrobello and printed by Petra (1612): *quid enim praeter ipsam sublimitatem ipso Longino sublimius? . . . ipsum*

very transference that, as we have seen, glimmers through Longinus' quotations. In Longinus' quotation of Homer's description of Ajax's battle with Zeus (*De sub.* 9.11), for instance, the Greek hero

μαίνεται, ὡς ὅτ᾽ Ἄρης ἐγχέσπαλος ἢ ὀλοὸν πῦρ
οὔρεσι μαίνηται, βαθέης ἐν τάρφεσιν ὕλης,
ἀφλοισμὸς δὲ περὶ στόμα γίγνεται.

stormily raves, as the spear-wielding War-god, or Fire, the destroyer,
stormily raves on the hills in the deep-lying thickets of woodland;
fringed are his lips with the foam-froth.   Hom. *Il.* 15.605–7

'Raving', with its Bacchic connotations of both effeminacy and inspiration, implies a loss on Ajax's part of autonomous, bounded identity, yet it is through this same action that Ajax becomes 'like the spear-wielding War-god' Ares or 'Fire, the destroyer', the relationship emphasised by the application of the same verb to both Ajax and his *comparanda*, its position at the start of line 605 and as the second word of line 606 lending a powerful rhythmic unity to the lines and to Ajax's earthly and supernatural similes.[98] At this point, however, the 'power-transference' starts to shift direction, as Homer is himself inspired by the majesty of the raving Ajax and, in turn, 'blows along' his representation of Ajax's agon through the 'forcefulness' of his language (οὔριος συνεμπνεῖ τοῖς ἀγῶσιν, *De sub.* 9.11). In Longinus' estimation, Homer's description of Ajax becomes, additionally, a self-description: it is Homer who truly μαίνεται (like all great poets he is to be counted a demigod, ἰσόθεος, *De sub.* 35.2),[99] appropriating the power of his subject matter to his own poetry which hence becomes sublime.[100] But the chain of transference does not stop there. As Pope points out,

---

typum atque exemplar sublimis et grandis orationis expressissimum; see Russell (1964) xlii–xliii. Ovid expressed a similar view of Lucretius: *carmina sublimis tunc sunt peritura Lucreti / exitio terras cum dabit una dies* (*Am.* 1.15.23); cf. Statius, *Silv.* 2.7.76 (*docti furor arduus Lucreti*), Fronto, *Ep.* 1.2 (*sublimis Lucretius*).

[98] Inspiration is a leitmotif of Longinus' treatise: *De sub.* 8.4, 9.2, 13.2–4, 14, 15.1, 16.2, 32.4, 33.5; contrast *De sub.* 3.2–5, 32.7, and see Innes (1995a) 324. The effeminising implications of inspiration are strongly suggested by the metaphors of impregnation at *De sub.* 9.2 and 13.2; see Schiesaro (2003) 129. In *The Grounds of Criticism in Poetry* (1704) John Dennis holds that the sublime 'commits a pleasing rape upon the very soul of the listener': Kirwan (2005) 17.

[99] Cf. *De sub.* 13.2, 16.2, 33.5, 36.1.   [100] Segal (1987), esp. 207–12.

by framing Homer's words with his own commentary, by literally incorporating them into his own text, Longinus effectively seizes their sublimity for himself. Gibbon makes the same point about Longinus' earlier conflated quotations from Homer's Battle of the Gods (*Il.* 21.388, 20.61–5)[101] asserting that Longinus' apostrophe of this scene is as sublime as the battle itself.[102] The movements of rupture and recuperation that the Homeric passage traces, whereby Hades, trembling, leaps with a bellow from his throne for fear the earth may splinter asunder, reverberate beyond the excerpt, its sublimity breaking into and being in turn recuperated by Longinus' own discourse: 'You see, friend, how the earth is split to its foundations, hell itself laid bare, the whole universe sundered and turned upside down; and meanwhile everything, heaven and hell, mortal and immortal alike, shares in the conflict and danger of that battle' (ἐπιβλέπεις, ἑταῖρε, ὡς ἀναρρηγνυμένης μὲν ἐκ βάθρων γῆς, αὐτοῦ δὲ γυμνουμένου ταρτάρου, ἀνατροπὴν δὲ ὅλου καὶ διάστασιν τοῦ κόσμου λαμβάνοντος, πάνθ᾽ ἅμα, οὐρανὸς ᾅδης, τὰ θνητὰ τὰ ἀθάνατα, ἅμα τῇ τότε συμπολεμεῖ καὶ συγκινδυνεύει μάχῃ, *De sub.* 9.6).

Longinus himself emphasises this phase of the relay when emphasising how imitation (μίμησις) of the great writers of the past can lead to sublimity: 'From the natural genius of those old writers there flows into the hearts of their admirers as it were an emanation from those holy mouths' (οὕτως ἀπὸ τῆς τῶν ἀρχαίων μεγαλοφυΐας εἰς τὰς τῶν ζηλούντων ἐκείνους ψυχὰς ὡς ἀπὸ ἱερῶν στομίων ἀπόρροιαί τινες φέρονται, *De sub.* 13.2). Herodotus, Stesichorus, Archilochus and Plato are all cited for the way they appropriated Homer 'for [their] own use' (13.3) and so attained sublimity. Longinus might well have added himself to the list. Reminding us of Ajax's 'mania' during his combat with Zeus, he pictures the sublime effect of the father-poet on his successors in terms of inspiration and ensuing contest. Like the Pythia

---

[101] The conflation only heightens the sublimity of the Longinian text, demonstrating Longinus' Homeric ability to 'force' and 'compress' words into unexpected, 'abnormal' union (cf. *De sub.* 10.6). Through his conflated quotation of Homer, Longinus agonistically demonstrates his sublime ability to assimilate the father-poet's sublimity. To adopt Bloom's terminology, he is 'misreading' the *Iliad*.

[102] See Murray (2000) xlix.

standing over the 'rift in the earth' that exhales the divine vapour (ῥῆγμά... γῆς ἀναπνέον... ἀτμὸν ἔνθεον), writers are often 'carried away by the inspiration of another' (ἀλλοτρίῳ θεοφοροῦνται πνεύματι), losing themselves as they submit to the rupturing of their autonomous discourse, thereby becoming 'impregnated with the divine power' (ἐγκύμονα τῆς δαιμονίου, *De sub.* 13.2) and inspired to new heights of creativity, 'shar[ing] the enthusiasm of these others' grandeur' (τῷ ἑτέρων συνενθουσιῶσι μεγέθει, *De sub.* 13.2; cf. συμπολεμεῖ καὶ συγκινδυνεύει, *De sub.* 9.6 above, and συνεμπνεῖ, *De sub.* 9.11 above, both of Homer; and later, of Demosthenes, συναποκινδυνεύειν ὑπ᾿ ἀγωνίας τῷ λέγοντι συναναγκάσας, *De sub.* 22.4). This submission, however, is soon converted into agonistic rivalry: Plato's philosophical and artistic greatness was only achieved because he strove 'with heart and soul, to contest the prize with Homer, like a young antagonist with one who had already won his spurs (ὡς ἀνταγωνιστὴς νέος πρὸς ἤδη τεθαυμασμένον), perhaps in too keen emulation, longing as it were to break a lance, and yet always to good purpose' (*De sub.* 13.4).[103] Those occasions when Plato is successful then put him on a par with Homer and make him, in turn, a potential source for our own achievement of sublimity through the same process (i.e. τὸ συνενθουσιᾶν τῷ λέγοντι, *De sub.* 32.4):[104] 'We too, then, when we are working at some passage that demands sublimity of thought and expression, should do well to form in our hearts the question, "How might Homer have said this same thing, how would Plato or Demosthenes have made it sublime?" (πῶς ἂν εἰ τύχοι ταὐτὸ τοῦθ᾿ Ὅμηρος εἶπεν, πῶς δ᾿ ἂν Πλάτων ἢ Δημοσθένης ὕψωσαν)' (*De sub.* 14.1).

From textual imagery and narrative to the text's author to the author's readers and rivals: the double movement of rupture and recuperation that characterises the sublime power-transfer

[103] So Whitmarsh (2001) 59–62: Longinus offers a 'knowingly oscillatory presentation of mimesis as both a "natural" relationship of filiation and a confrontational struggle. In its subtle self-contradictions, *On the Sublime* enacts the manifold complexities of the imitative process. The act of allusion to the literature of the past simultaneously exalts it and seeks to neutralise its superiority' (p. 62).
[104] Innes (1995a) 324.

61

persistently shifts direction.[105] Hertz has shown how this instability determines the very structure of Longinus' treatise, as the interplay between text and quotation spills over into the play between consecutive quotations. Longinus' argument does not so much progress by logical as by associative steps, the slide between the standard critical distinctions of writer and subject matter, text and interpretation, author and reader mirroring the treatise's slide from literary fragment to literary fragment:[106] 'reading along,' as Hertz puts it, 'one has the sense of moving through a verbal medium increasingly rich in repetitions and glancing analogies, the thematic equivalent of slant rhymes'.[107]

And we might make a further Longinian move of our own here, for Hertz's comment could be applied to the whole tradition of speculation on the concept of the sublime. Between the theorisations of Longinus, Burke and Kant (and beyond, for example to the more recent formulations of Lyotard and the French poststructuralists)[108] patterns of repetition, conceptual echoes and structural analogies proliferate. At the same time, plotting the precise relation between these analogies is no straightforward task. How, for instance, does the sublime transform from a function of Lucretian atomism into its Longinian instantiation as an index of 'great writing' and then again into its eighteenth-century incarnation as a label for the potential affective qualities of particular natural landscapes or dangerous phenomena? (And how, to anticipate my next section momentarily, did it mutate again in the late twentieth century into a means of thinking a post-modern ethics of 'difference'?) A psychoanalytic, 'Oedipal' reading of the sublime,

---

[105] Russell (1981a) 82 recognises this dynamic in simplified form but does not develop the observation: 'So we have two stages: the excitation of the writer's mind by emotion, and the consequent excitation of the reader's, which is the purpose of the whole procedure' (cf. p. 110). To understand the transference of the sublime as operative only across these two stages is to deny its radically expansive potential.

[106] Hertz (1978/1985) 14 suggestively compares Longinus' aesthetic of the quotation with that of Walter Benjamin. Cf. Stewart (1984) 19 on practices of quotation, 133–50 on the appeal of the souvenir, and on the 'nostalgia' that governs both.

[107] Hertz (1978/1985) 4. On the turns and elisions of Longinus' discourse, see also Walsh (1988), esp. 254–7: for Longinus, 'likeness usually invites discrimination and (conversely) divisions frequently become blurred' (p. 255); the same can be said of Lucan, see Chapter 4. Cf. Russell (1981b); Deguy (1993) 11–12, 14–16; Innes (1995c/2006); Too (1998) 195–9; Whitmarsh (2001) 61, 64.

[108] See the essays in Librett (1993).

which understands its 'logic' in terms of a transfer of power, and which situates this transfer at the heart of the creative agon, offers one possible explanation. Each theorist, as the newest link in the discursive chain, finds himself in thrall to his father-predecessor(s), his analysis inescapably coloured by prior pronouncements, yet through this very thraldom each succeeds in 'turning' the sublime so that it speaks to his own distinct concerns and aims. This dynamic, moreover, is inscribed right at the beginning of the extant tradition. The *Peri hupsous* opens with a reference to, and repeatedly positions itself against, Caecilius of Caleacte's treatise on the sublime:[109] the foundational theorisation of the sublime, the father-text in relation to which subsequent analyses obsessively claim or disavow allegiance, turns out – as soon as we begin reading it – to be simply another link in the concept's transferential chain.[110] Further: Longinus' identification of the motor behind this process, his paradoxical construction of μίμησις, imitation, as inspiration, may itself be understood as a sublime reconfiguration of what imitation means.[111] Again, Longinus' text emerges as a performance of the sublimity to which it insistently points.

Liberation and tyranny: the politics of the sublime

The drama of subjectivity brought out by a psychoanalytic reading of the sublime prompts consideration of the sublime's ethical and political dimensions. As Paul Fry puts it, referring in particular to Longinus, the sublime 'covertly transfers power from the oppressor to the oppressed' yet it is also a 'rule of "transport" in the sublime . . . that to have power one must be enslaved, possessed by another'.[112] I now turn to explore this ambivalence in more detail.[113]

[109] *De sub.* 1.1, 4.2, 8.1–4, 31.1, 32.1, 32.8.
[110] Porter (2007) 174–6 and (2010) 158–67, 453–523 offers a refreshingly wide view of Longinus' possible antecedents; also Porter (forthcoming): 'Longinus set out to hijack a tradition, not to encapsulate it.' Cf. Conte (1996) 43 n. 8; Innes (2002).
[111] On the tendentiousness of Longinus' treatment of imitation, see Innes (1985) 647. Cf. Russell (1981a) 99–113.
[112] Fry (1983) 64–5.
[113] The ambiguities of the sublime reach into other discourses too, most notably epistemology. Sedley (2005) for instance, with reference to Montaigne and Milton, argues

Longinus asserts that 'the true sublime naturally elevates us' (*De sub.* 7.2), that it is 'the echo of a noble mind' (*De sub.* 9.2); contrariwise, 'it is impossible that those whose thoughts and habits all their lives long are petty and servile should produce anything wonderful, worthy of immortal life' (*De sub.* 9.3).[114] Kant follows suit, arguing that sublime objects 'elevate the strength of our soul above its usual level'.[115] Lyotard has recently given these morally beneficial constructions of sublimity fresh impetus by claiming the sublime in art as a crucial site of anti-capitalist resistance.[116] His understanding of the sublime is self-confessedly Kantian: the sublime sentiment, he writes, 'takes place . . . when the imagination fails to present an object which might, if only in principle, come to match a concept'.[117] His first two examples, moreover, as they gesture respectively towards cosmology and atomism, remind us of both Longinus (e.g. *De sub.* 35.3) and Lucretius: 'We have the Idea of the world (the totality of what is), but we do not have the capacity to show an example of it. We have the Idea of the simple (that which cannot be broken down, decomposed), but we cannot illustrate it with a sensible object which would be a "case" of it.'[118] What might this mean when translated into artistic terms? 'To make visible that there is something which can be conceived and which can neither be seen nor made visible: this is what is at stake in modern painting.'[119] Lyotard elaborates: the sublime artwork 'will of course "present" something though negatively; it will therefore avoid figuration or representation . . . it will enable

---

for the sublime as a spur towards, and consequence of, philosophical scepticism. Conte (1994), by contrast, notes that for Lucretius the sublime represents a path to true knowledge: 'The rhetoric of marvel has been replaced by a rhetoric of necessity (*necesse est* – [an] eminent formula of Lucretian argument), which in fact is the contrary of the miraculous; and this inevitably produces a sense of exaltation on the part of the individual, who becomes conscious of his own intellectual greatness' (p. 21); cf. Ankersmit (2005) 338 on how 'the logical space enabling the epistemologist to discuss experience and the conditions of the possibility of experience is . . . identical with the one where the experience of . . . the sublime may manifest [itself]'.

[114] The same thought animates the discussion of the effects of political and moral freedom with which the *Peri hupsous* closes (*De sub.* 44): see Segal (1959); Fantham (1978); Whitmarsh (2001) 67–71. Longinus frames sublimity in moral terms throughout his treatise: Russell (1981a) 8, 82. Cf. Too (1998) 5–12, 202–12 on the discourse of sublimity, and of ancient literary criticism in general, as a tool of social distinction.

[115] Kant (2003) 144.   [116] See e.g. Lyotard (1984) 77–82, (1991) 104–7.

[117] Lyotard (1984) 78. For a full exposition of his reading of Kant, see Lyotard (1994).

[118] Lyotard (1984) 78.   [119] Ibid.

us to see only by making it impossible to see; it will please only by causing pain'.[120] Lyotard adduces, by way of example, the colour-bleached 'squares' of the Russian Suprematist painter Malevich; his later writings display a fascination with the huge, abstract, 'zipped' canvases of Barnett Newman.[121] (We will take up these ideas again in Chapter 2.)

Lyotard's interest in the sublime is avowedly political in intent.[122] His reading of Kant functions as a counterweight to what he regards as the deceptions conjured by universalising metanar-ratives and myths of transcendent subjectivity. As such, paradox-ically, it is an interpretation that dismantles the supremacy of the rational which the Kantian sublime asserts. In doing so, however, it orients us towards the redemptive potential of the sublime, offering a 'theorisation of the particular' that upholds the claims of 'inex-orable alterity', alerting us to what might lie beyond established discursive structures.[123] As Christine Battersby puts it, the Lyotar-dian sublime constitutes a means of 'opening up the differences within Western modernity that are covered over by notions of a universal good or the culture of consensus'.[124] In its stress on the claims of the individual and the specific against the absolute and the totalising, it provides 'a useful way to think about how one both registers multicultural differences and multiple narratives, whilst also refusing any move that suggests that we are stuck with moral relativism and are bereft of principles that could provide the basis of condemning mass murder'.[125] Post-modern attacks on humanist universalisms are regularly taxed with ethical passivity: if all ide-ological positions are simply constructions, it is alleged, we have no criteria for judging between them; 'difference', the watchword of the well-meaning, morphs into a sinister homogeneity. While retaining commitment to pluralism and 'the other', the Lyotardian

---

[120] Ibid. Cf. Adorno (1984) 280, cited by Nancy (1993b) 26: 'The Kantian theory of the sublime describes . . . an art which shudders within itself: it suspends itself in the name of the content of truth deprived of appearance, but without, qua art, renouncing its character as appearance.'

[121] See the essays 'Newman: The Instant' and 'The Sublime and the Avant-Garde' in Lyotard (1991) 78–88 and 89–107.

[122] For his reading of Kant's own 'interest' in the sublime, see Lyotard (1993).

[123] See Hitchcock (2008) 178.   [124] Battersby (2007) 40.

[125] Battersby (2007) 41.

sublime sidesteps this trap. In its stubborn refusal to accept any ultimate reconciliation between concept and object, it pits itself firmly against all totalitarian or otherwise repressive structures that would attempt to close down the operations of difference, to identify concept and object and hence deny the claims of those whose position exceeds discursive constraints.[126] As Jacques Rancière summarises, the Kantian sublime is 'an encounter with the unpresentable that cripples all thought'; by making art a witness to this encounter Lyotard also makes art 'a witness for the prosecution against the arrogance of the grand aesthetico-political endeavour to have "thought" become "world"'.[127]

Lyotard's case is, specifically, against what he calls the Hegelian desire for a 'reconciliation between language games', a desire he labels 'transcendental illusion'.[128] This way, moreover, leads to terror:

The nineteenth and twentieth centuries have given us as much terror as we can take. We have paid a high enough price for the nostalgia of the whole and the one, for the reconciliation of the concept and the sensible, of the transparent and the communicable experience. Under the general demand for slackening and for appeasement, we can hear the mutterings of the desire for a return of terror, for the realisation of the fantasy to seize reality.[129]

Lyotard died in 1998 and so did not witness the events of 11 September 2001. The prophetic force of his words, however, indirectly alerts us to a very different way of interpreting the sublime, for the attack on the World Trade Center has itself been understood as a sublime event.[130] While Lyotard's association of terror with totalisation would seem to exclude the sentiment of the sublime, it was precisely this sentiment that the composer Karlheinz Stockhausen, speaking shortly after the attack, invoked when he reportedly described the event as 'the greatest work of art imaginable for the whole cosmos'. For Stockhausen, the exploding

---

[126] Cf. Ray (2005) 13 (and *passim*) on Adorno's concept of 'truth' as a form of Marxist sublimity: 'The "truth" of culture . . . is its desire to reach beyond the world "that is the case". Truth can never be merely a positivist correspondence between claims or descriptions and a factual world. For that world itself, the social given, remains accountable to the virtual utopia that never ceases to haunt and indict it from within.'

[127] Rancière (2004) 10.   [128] Lyotard (1984) 81.   [129] Lyotard (1984) 82.

[130] See e.g. Weigel (2001); Sharpe (2002); Žižek (2002); Shaw (2006) 2, 128–9, 140; Foster (2011).

towers induced a 'jump out of security, out of the everyday, out of life':

You have people who are that focused on a performance and then 5,000 people are dispatched to the afterlife, in a single moment. I couldn't do that. By comparison, we composers are nothing ... Artists, too, sometimes try to go beyond the limits of what is feasible and conceivable, so that we wake up, so that we open ourselves to another world.[131]

Battersby initially acknowledges this face of sublimity[132] but swiftly sidelines it in favour of Lyotard's post-modern Kantianism. I do not think we can avoid it so easily. Stockhausen's aestheticisation of the 9/11 attacks received widespread condemnation in the media. It is, however, this very moral questionability by which the sublime is marked.

Burke's emphasis on terror provides a theoretical correlate to Stockhausen's response: in the *Enquiry*'s emphasis on the subject's distance from danger (i.e. his status as a *spectator*) and on the peculiar pleasure to which this danger gives rise we can detect the same aestheticising tendency for which Stockhausen was attacked. As Burke points out, Longinus is also alive to this side of the sublime: 'what Longinus has observed of that glorying and sense of inward greatness, that always fills the reader of such passages in poets and orators as are sublime', stems from that same 'swelling' that arises in us 'when without danger we are conversant with terrible objects' (cf. *De sub.* 7.2).[133] Burke and Longinus remind us, as does Kant, that the sublime is a subjective state, a mental disposition, produced by encounters with particular objects. In contradistinction to Kant (and Lyotard), however, Longinus and Burke recognise that this elevated state can be triggered by morally problematic objects. Indeed, it possesses no determinate relationship with morality at all. As one of Burke's sources of sublime terror is 'a power in some way superior' to ourselves,[134] so Longinus emphasises the importance of 'power and irresistible might' (βίαν ἄμαχον, *De sub.* 1.4) in affecting the reader. It is for this reason that Demosthenes is one of Longinus' heroes: 'with his violence, yes, and

---

[131] From the transcript of a press conference given in Hamburg by Stockhausen on 16 September 2001: see www.stockhausen.org/hamburg.pdf p. 77 (last accessed 22/9/2012); see Battersby (2007) 21–2 for the English translation.
[132] Battersby (2007) 21–38.   [133] Burke (1990) 46–7.   [134] Burke (1990) 60.

his speed, his force, his terrific power of rhetoric, [he] burns, as it were, and scatters everything before him, and may therefore be compared to a flash of lightning or thunderbolt' (διὰ τὸ μετὰ βίας ἕκαστα ἔτι δὲ τάχους ῥώμης δεινότητος οἷον καίειν τε ἅμα καὶ διαρπάζειν σκηπτῷ τινι παρεικάζοιτ᾽ ἂν ἢ κηραυνῷ, *De sub.* 12.4, cf. the panic, φόβος, and pleasurable astonishment that Demosthenes' hyperbata cause in the listener, *De sub.* 22.4). Here is the orator become explosive pyrotechnician: far from condemning the violence of his rhetorical onslaught, his audience positively delight in its fearful, spectacular power. This gives an unsettling colour to Longinus' subsequent Lucretian statement that 'the whole universe is not enough to satisfy the speculative intelligence of human thought; our ideas often pass beyond the limits that confine us' (*De sub.* 35.3). As in Stockhausen's view of the flaming World Trade Center – an event that goes 'beyond the limits of what is feasible and conceivable, so that we wake up, so that we open ourselves to another world' – violence combines with the transgression of established limits to edge us towards transcendence.

Burke's identification of sublimity with unlimited power and the terror that such power can produce came back to haunt him as, wrestling with the spectacle of the French Revolution, he realised the full political implications of his advocacy of the sublime. Where Burke's politics were staunchly conservative, the firebrand aesthetic of the sublime seemed to align him with the Jacobin proponents of 'The Terror'. This real-life manifestation of Burke's sublime laid bare its latent affinities with tyranny, horror and extreme violence. In his *Reflections on the Revolution in France* (1790) the sublime is barely mentioned; it is not the distance of the sublime that Burke now seeks but distance from the concept of the sublime itself.[135]

Yet it is at this point that the ethico-political dimensions of the sublime begin again to destabilise. As well as 9/11 and the French Revolution, the category of the sublime has also been used in critical discourse to frame and negotiate the twin, perhaps defining, atrocities of the twentieth century: the Holocaust and the obliteration of Hiroshima by the first atomic bomb. We have seen

---

[135] See further Paulson (1980); Furniss (1993) 134–7; Shaw (2006) 63–71.

how, according to the Lucretian–Kantian schema, atomic physics may be regarded as the source of a positive sublimity, in which we achieve renewed awareness of the rational or 'supersensible' powers of the human mind and, hence, of human dignity and greatness. But what happens when, through these same rational human faculties, atomic force is harnessed to overtly destructive military ends, when terror ousts enlightenment? Gene Ray, in his recent analysis of the twentieth-century sublime, *Terror and the Sublime in Art and Critical Theory from Auschwitz to Hiroshima to September 11* (2005), advances two possible responses. Discussing the famous wristwatch whose hands remain frozen at 8:15:38 on 6 August 1945, the precise moment of the Hiroshima blast, he argues that its image may produce 'an active passivity that no longer resists the most extreme violence, but actually savours it as the mark of exceptionalism'.[136] This is precisely the reader-response, exemplified for Ray by the use of the image in a textbook glorifying US nuclearism, to which Stockhausen succumbed after 9/11 and which Burke belatedly registered when writing the *Reflections*.[137] But Ray also limns another possible reaction to this sublimity, very different in its effects, though its structure is analogous. In this alternative case, the traumatic violence of Hiroshima becomes sublime by instigating in us 'a permanent, ghastly latency, compounded by the anguish of shame'.[138] As in the former scenario, the sublimely terrifying, traumatic event overwhelms us but, as it does so, instead of producing assent and identification, it gives rise to a movement of resistance and retaliation. Here, then, is a model that confronts the sublime's co-implication with terror and violence yet which manages to recuperate this involvement for positive ethical ends.

Reading deconstructively, Ray detects the traces of this model, what we might call the 'traumatic sublime', in Kant's theorisation of sublimity. In 1755 a severe earthquake struck Lisbon, sending metaphorical shockwaves around Europe. Although this event is

---

[136] Ray (2005) 97.
[137] On the American 'nuclear sublime', see further Wilson (1991) 228–66.
[138] Ray (2005) 5. Cf. Roth (1995) 201–11 on Alain Resnais' film *Hiroshima mon amour* (1959) and on how the traumatic past can resist representation and yet 'pressure our capacity to act in the present' (p. 210).

not mentioned in Kant's third *Critique*, Ray argues that its terrifying impact provides the unacknowledged inspiration for the 'agitation' of the mind that Kant's natural sublime provokes.[139] Indeed, it is precisely the absence of reference to the earthquake that suggests it is the truly sublime event behind Kant's theorisation: negative presentation is, after all, as Lyotard points out, the only form of presentation that the Kantian sublime truly admits. While, therefore, Kant intends the sublime to work ideologically to reinforce metaphysical optimism, its inherently rupturing, excessive properties – as evidenced by the Lisbon earthquake, the absent presence in his text – militate against this. Despite this crack in the structure of the Kantian sublime, however, Ray understands this metaphysically pessimistic sublime as a fundamentally twentieth-century development. The stubborn welling of resistance, the sublime experience of atrocity as, at best, a protreptic towards 'mourning' and social transformation, is what we now, after 1945, in the post-Holocaust nuclear age, are left with in place of Kantian exaltation.

A similar analytical operation, however, can be performed on Burke's pre-Kantian sublime. Burke's theory, as he himself came to see, can be read as an endorsement of terror and political violence. Yet it also prepares the ground for the resurgence of those very subjects that such violence would seek to oppress. As Luke Gibbons has argued, the sublime here intersects with discourses about colonialism: 'much of Burke's abiding concerns with colonial aggression ... are bound up with his acute awareness of the capacity of the servant to rise up against intolerable abuses of state power'.[140] Where in the experience of the natural sublime the subject feels some of nature's terrible might accrue to himself, in the 'colonial sublime' the subject, analogously, finds in the very power of his oppressor the inspiration to jolt himself into action.[141] The 'theatrics of terror',[142] far from providing their audience with guilty, Stockhausian aesthetic pleasure, or

---

[139] Ray (2005) 26–30. [140] Gibbons (2003) 3.
[141] So also Haywood (2006) 5 on how political texts of the Romantic period explore 'spectacular violence [as] a manifestation of abusive power rebounding on itself'.
[142] I borrow this phrase from Iain Boal's paper, 'The Sublime and the Politics of Terror', delivered at the Tate Britain symposium on 'The Sublime Now', 19–20 October 2007.

numbing them into submission and identification, on this interpretation galvanise a powerful retaliatory response.

In different ways, then, from its first systematic formulation to its most recent and radical theorisations, the sublime, on the one hand, has promised to cast off our existential shackles and baptise us anew. It offers to transfigure limited, blinkered mortality into a supra-mortal largeness, unfettered and dynamic. Yet, on the other hand, the sublime has also been understood, often simultaneously and by the same writer, as a function of, and encouragement towards, tyranny, violent aggression and totalitarianism. As Ban Wang puts it, analysing the role of the sublime in twentieth-century Communist China, 'the aesthetic offers emancipatory alternatives to an oppressive political structure' yet, at the same time, it can be deployed by the state 'to anchor power and laws all the more securely in the sensibilities of its subjects'.[143] The sublime is intrinsically 'double-edged', displaying the potential 'to liberate or to oppress'.[144] More than this, for these twin ethico-political constructions of sublimity are neither as distinct nor as stable as Wang's dichotomy suggests: they constantly threaten to collapse into each other, always ready to overstep their respective margins.

[143] Wang (1997) 8. Cf. Too (1998) 216.   [144] Wang (1997) 11–12.

CHAPTER 2

PRESENTATION, THE SUBLIME
AND THE *BELLUM CIVILE*

Introduction

The *Bellum civile*, with its ferocious anti-hero Caesar and its narrator's repeated laments for Rome's lost *libertas*, offers an extended
and highly instructive examination of the sublime's political and
ethical duality. Where, as we have seen, the sublime is typically viewed in association with *either* freedom *or* tyranny, Lucan
explores its connections with both. In order, however, to understand the implications for both Lucan and us as readers of the
particular ways in which the *Bellum civile* configures the sublime
and the political, we need first to describe the current of sublimity
in which the *Bellum civile* declares itself to participate. Drawing upon our previous examination of the logic of the sublime,
the present chapter models this sublime movement as a form of
transference: Lucan presents his subject of civil war as something
sublime, beyond imagining; this sublimity of theme directs us to
consider how the poem presents itself, in its very linguistic substance, as a sublime thing and how in turn it projects this sublimity
onto us as readers; completing the process, mirroring and anticipating the projected experience of the reader, is the sublimity
claimed by the poem's narrator in response to his overwhelming
subject, metapoetically represented in the figures of the Bacchic
matrona, the Pythian priestess Phemonoe and the witch Erictho.
This transferential current, once established, provides a frame for
the discussion in the following chapters of Caesar and of Pompey. Lucan's presentation of each emerges as a particular means
of ethically modelling the sublime experience that is claimed as
both the source and primary effect of the poem. As such, expanding upon the roles of Erictho, Phemonoe and the *matrona*, both
figures become potential images for both poet and reader.

Examination of the *Bellum civile*'s own sublimity as a poem also prompts reflection upon the artistic challenge posed by the sublime. As Lyotard and others have argued, taking their cue from Kant, the sublime raises the question of how to present what exceeds presentation.[1] Indeed, this has often been considered its fundamental problematic: sublimity, after all, precisely denotes that situation in which the imagination is beggared and words fail. Underlying this chapter's exploration of the *Bellum civile*'s participation in the sublime, therefore, lies the vexed issue of how sublimity can be articulated in the first place and what it might mean to succeed in doing so. When we find ourselves unable to match concept to object, when experience leaves us speechless, how do we set about communicating our failure? The *Bellum civile* offers one attempt at an answer.

discors machina: Lucan's sublime subject

For Lucan's narrator, Rome's civil war marks the end of history, the end of time – literally the end of the world. As the armies engage at the climactic battle of Pharsalus he cries, 'These sword-hands will achieve things that no future age can make good [nor humankind repair in all the years], though it be free from warfare' (*hae facient dextrae quidquid non expleat aetas / [ulla nec humanum reparet genus omnibus annis]/ ut vacet a ferro*, 7.387–389); once the fighting is done he despairingly declares, 'for all the world's eternity we are prostrated' (*in totum mundi prosternimur aevum*, 7.640). The idea that Rome's, and hence the world's, 'final hour' has come is introduced right at the start of the poem:

> fert animus causas tantarum expromere rerum,
> inmensumque aperitur opus, quid in arma furentem
> inpulerit populum, quid pacem excusserit orbi.
> invida fatorum series summisque negatum   70
> stare diu nimioque graves sub pondere lapsus
> nec se Roma ferens. sic, cum conpage soluta
> saecula tot mundi suprema coegerit hora

---

[1] Lyotard (1984) 78 and (1991) 101–4, 124–8. Cf. Derrida (1987) 131–4; Žižek (1989) 201–7; Lacoue-Labarthe (1993) 74, 80–1, 86; Nancy (1993b) 27–43.

antiquum repetens iterum chaos, [omnia mixtis
sidera sideribus concurrent,] ignea pontum   75
astra petent, tellus extendere litora nolet
excutietque fretum, fratri contraria Phoebe
ibit et obliquum bigas agitare per orbem
indignata diem poscet sibi, totaque discors
machina divolsi turbabit foedera mundi.   80
in se magna ruunt: laetis hunc numina rebus
crescendi posuere modum.

My spirit leads me to reveal the causes of such great events,
and an immense task is opened up – to tell what drove
a maddened people to war, to tell what cast out peace from the world.
It was the envious chain of destiny, impossibility of the very high
standing long, huge collapses under too much weight,
Rome's inability to bear herself. So, when the final hour
brings to an end the long ages of the universe, its structure dissolved,
reverting to primeval chaos, then fiery stars will plunge
into the sea, the earth will be unwilling to stretch flat her shores
and will shake the water off, Phoebe will confront
her brother and for herself demand the day, resentful
of driving her chariot along its slanting orbit, and the whole
discordant mechanism of universe torn apart will disrupt its own laws.
Mighty structures collapse on to themselves: for prosperity the powers
have set this limit to growth.   1.67–82[2]

With this vision of apocalypse or final conflagration, what the Stoics termed *ekpyrosis*,[3] Lucan here claims his poem's theme, and by
implication his poem itself, as something truly awesome, terrifyingly spectacular, sublime. In Kantian terms, Lucan's apocalypse
is sublime both mathematically (it is the entire cosmos that will
be engulfed) and dynamically (the cataclysm's force will cause the
stars to hurtle into the waves and the earth to shake off the sea; 'the

[2] On this passage see in particular the compelling observations of Johnson (1987) 13–
18, arguing for the central role of the *discors machina* in Lucan's poem, although it is
curious that on p. 12 he denies Lucan's sublimity. Compare Martindale (2005) 231–2,
who comments that 'Lucan always writes well about the end of things' and perceives in
his poetry 'a kind of maimed sublimity'. See also Cheney (2009) 46 on the sublimity of
Marlowe's translation of these lines.
[3] Lapidge (1979/2010) examines the relations between Stoicism and 'Lucan's imagery
of cosmic dissolution'; see especially pp. 309–12 on *Lucan* 1.67–82. For more general
discussion of the Stoic dimensions of the *Bellum civile*, typically centred on the figure
of Cato, see e.g. Marti (1945); George (1991); D'Alessandro Behr (2007), esp. 87–112;
Roche (2009) 30–6.

whole / discordant mechanism of universe torn apart will disrupt its own laws', the juxtaposition of *divolsi turbabit* bringing home this upheaval's power).

By way of explanation for both cataclysm and Rome's civil war, we are told that the powers above have imposed a limit (*modum*) on the prosperity of all things (82). Yet in effecting this *modus* the cataclysm itself – and by implication the civil war – bursts all established bounds; and in so doing it also exceeds our imaginative powers, removing previously known constants from the world, forcing our minds beyond the limits of the conceivable.[4] Longinus, we remember, observes that 'the whole universe is not enough to satisfy the speculative intelligence of human thought; our ideas often pass beyond the limits that confine us' (*De sub.* 35.3). Lucan dramatises the idea: in thinking beyond the conceivable, he and hence we as readers are drawn literally to envisage the end of the world.

A comparable image occurs at the end of the *De rerum natura*'s first book, as Lucretius thrusts the apocalyptic implications of the mind's sublime flight beyond the *moenia mundi* (1.73, 3.16) startlingly into view: if the theory is true that air and fire have a natural tendency to move upwards, there is a danger

> ne volucri ritu flammarum moenia mundi
> diffugiant subito magnum per inane soluta
> et ne cetera consimili ratione sequantur,
> neve ruant caeli tonitralia templa superne,　　　　　1105
> terraque se pedibus raptim subducat et omnis
> inter permixtas rerum caelique ruinas
> corpora solventes abeat per inane profundum,
> temporis ut puncto nil extet reliquiarum
> desertum praeter spatium et primordia caeca.　　　　　1110

> lest the walls of the world suddenly be dissolved and flee apart
> after the fashion of flying flames through the void,
> and the rest follow in like manner,
> the thundering regions of the sky rush upwards,
> the earth swiftly slip from under our feet,
> and amidst the commingled ruin of sky and all things,

---

[4] So Conte (1966/2010) 57 of *Lucan* 1.8 (*quis furor, o cives, quae tanta licentia ferri?*): 'the horror of the inconceivable'.

letting their elements go free, utterly depart through the empty profound,
so that in one moment of time not a wrack be left behind
except desert space and invisible elements.   Lucr. I.1102–105[5]

But, layering the ironies, Lucan goes beyond Lucretius. Where in
the *De rerum natura* apocalypse is posited as the logical consequence of an erroneous scientific theory and therefore remains in
the realm of the counterfactual, in the *Bellum civile* it is framed
as a comparison (*sic...*), mapping what is unimaginable and in
the future onto an event that for the poet is all too imaginable,
was in fact inevitable (*inuida fatorum series*; *in se magna ruunt*) –
indeed has already happened. This presentation of Rome's civil war
as boundary-confounding, unpresentable apocalypse is a paradox
whose implications are explored throughout the rest of the poem:
having at the outset established his theme of civil war as, like
the apocalypse, an event beyond presentation, Lucan is then faced
with the question of how civil war *can* be presented.

Before turning to consider Lucan's responses to this conundrum,
I want to note the status of *discordia* – the driving principle behind
Lucan's *discors machina* (1.79–80) and accordingly of its analogue (or consequence), civil war – as an inherently sublime thing.
Longinus considers Homer's personification of Eris ('Discord',
Il. 4.440–5) sublime, the expanse between her head and feet mea-
suring 'the distance (τὸ... διάστημα) between earth and heaven'
(*De sub.* 9.4): Eris' sublimity derives simultaneously from her
vast size and from Homer's evaluation of this size in terms of a
gap, a void – empty space. As Porter points out, these same sublime features motivate Longinus' exclamations in the immediately
following sections of the *Peri hupsous* upon a whole series of
Homeric passages:[6] heaven's mighty horses (*Il.* 5.770–2), whose
leap, stretching as far as a man can see across the ocean to the
horizon, Homer must measure with a 'cosmic interval' (κοσμικῷ

---

[5] On this passage, see Martindale (2005) 190–1. Lucretius' picture of apocalypse is introduced as a refutation of the theory of the centrifugal force of fire; the reference to those
same *moenia mundi* that Epicurus surmounted (1.1102, cf. 1.73, 3.16), however, and the
visual power of Lucretius' language, suggest that the passage also reveals a metaphorical,
ethical truth about Lucretian atomism and its consequences.

[6] See Porter (2010) 512–13; for further instances of the sublime in the *Iliad*, see
ibid. 476–9.

διαστήματι) on account of its supreme grandeur (τὴν ὑπερβολὴν τοῦ μεγέθους, *De sub.* 9.5); Poseidon's approach through the sea (*Il.* 13.18, 20.60, 13.19, 13.27–9), at which all the earth trembles and the sea divides (διΐστατο, *De sub.* 9.8); and Homer's marvellous (ὑπερφυᾶ) Battle of the Gods, where, as in the Lucanian apocalypse, we see 'the whole universe sundered and turned upside down' (ἀνατροπὴν δὲ ὅλου καὶ διάστασιν τοῦ κόσμου λαμβάνοντος, *De sub.* 9.6):

ἀμφὶ δὲ σάλπιγξεν μέγας οὐρανὸς Οὔλυμπός τε.	21.388
ἔδδεισεν δ' ὑπένερθεν ἄναξ ἐνέρων Ἀϊδωνεύς,	20.61
δείσας δ' ἐκ θρόνου ἆλτο καὶ ἴαχε, μή οἱ ἔπειτα	
γαῖαν ἀναρρήξειε Ποσειδάων ἐνοσίχθων,	
οἰκία δὲ θνητοῖσι καὶ ἀθανάτοισι φανείη,	
σμερδαλέ εὐρώεντα, τά τε στυγέουσι θεοί περ.	20.65

Blared round about like a trumpet the firmament vast and Olympus;
shuddering down in the depths, the king of the dead, Aïdoneus,
sprang from his throne with a shuddering cry, for fear the earthshaker, Poseidon,
might soon splinter asunder the earth, and his mansions lie open,
clear to the eyes of immortals and mortals alike all uncovered,
grim and dreary and dank, which the very gods see with abhorrence.

Hom. *Il.* 21.388, 20.61–5

It is not, then, the mere fact that Longinus considers Eris a sublime thing that impacts upon our response to Lucanian *discordia* but that, for Longinus, Eris' sublimity is analogous to that of a rupture in the cosmos (which in the third of these Homeric examples is itself the product of divine discord). This series of Longinian passages, in other words, is guided by the same associative principles of scale and vacuity as underpin Lucan's comparison of civil war and apocalypse.

Moreover, in his comment on Homer's divine horses, Longinus alerts us to the tension within all attempts to present such sublimity. 'So supreme is the grandeur of [Homer's comparison], one might well say that if the horses of heaven take two consecutive strides there will then be no place found for them in the world' (τίς οὖν οὐκ ἂν εἰκότως διὰ τὴν ὑπερβολὴν τοῦ μεγέθους ἐπιφθέγξαιτο, ὅτι ἂν δὶς ἑξῆς ὀφορμήσωσιν οἱ τῶν θεῶν ἵπποι, οὐκέθ' εὑρήσουσιν ἐν κόσμῳ τόπον; *De sub.* 9.5). Casting our minds forward to his later observation that 'the whole universe is not enough to satisfy

77

the speculative intelligence of human thought' (*De sub.* 35.3), Longinus here allows us to read the leap of Homer's divine horses as an image for the mind's vaulting potential. But the image is one that, like (the image of) the universe at its end, collapses in upon itself. Homer's horses, and our minds, need take only two strides to find themselves without a place in this world. As Lucan's apocalypse, by bringing the limits of the conceivable into question, ironically works to deconstruct the possibility of the civil war's presentation, so Longinus turns the Homeric comparison between heaven's horses and a man's gaze into an allegory of the problem of presenting the non-presentable – and, from the associative thread of quotations in *De sub.* 9, we infer that Homer's Eris, precisely because of her sublime dimensions, is caught in the same bind.

Burke picks up in his *Enquiry* on Longinus' appreciation of Eris' sublimity. He lists 'judicious obscurity' as second only to and an adjunct of the sublime's primary motor, 'terror': 'to make any thing very terrible, obscurity seems in general to be necessary',[7] for

hardly any thing can strike the mind with its greatness, which does not make some sort of approach towards infinity; which nothing can do whilst we are able to perceive its bounds; but to see an object distinctly, and to perceive its bounds, is one and the same thing. A clear idea is therefore another name for a little idea.[8]

According to Burke, literary personifications convey such sublime obscurity especially effectively because they give vivid, tangible form to abstract, non-material and therefore boundless things: 'In all these subjects poetry is very happy. Its apparitions, its chimeras, its harpies, its allegorical figures, are grand and affecting.'[9] Burke's examples include Milton's personification of Death (*Paradise Lost* 2.666–73), an image full of 'gloomy pomp' in which 'all is dark, uncertain, confused, terrible, and sublime to the last degree',[10] as well as Lucretius' *Religio*,[11] Virgil's *Fama* – and, following Longinus, Homer's Eris.[12] As they 'approach towards infinity', thereby preventing us from perceiving their 'bounds', all are presentations of things that (in their terribleness) defy presentation. The 'obscurity' of the sublime, then, helps us to understand Burke's privileging of words over pictures: in their

7 Burke (1990) 54.   8 Burke (1990) 58.   9 Burke (1990) 59.
10 Burke (1990) 55.   11 Burke (1990) 157.   12 Burke (1990) 59.

ability to transcend the requirements of clarity and delineation imposed by visual figuration, indeed in their ability to suggest the very disintegration of the images they construct, words are endowed with a unique power to convey what can at best be dimly imagined, to approach the infinite, to contend with excess.[13] As for Longinus, the question of the presentation of the sublime, again exemplified by the Homeric Eris, persists.

Taking his cue from Burke's examination of 'obscurity', Philip Hardie has recently provided a counterpart to Longinus' discussion of the sublimity of Eris with his analysis of Ennius' *Discordia*: 'perhaps the original embodiment in Roman poetry of the monstrous sublime', it is *Discordia* who provides the 'seedbed'[14] both for Lucretius' description of *Religio* defeated by Epicurus (Lucr. 1.70–73) and for Virgil's *Fama* (*Aen.* 4.173–218), as well as for a range of related figures in the *Aeneid*, including Atlas (*Aen.* 4.246–51) and Aetna (*Aen.* 3.571–82).[15] Hardie's observations are related partly to the sublime action of Ennius' *Discordia* in breaking open the Gates of War (*Ann.* 225–6 Skutsch), but it is Ennius' description of *Discordia* as 'a maiden in a military cloak, born with hellish body, of equal proportion with water and fire, air, and heavy earth' (*corpore Tartarino prognata Paluda virago / cui par imber et ignis, spiritus et gravis terra*, *Ann.* 220–1 Skutsch, trans. Hardie (2009a) 99) that provides the connection with Burkeian obscurity: in her several conflicting elements and in the difficulties she presents to clear visualisation, *Discordia* mirrors Virgil's description of Jupiter's thunderbolt (*Aen.* 8.429–32), a passage admired by Burke as an example of how 'words may affect without raising images', its sublimity the product of its 'extraordinary composition'.[16]

Ennius' *Discordia* brings us back to Lucan. The *Bellum civile*'s exploration of the theme so influentially personified in Ennius' poem takes a startling turn early in Book 2 as, following the previous book's dire catalogue of portents heralding the coming strife,

---

[13] Cf. Lyotard (1991) 84–6, 100–3: abstract expressionism is another matter. The challenge posed by the sublime is convincingly met in the work of, for instance, Braque or Newman; it is figurative representation that the sublime discredits.

[14] Hardie (2009a) 101, 103.   [15] Hardie (2009a) 80–1, 88–92, 96.

[16] Burke (1990) 156; see Hardie (2009a) 97–8.

a nameless old man remembers the earlier civil conflict between Marius and Sulla: the cycle of carnage is beginning again. The old man's speech ends with the murder of Marius Gratidianus. As the episode strains our conception of the violence that humans can inflict upon one other, its horror reaches into the sublime:[17]

'cum iam tabe fluunt confusaque tempore multo
amisere notas, miserorum dextra parentum
colligit et pavido subducit cognita furto.
meque ipsum memini, caesi deformia fratris
ora rogo cupidum vetitisque inponere flammis,   170
omnia Sullanae lustrasse cadavera pacis
perque omnis truncos, cum qua cervice recisum
conveniat, quaesisse, caput. quid sanguine manes
placatos Catuli referam? cum victima tristis
inferias Marius forsan nolentibus umbris   175
pendit inexpleto non fanda piacula busto,
cum laceros artus aequataque volnera membris
vidimus et toto quamvis in corpore caeso
nil animae letale datum, moremque nefandae
dirum saevitiae, pereuntis parcere morti.   180
avolsae cecidere manus exsectaque lingua
palpitat et muto vacuum ferit aera motu.
hic aures, alius spiramina naris aduncae
amputat, ille cavis evolvit sedibus orbes
ultimaque effodit spectatis lumina membris.   185
vix erit ulla fides tam saevi criminis, unum
tot poenas cepisse caput. sic mole ruinae
fracta sub ingenti miscentur pondere membra,
nec magis informes veniunt ad litora trunci
qui medio periere freto.'   190

'Already the corpses, melting with decay and blurred with time's
long passage, have lost their features; only now do miserable parents
gather and steal in fearful theft the parts they recognise.
I recall how I myself, keen to place my slain brother's
disfigured face on the pyre's forbidden flames,
examined all the corpses of Sulla's peace
and searched through all the headless bodies for a neck
to match the severed head. Why tell of the ghost
of Catulus appeased with blood? – when as a victim Marius,

---

[17] And the grotesque. The two aesthetic concepts often overlap: see e.g. Hardie (2009a) 116–25 on 'the sublime and grotesque body of the poet'.

with the shades perhaps not liking the bitter offerings,
made a sacrifice unspeakable to a tomb never satisfied,
when we saw mangled limbs, each with a wound,
and no death-blow dealt although the entire body
was gashed; we saw the dreadful practice
of unutterable cruelty – to keep alive the dying man.
Down fell the hands, torn off; the cut-out tongue
quivered, beating empty air with noiseless movement.
One cut off his ears, another the hooked nose's nostrils;
a third tears out the eyeballs from their hollow sockets
and, compelling him to view his body, finally gouges out his eyes.
Hardly will a crime so savage be believed, that one man
can incur so many tortures. Limbs look like this when crushed
and smashed by falling building's mass beneath the mighty weight;
no worse disfigured do headless corpses come to shore,
perished in mid-sea.'   2.166–190

In its abject savagery, in its position as the culmination of the
catalogue of atrocities perpetrated during the civil war between
Marius and Sulla, and in that earlier conflict's role as precursor
and model for the civil war between Caesar and Pompey,[18] the
episode takes on an emblematic, originary status within Lucan's
examination of *discordia* and of *discordia*'s effects on bodies both
literal and metaphorical. The episode's conclusion resonates with
particular power: the crushing force of a great weight (2.187–8)
is precisely what is said to cause Rome's collapse in Book 1's
comparison with apocalypse (*nimioque graves sub pondere lap-
sus*, 1.71); the headless corpse washed up on the shore (2.189–90)
looks towards the end of the poem and Pompey's murder (8.698,
cf. 1.140, 1.685–6). Moreover, as Hardie has shown, the phrase
spiramina naris aduncae (2.182) contains an allusion to a phrase
used of *Discordia* by Ennius, *spiramina Naris ad undas* (*Ann.* 222
Skutsch): from Gratidianus' corpse the ghost of Ennian *Discordia* emerges; Gratidianus' dismembered body comes to stand for
the *discordia* of Lucan's own fractured poem.[19] And *discordia*, as

18 See Henderson (1987/2010) 445–50.
19 Hardie (2009a) 122. Hardie (ibid. 119–21) reminds us that the metapoetic potential of
Ennius' *Discordia* is limned by Horace's identification of the *disiecti membra poetae*
(Hor. *S.* 1.4.56–62) in Ennius' *postquam Discordia taetra / belli ferratos postis por-
tasque refregit* (*Ann.* 225–6 Skutsch); cf. Gowers (2007) 26–36 on Ennius' conception
of his own (sublime) poetic *corpus*.

we have seen it conceptualised by Ennius, is a multiple, obscure, sublimely unpresentable thing. At the level both of immediate, horrifying signified and of intertextual referent, Gratidianus' murder thus points to the sublimity of Lucan's subject, reflecting at the start of Book 2 the image conveyed by the simile of apocalypse at the opening of Book 1. Indeed, the sublimity shared by these passages has already been adumbrated in the course of Lucan's first book. As Rome's populace flees Caesar's advance, terrible omens appear: comets, lightning, an eclipse, the eruption of Aetna, blood-red seas, earthquakes, tidal waves, animals with powers of human speech, mutant babies, a flying Fury and ghostly armies on the move (1.522–83). As they manifest a world turned upside down, these portents index the same cosmic *discordia* represented by the apocalyptic upheavals at 1.72–80;[20] the list concludes with the appearance of the shades of Sulla and Marius (1.580–3).

Presenting the unpresentable: the *Bellum civile* as sublime object

If, then, *discordia* is to be considered a sublime thing, how does Lucan approach the paradox of sublime presentation that it poses? John Henderson's groundbreaking article 'Lucan/The word at war', along with Jamie Masters' subsequent monograph, offered powerful answers, demonstrating how Lucan's epic enacts what it is about, how its theme of civil war, of divided wholes and united opposites, goes all the way down, rupturing the narratorial perspective, permeating the poem's very syntax and vocabulary.[21] In dialogue with Longinus, I want here to suggest another way in

---

[20] The second passage typically gives the inversions of the first an intensifying twist: compare in particular 1.75–6 with 1.526–9 (the stars), 1.76–7 with 1.552–5 (the earth and ocean), and 1.77–9 with 1.538–44 (the sun and moon). The whole unearthly sequence fits well with the Burkeian sublime's feeling for the extraordinary and the supernatural. With the *ingens Erinys* (1.572–7) compare also Euripides, *Orestes* 255–7 and 264–5, quoted at *De sub.* 15.2 and 15.8.

[21] Appreciation of Lucan's bravura poetic talent has been commonplace for some time now: besides Henderson (1987/2010), esp. 455–66 and Masters (1992) *passim*, see e.g. Bonner (1966/2010); Morford (1967); Martindale (1976); Roche (2009) 47–64.

which we may see Lucan responding linguistically to the challenge of the sublime.[22]

Space does not permit analysis of the linguistic characteristics of the entire poem. Instead, as an example representative of Lucan's hothouse technique, let us turn again to the emblematic description of Gratidianus' murder, quoted above. How does it convey the horror of the events it recounts? The passage opens with hypallage, one of Lucan's favourite tropes: *dextra* takes the place of *parentes* as the subject of lines 167–8; grammatically, it is this disembodied hand, not the parents, that goes about the grisly task of gathering the dead's limbs, thereby extending the theme of dismemberment to include even those still living. This is followed by the sudden, startling use of the first person: the phrase *meque ipsum memini* stands at the start of its line and sentence, each of the three words hammering home the old man's status as eyewitness, reinforcing each other through assonance and alliteration. This leads into a sentence remarkable for its length and tortured hyperbata. *caesi deformia fratris* forms a metrical unit balancing the first half of line 169, contrasting speaker and brother, even as this brutally simple opposition itself contrasts with a syntax so distorted that it manages to enact the funereal action being described: *meque ipsum*, expanded by the phrase *caesi deformia fratris / ora rogo cupidum vetitisque inponere flammis*, forms the subject of *lustrasse* and *quaesisse*; *caput*, emphatically placed at the end of the sentence, is literally severed from its adjective *recisum*, leaving the two preceding verbs, *conveniat* and *quaesisse*, to rub uncomfortably against each other. The breathless, distressed rush of this sentence is followed by an abrupt rhetorical question in 173–4 and then another instance of hypallage (175), Gratidianus becoming both *victima* and the subject of the sentence, syntactically transforming

---

[22] The following discussion takes its cue from the observations of Porter (forthcoming) on the role of textual materiality within the Longinian sublime. For a diametrically opposite view of Longinus' linguistic prescriptions, see Hunter (2009) 134–41: 'style which calls attention to itself ("mannered") . . . is felt to distract the audience from their concentration on what is being described' (p. 135); 'because of the intellectual demands of such writing, the audience never "gives itself" completely to it, in the way in which we respond to the sublime' (p. 138). Such a reading ignores Longinus' interest in the sublimity of language *as language*, independent of any necessary referent. See also Schiesaro (2003) 130–2.

into his own executioner. The graphic visualisation (*vidimus*) of Gratidianus' mangled body, one wound for each limb, glosses the effect of the passage's stylistic hypertrophy. Lines 177–80 offer hyperbole and paradox, repeating in three variant forms the idea of sparing the dead from dying, while lines 181–5 constitute one of the poem's most extraordinary examples of depersonalisation and the horror of the abject. Not only is Gratidianus' body pulled apart, but its constituent parts then seem to acquire a life of their own: *manus* is the subject of *cecidere*, the tongue keeps twitching. Line 185, in its density of expression, juxtaposition of active and passive (*effodit/spectatis*) and play with spectatorship and perspective (*spectatis/lumina*), caps both conceits: one of Gratidianus' killers gouges out his eyes even as (by these same disembodied eyeballs) his severed limbs 'are looked upon'. *vix erit ulla fides tam saevi criminis* ('hardly will a crime so savage be believed', 186) – nor can we quite believe Lucan's virtuosity.

How does all this relate to Longinus' prescriptions? Longinus acknowledges that his aesthetic is one of hyperbole (*De sub.* 38), characterised like the Lucanian baroque by startling, violent figures, diction and syntax.[23] Longinus dwells at length, for instance, on the conduciveness of hyperbata to sublimity, citing – and imitating – the way in which Demosthenes, one of his favourite authors,

πολλάκις γὰρ τὸν νοῦν ὃν ὥρμησεν εἰπεῖν ἀνακρεμάσας καὶ μεταξύ πως εἰς ἀλλόφυλον καὶ ἀπεοικυῖαν τάξιν ἄλλ' ἐπ' ἄλλοις διὰ μέσου καὶ ἔξωθέν ποθεν ἐπεισκυκλῶν εἰς φόβον ἐμβαλὼν τὸν ἀκροατὴν ὡς ἐπὶ παντελεῖ τοῦ λόγου διαπτώσει καὶ συναποκινδυνεύειν ὑπ' ἀγωνίας τῷ λέγοντι συναναγκάσας, εἶτα παραλόγως διὰ μακροῦ τὸ πάλαι ζητούμενον εὐκαίρως ἐπὶ τέλει που προσαποδούς, αὐτῷ τῷ κατὰ τὰς ὑπερβάσεις παραβόλῳ καὶ ἀκροσφαλεῖ πολὺ μᾶλλον ἐκπλήττει.

often suspends the sense which he has begun to express, and in the interval manages to bring forward one extraneous idea after another in a strange and unlikely order, making the audience terrified of a total collapse of the sentence, and compelling them from sheer excitement to share the speaker's risk: then unexpectedly, after a great interval, the long-lost phrase turns up pat at the end, so that he astounds them all the more by the very recklessness and audacity of the transpositions. *De sub.* 22.4

---

[23] Cf. Fantham (1992) 39: hyperbole is 'almost [Lucan's] natural mode of thought'.

So in the passage from the *Bellum civile* we have been considering, it is the 'long-lost' *caput* that turns up at the end of the sentence (if not at the end of the old man's search) in line 173. Lines 187–8 (*sic mole ruinae / fracta sub ingenti miscentur pondere membra*) even provide an image of the 'collapse' with which hyperbaton dallies. Like hyperbata, Longinus says, sudden changes of person can 'make the audience feel themselves set in the thick of the danger' (ἐν μέσοις τοῖς κινδύνοις ποιοῦσα τὸν ἀκροατὴν δοκεῖν στρέφεσθαι, *De sub.* 26.1), while he also praises Demosthenes for his 'inspiration and quick play of question and answer and his way of confronting his own words as if they were someone else's' (τὸ ἔνθουν καὶ ὀξύρροπον τῆς πεύσεως καὶ ἀποκρίσεως καὶ τὸ πρὸς ἑαυτὸν ὡς πρὸς ἕτερον ἀνθυπαντᾶν), thereby making his speech 'not only loftier but also more convincing' (οὐ μόνον ὑψηλότερον... ἀλλὰ καὶ πιστότερον) (*De sub.* 18.1). So in the old man's speech emphatic use of the first person alternates with third-person description, while, as we will see later in Chapter 4, his angry rhetorical questions echo those of the poem's own narrator: are we witnessing a form of ventriloquism? Is Lucan's narrator here 'confronting his own words as if they were someone else's'?

Even more important for Longinus are the effects of metaphor and of bold imagery in general: 'figurative writing', as he puts it, 'has a natural grandeur and... metaphors make for sublimity (ὑψηλοποιὸν αἱ μεταφοραί): emotional and descriptive passages are most glad of them' (*De sub.* 32.6). It is worth considering under this rubric the comparable effect of Lucanian hypallage. Conte has recently argued for this trope as a marker of sublimity in the *Aeneid*.[24] Its abrasive, jarring effects are even more pronounced in the *Bellum civile*: hypallage becomes a means whereby even the words of the poem are at war with one other. Like metaphor, hypallage is predicated on the association of previously distinct elements or, looked at the other way around, on the destabilisation of conventional relationships between signifier and signified, of previously associated elements. This interplay between dissolution and wholeness is also what attracts Longinus to Sappho's

---

[24] Conte (2007) 58–122.

Φαίνεταί μοι: 'Is it not wonderful how she summons at the same time, soul, body, hearing, tongue, sight, skin, all as though they had wandered off apart from herself?' (*De sub.* 10.3). It is through the very breaking of her tongue (ἀλλὰ κὰμ μὲν γλῶσσα ἔαγε), through the dearticulation of her body parts, that the speaker paradoxically gains her poetic voice and persona. Turning back to Lucan, we may notice similarities, despite its very different context, with the description of Gratidianus' fate. As Sappho's body parts become alienated from her, so that she seems 'on the brink of death' (τεθνάκην δ' ὀλίγω 'πιδεύης), so Gratidianus meets his end by being literally dismembered. The salient features in both cases are ears, eyes and tongue. The effect of the two passages is obviously not identical. Gratidianus does not enumerate his injuries himself. Moreover, Lucan's *ultima* in line 185 is indeed final: unlike the Sapphic subject who declares ἀλλὰ πᾶν τόλματον, Gratidianus is unable to endure. There is no straightforward sense in which Gratidianus' ruptured body achieves restitution. But let us remind ourselves why Longinus says he so admires Sappho's poem. It is sublime because of the way in which Sappho's 'selection', accumulation and 'combination' of details (*De sub.* 10.1) vivifies it, makes it 'dense', turning it into an object which truly speaks to its reader. The choice and arrangement of detail in Lucan's description of Gratidianus' dismemberment has, I suggest, a comparable effect, the separation of the body parts, and the separate acts of violence, contrasting with the balanced, interlocking architecture of the sentence, its alternation of verbal enjambement and end- or sense-stopped lines set off by a final self-contained clause in line 185. Like Sappho's poem, these lines achieve a hard, almost tangible, density through a Longinian agglomeration of detail.

Bellum civile 2.166–90 offers an illustration of the connections between the poem's linguistic characteristics and those associated by Longinus with sublime writing.[25] But do such connections in

---

[25] Compare Norbrook's characterisation of Milton's language in the *Areopagitica* and in *Paradise Lost* as Longinian *and* Lucanian: 'like Lucan, Milton is enacting in his language a breakdown of concord, emulating Longinus' prescriptions for a mode of

themselves tell us very much? What is it that makes these particular language usages sublime? The sublime, we remember, should not be confused with the *genus grande* or in fact with any prescribed style of writing. Rather, as Gilby proposes, we should understand the sublime as a particular experience of language: 'the "sublime" of [Longinus'] title is always an encounter . . . Language is sublime when it gives us, as readers or listeners, such a deep understanding of what its author communicates that the words seem somehow to have come from within ourselves.'[26] Following Porter's lead, we may take this idea of the sublime as a heightened form of communication a stage further. 'The sublime', he argues, 'brings about an abrupt confrontation with the materiality of texts':[27] 'language must become (more fully) a body, must be made into a more coherent substance and soul, before it can become voiced and finally sublime' or, as Longinus puts it, just as 'sublime words . . . when they form a body (σωματοποιούμενα) . . . become endowed with voice' (*De sub.* 40.1), so the choice of correct and magnificent words 'gives things life and makes them speak' (ψυχήν τινα τοῖς πράγμασι φωνητικὴν ἐντιθεῖσα, 30.1). It is this communicational power, vested in sublime writing *as writing*, that unites the figures and examples adduced by Longinus and, I suggest, that underpins Lucan's jagged, intractable use of language. In each case, language manages to achieve a unique substantiality, to assert its presence *as* language, and thereby, paradoxically, to transcend its status as mere 'words on the page', becoming instead something truly alive. It is not, then, Lucan's particular choice of tropes that makes the passage from Book 2 (for instance) sublime, but rather the way in which these tropes endow his text with a harsh, heated life of its own. Their density and extravagance interposes a barrier between the lines and our immediate understanding of them. At the same time, it is this very barrier that opens the gates to sublimity: in our struggle to grasp fully Lucan's words, they achieve resonance and vitality.

---

writing that gains sublimity by verging on disorder' (Norbrook 1999: 448; cf. ibid. 134–9).
[26] Gilby (2006) 1.   [27] Porter (forthcoming).

attonitique omnes: readerly sublimity

This sublime 'thickening' of linguistic texture is reinforced by the Lucanian narrator's purposeful orchestration of the sublimity of our response to his poem. The *Bellum civile* is famous for its repeated assertions of the impossibility of narrating the *nefas*, the unspeakability, of civil war.[28] The most striking of these assertions occurs in Book 7: in the middle of the description of the critical battle of Pharsalus, the narrator suddenly exclaims, amplifying the old man's earlier question, *quid sanguine manes / placatos Catuli referam?* (2.173–4):

> hanc fuge, mens, partem belli tenebrisque relinque,
> nullaque tantorum discat me vate malorum,
> quam multum bellis liceat civilibus, aetas.
> a potius pereant lacrimae pereantque querellae: 555
> quidquid in hac acie gessisti, Roma, tacebo.

> Mind of mine, shun this part of battle and leave it to darkness
> and from my words let no age learn of horrors
> so immense, of how much is licensed in civil war.
> Better that these tears and protests go unheard:
> whatever you did in this battle, Rome, I shall not tell.

> 7.552–6[29]

With his next breath, however, he continues with his story. Indeed, the following line (557) begins with the emphatic words *hic Caesar*: no sooner has our narrator refused to narrate than Caesar comes barrelling back onto the scene, hurling his *hic*, his 'here and now', in the face of *nulla aetas*. The shocking immediacy of the *Bellum civile*'s narrative reasserts its pull. Now Longinus, discussing the sublime effects of such immediacy, what he calls ἐνάργεια, and, in particular, of asyndeta and repetition, quotes a passage from Demosthenes (*Oration* 21.72) in which the orator asserts that the behaviour of his opponent Midias was so violent that 'nobody could convey the horror of it simply by reporting it' (οὐδεὶς ἂν ταῦτα ἀπαγγέλλων δύναιτο τὸ δεινὸν παραστῆσαι,

---

[28] See e.g. O'Higgins (1988) 215–17; Feeney (1991) 276–83; Masters (1992) 5–6.
[29] On this declaration, see in particular Johnson (1987) 98–9; Masters (1992) 148; Ormand (1994/2010) 343.

De sub. 20.3). Accordingly, instead of just stating what happened, Demosthenes is forced, like Lucan, to vivify his language, to fire it so that it itself becomes an experience of violence for his listeners.[30] It is this contrast, between the unpresentability of his subject matter and its successful *materialisation* (rather than simple description), which lies at the heart of Lucan's sublime. By having his narrator refuse to narrate his poem, he calls attention to the sublimity of his endeavour to present the unpresentable. He explains, as it were, the logic behind his rebarbative stylistics, alerting us to the presence of the sublime.

This dynamic of blockage and recuperation recalls Kant's formulation of the sublime as 'a momentary inhibition of the vital powers and the immediately following and all the more powerful outpouring of them'.[31] If, as we have seen, Lucan is concerned to emphasise the moment of inhibition, he is equally careful to encourage the subsequent rush, to remind us of the work his language is doing and of the communicative effect it is meant to have. Apostrophe provides him with a crucial means of achieving this aim. One of the *Bellum civile*'s defining features, apostrophe is directed variously at Caesar, Pompey and Cato, as well as minor characters such as Vulteius and Scaeva, apportioning blame and praise as the narrator sees fit.[32] Such narratorial outbursts serve to engage and direct readerly response, but even more striking in this regard are those moments when the narrator includes us, the poem's readers, in his assertions, when he turns, as it were, to speak straight to camera.[33] The best-known example again occurs in Book 7 as, on the eve of Pharsalus, the narrator tells Pompey:

> haec et apud seras gentes populosque nepotum,
> sive sua tantum venient in saecula fama
> sive aliquid magnis nostri quoque cura laboris

---

[30] Cf. Leigh (1997) 11–14 on the *Bellum civile*'s achievement of Longinian ἐνάργεια.

[31] Kant (2003) 128–9.

[32] On Lucan's use of apostrophe, see Marti (1975) 82–9; Ahl (1976) 151; Williams (1978) 234; Lausberg (1985) 1571; Johnson (1987) 7; Martindale (1993) 67–8; Leigh (1997) 307–10; Bartsch (1997) 93–8; D'Alessandro Behr (2007) 33–161 offers the most comprehensive treatment.

[33] See Ormand (1994/2010) 327–30.

nominibus prodesse potest, cum bella legentur,   210
spesque metusque simul perituraque vota movebunt,
attonitique omnes veluti venientia fata,
non transmissa, legent et adhuc tibi, Magne, favebunt.

Even among later races and the people of posterity, these events –
whether they come down to future ages by their own fame alone
or whether my devotion also and my toil can do anything
for mighty names – will stir both hopes and fears together
and useless prayers when the battle is read;
all will be stunned as they read the destinies, as if
to come, not past and, Magnus, still they will side with you.

                                                    7.207–13

'Astonishment' is identified by both Burke and Kant as one of sublimity's fundamental affects.[34] Here, our astonishment (*attoniti*, 212) is produced by the vividness, the present-ness of Lucan's text, as it causes us to treat what history has already accomplished, what is *transmissa*, as though it were still in the future, *venientia*. As Longinus prescribes, the poem's sublimity will lift us from our immediate circumstances, will transport us out of ourselves: εἰς ἔκστασιν ἄγει τὰ ὑπερφυᾶ (*De sub.* 1.4). More than this: the *Bellum civile*, we are told, manages to pull off that most extraordinary of all sublime feats. So powerful is the communicative force of the poem that, when we read it (*cum bella legentur*), we will experience the mingled hope and fear (*spesque metusque*) that, we are told later at line 386 (and have already learned at 6.419, a line that also begins with the words *spemque metumque*), drives the combatants themselves. We are truly, in Longinus' words, 'uplifted . . . as if we had ourselves produced the very thing we heard' (*De sub.* 7.2). That intersubjectivity which is the hallmark of all sublime experience, wherein the boundaries between sublime object and sublime subject blur and collapse, is, we are assured, generated by Lucan's epic.[35]

We encounter a comparable assertion of communicative sublimity during Caesar's visit to Troy in Book 9. Turning to the future dictator, the narrator declares:

---

[34] Burke (1990) 123; Kant (2003) 152.
[35] D'Alessandro Behr (2007) 76–7, 165; cf. Bartsch (1997) 140–9.

o sacer et magnus vatum labor! omnia fato   980
eripis et populis donas mortalibus aevum.
invidia sacrae, Caesar, ne tangere famae;
nam, siquid Latiis fas est promittere Musis,
quantum Zmyrnaei durabunt vatis honores,
venturi me teque legent; Pharsalia nostra   985
vivet, et a nullo tenebris damnabimur aevo.

O how sacred and immense the task of bards! You snatch everything
from death and to mortals you give immortality.
Caesar, do not be touched by envy of their sacred fame;
since, if for Latian Muses it is right to promise anything,
as long as honours of the Smyrnaean bard [i.e. Homer] endure,
the future ages will read me and you; our Pharsalia
shall live and we shall be condemned to darkness by no era.

9.980–6

Wrapped into an apostrophe to one of the poem's central characters, we once more find ourselves thrust into the poem's frame.
Putting aside for a moment the questions raised by *me teque* and
nostra, I want to draw attention here to the emphatic location of
vivet at the start of line 986, assuring us that the poem will achieve
Longinian life, embodied (σωματοποιούμενα as Longinus has it,
De sub. 40.1) and fully voiced. Most significantly, the narrator's
statement suggests that this embodiment will come about through
the agency of the poem's readers: *Pharsalia nostra* will not die
precisely *because* future generations will read it.[36] We will, again,
'produce the very thing we have heard'.[37]

Longinus emphasises that nothing 'can really be the true sublime if its effect does not outlast the moment of utterance; for
what is truly great bears repeated consideration; it is difficult,
if not impossible, to resist its effect; and the memory of it is
stubborn and indelible' (οὐκ ἂν ἔτ' ἀληθὲς ὕψος εἴη μέχρι μόνης
τῆς ἀκοῆς σῳζόμενον. τοῦτο γὰρ τῷ ὄντι μέγα, οὗ πολλὴ μὲν ἡ
ἀναθεώρησις, δύσκολος δέ, μᾶλλον δ' ἀδύνατος ἡ κατεξανάστασις,

---

[36] So Deguy (1993) 10: 'The poet is the witness who passes on the legacy of [his subject's]
     eternal final word. The witness – poet, historian, novelist – has heard the supplication
     at the implacable knees of death. He inscribes its trace on the gravestone of the page.'
[37] Cf. Norbrook (1999) 32 and Cheney (2009) 174 on the sublimity of Luc. 9.980–6. See
     also Bartsch (1997) 131–7.

ἰσχυρὰ δὲ ἡ μνήμη καὶ δυσεξάλειπτος, *De sub.* 7.3).[38] The assertion *Pharsalia nostra / vivet* is driven by a similar awareness. The
temporality of the sublime, like that of Lucan's epic, is so emphatically, so expansively rooted in the present that it swallows up the
future, its lightning-flash immediacy so brilliant that it spans the
centuries. It is a concern that is connected with the *Bellum civile*'s
theme of on-going, never-ending war with Caesar. We have already
looked at Book 7's assertion that the poem will make us react to
Pharsalus as if the battle were still to come, *venientia*. So later,
once the battle is done, we are told that there will be 'that pair
of rivals always with us – Liberty and Caesar' (*par quod semper
habemus, / libertas et Caesar*, 7.695–6). Why will there always
be *libertas et Caesar*? One reason, surely, is to be found in the
poem's sublime communicational force, its ability to *present*, to
make present, the unpresentable subject of civil war. Through the
uncomfortable materiality of its language, its ἐνάργεια, the poem
asserts its power literally to realise the unrealisable, to turn back the
clocks to a time before the outcome of the civil war was decided.
Towards the end of Book 1, the astrologer Figulus prays:

> 'et superos quid prodest poscere finem?
> cum domino pax ista venit. duc, Roma, malorum   670
> continuam seriem clademque in tempora multa
> extrahe civili tantum iam libera bello.'

> 'And what use is it to ask the gods to end it?
> The peace we long for brings a master. Rome, prolong your chain
> of disaster without a break and protract calamity
> for lengthy ages: only now in civil war are you free.'   1.669–72

Lucan's poem, which ends (apparently) unfinished, with Caesar
under siege, itself enacts this longed-for endlessness.[39] It is part of
its sublimity.

---

[38] The idea that sublimity involves transcendence of the present is fundamental to Longinus' thinking, and recurs throughout his treatise: *De sub.* 1.3, 4.7, 9.3, 14.3, 36.2, 44.1,
44.9; see Whitmarsh (2001) 65 and cf. Schiesaro (2003) 129. The concept of artistic
fame also formed part of eighteenth-century thinking about the sublime: in *An Essay on
the Sublime* (1747), Baillie declares that 'to be praised not only by the present generation, but through the revolving circle of ages down to latest posterity, is stretching our
expectations and our ideas to an immensity; and from this the sublime of the passion
itself arises' (Ashfield and De Bolla (1996) 93–4, cited by Hardie (2009a) 84).
[39] See Masters (1992) 216–59; Quint (1993) 147–57.

Matrona, Pythia and witch: narratorial sublimity

Lucan, then, in his concern to make his text truly communicate with its readers, not merely aims for a Longinian thickening of language but also through his narrator repeatedly insists upon his text's sublime vivification, framing it in terms of the tension between unpresentability and immediate (as well as on-going, future) presence, presentation. Implicit in my observations has been the positive ethical value of this aesthetic. The *Bellum civile* mobilises the sublime as a means of resistance to Caesarism and its atrocities. For Lucan, the sublime offers a means of fully encountering the unspeakable horror of civil war. Presenting the unpresentable becomes a way of negotiating social or political trauma. To adopt Lyotard's phraseology, the *Bellum civile* is an artwork that denies itself, and us, 'the solace of good forms':[40] it refuses the ease of conventional syntax, striving instead for a fuller, because harder, mode of communication. This kind of sublimity refocuses the spiritual elevation promised by Kant, converting it into a force that enables us to contend with the horrific in all its overwhelming power, to commemorate trauma in a way that, contrary to direct, conventional forms of commemoration, prevents its reification, its insertion into a naturalised, acceptable story of 'the way things are'.

While its narrator insistently proclaims the effect of this peculiar mode of commemoration on the *Bellum civile*'s readers, the poem also conjures for us two powerful metapoetic images of the sublime experience that is claimed by the narrator in response to the civil war and that forms the motivating force behind the poem's commemorative efforts. The first such instance is provided by the Bacchic *matrona*, whose whirling flight through Rome, as it closes the first book of the epic, casts shadows backwards and forwards across that book and the remainder of the poem:[41]

---

[40] Lyotard (1984) 81. Cf. Lyotard (1991) 125: 'When the point is to try to present that there is something that is not presentable, you have to make presentation suffer.'

[41] It should be noted that Longinus finds fault with writers who allow themselves to be 'carried away by a sort of Bacchic possession (ὑπὸ βακχείας τινὸς'), temporarily aligning himself with those critics who censure Plato, for example, for his use of 'harsh and intemperate metaphor and allegorical bombast' (*De sub.* 32.7, cf. 3.5 on 'what

nam, qualis vertice Pindi
Edonis Ogygio decurrit plena Lyaeo   675
talis et attonitam rapitur matrona per urbem
vocibus his prodens urguentem pectora Phoebum:
'quo feror, o Paean? qua me super aethera raptam
constituis terra? video Pangaea nivosis
cana iugis latosque Haemi sub rupe Philippos.   680
quis furor hic, o Phoebe, doce, quo tela manusque
Romanae miscent acies bellumque sine hoste est.
quo diversa feror? primos me ducis in ortus,
qua mare Lagei mutatur gurgite Nili:
hunc ego, fluminea deformis truncus harena   685
qui iacet, agnosco. dubiam super aequora Syrtim
arentemque feror Libyen, quo tristis Enyo
transtulit Emathias acies. nunc desuper Alpis
nubiferae colles atque aeriam Pyrenen
abripimur. patriae sedes remeamus in urbis   690
inpiaque in medio peraguntur bella senatu.
consurgunt partes iterum, totumque per orbem
rursus eo. nova da mihi cernere litora ponti
telluremque novam: vidi iam, Phoebe, Philippos.'
haec ait, et lasso iacuit deserta furore.   695

As the Bacchante races down
from Pindus's summit, filled with Lyaeus of Ogygia,
so a matron sweeps through stunned Rome, revealing
with these words that Phoebus is harrying her breast:
'O Paean, where are you taking me? You whisk me over the ether;
where do you set me down? I see Pangaea white
with snow-clad ridges and broad Philippi under Haemus' crag.
What madness this, O Phoebus, tell: why do Roman battle-lines
contend with hands and weapons? Why war without an enemy?
Where else now are you taking me? You lead me eastwards,

Theodorus used to call the pseudo-bacchanalian (παρένθυρσον)'). Our reading of such statements, however, needs to take into account the polemical positioning of the *Peri hupsous*: both the preceding praise of Plato (*De sub.* 32.5–6) and the immediately subsequent attack on Caecilius for privileging Lysias (*De sub.* 32.8, cf. 35.1) frame *De sub.* 32.7 as a carefully modulated turn within Longinus' on-going attempt to navigate the waters of contemporary academic debate. As the treatise's recurrent emphasis on inspiration makes clear, it is not Bacchic possession per se but the results to which on occasion it leads Plato (cf. *De sub.* 4.4, 29.1) that are to be avoided; elsewhere, Plato is held up by Longinus as a paradigm of sublimity precisely because of his openness to inspiration (*De sub.* 13, cf. 14.1, 28.2). Note too the connotations of the Bacchic in Homer's sublime image of Ajax (μαίνεται, *De sub.* 9.11), discussed in Chapter 1. Cf. Russell (1981a) 69–83 on the tradition of poetic 'possession', esp. pp. 81–3 on Longinian *enthousiasmos*.

where sea is dyed by Egyptian Nile's flood:
him I recognise, lying on the river sands,
an unsightly headless corpse. I am taken over seas to shifting
Syrtes and to parched Libya: this is where grim Enyo
has shifted Emathia's battle-lines. Now I am hurried
over mountains of the cloud-capped Alps and soaring
Pyrenees. Back I come to the abodes of my native Rome,
to impious war waged in the Senate's midst.
The factions rise again, again I travel through
all the world. Let me gaze on different sea-shores,
different land: already have I seen Philippi, Phoebus.'
So she spoke and then collapsed, abandoned by exhausted frenzy.

1.674–95

The *matrona*'s metapoetic status is well established: driven
onwards by Apollo, she is also likened to one of Bacchus' fren-
zied followers (1.674–7), both divinities having been mentioned as
potential sources of inspiration in the narrator's prayer to Nero at
the beginning of the book (1.63–5);[42] the passage recalls Horace's
Ode 3.25.8–14, in which the speaker compares his own Bacchic
inspiration to that of a Maenad[43]; the flight takes in the twin cli-
maxes of the *Bellum civile*, the battle of Pharsalus (1.679–82) and
the decapitation of Pompey (1.683–6), as well as Cato's march
through the Libyan desert (1.686–7) and other critical events in
the war which are beyond the scope of the extant poem (the battles
of Thapsus and Munda 1.686–90, Caesar's assassination 1.690–
1, the battle of Philippi 1.694) but which scholars have variously
argued formed part of Lucan's overall plan for the work;[44] as
Bernard Dick has argued, the *matrona*'s vatic vision, a continua-
tion of the predictions of Arruns (1.584–638) and Figulus (1.639–
72), is itself continued in mutant vein at the start of the next book
by the narrator (who has already identified himself as a *vates*,
1.63)[45] as he laments the portents revealed by *praescia natura*
(2.3).[46]

[42] Feeney (1991) 275; Hardie (1993) 107–8.
[43] Bohnenkamp (1979); Masters (1992) 136 n. 100.   [44] See Dick (1963) 40–1.
[45] Cf. Luc. 7.553, 9.980. On Lucan's self-presentation as a *vates*, see O'Higgins (1988)
      (who, however, does not discuss the Bacchic *matrona*).
[46] Dick (1963) 41.

And these metapoetic features also mark the *matrona*'s transport as distinctively sublime.[47] The prophetess is overwhelmed, mastered by the irresistible force of the god (*urguentem pectora Phoebum*, 1.677); at the same time, where the Bacchante to whom she is compared hurtles down (*decurrit*, 1.675) from Mount Pindus, the *matrona* is borne onwards and upwards (*rapitur, raptam, feror* repeated three times, *abripimur*),[48] soaring *super aethera* (1.678), *super aequora* (1.686), over the peaks of Pangaea and Haemus, the Alps and the Pyrenees, the impact of this sudden afflatus accentuated by her initial barrage of frantic questions and by the sublimity of the passage's Horatian intertext.[49] Once aloft, as she surveys the future events of the civil war, she sees the whole world, *totum . . . orbem* (1.692), a truly sublime prospect. Perhaps most sublime of all, once we have noted how the narrator at the start of Book 2 maintains (at least briefly) the *matrona*'s prophetic role, is the way in which the transport of the *matrona* reaches out beyond the lines which describe it to span the space between Books 1 and 2: the text's own structure, its very physical form, comes to enact that sublime movement between the gap (a collapse or stoppage, as the *matrona* in the last line of Book 1 *lasso iacuit deserta furore*, 'collapsed, abandoned by exhausted frenzy') and the surmounting of that gap, a movement which, we have seen, Longinus discerns for instance within Homer's depiction of Eris.

But there is more: the Bacchic *matrona*'s sublimity is framed not merely in metapoetic terms but, specifically, as a response to the overwhelming event of civil war. Another name for the *Bellum civile*'s subject of *discordia* is of course *furor*: the *matrona*'s question *quis furor hic . . . ?* (1.681) offers a clear echo of the narrator's question in the opening lines of the poem, *quis furor, o cives, quae*

---

[47] Cf. Cheney (2009) 48–9 on Marlowe's translation – and appropriation – of the *matrona*'s sublimity in *Lucan's First Book*.

[48] Roche (2009) ad 1.676 notes the paradox of Bacchic activity within the city (*urbem*) instead of the wilderness. The frisson underlines the extraordinary nature of the *matrona*'s transport.

[49] On the Lucretian appeal of the sublime for Horace in *Carm.* 3.25.8–14, see Hardie (2009c) 220–1. Cf. Schiesaro (2003) 51 on the Bacchic sublimity of Seneca's Atreus at *Thy.* 260–2.

tanta licentia ferri? (1.8).[50] *furor* is also what fills the possessed
matrona, as the emphatic positioning of *furore* as the last word of
the book (1.695) and as the punning repetitions in the passage of
the verb *feror* remind us.[51] The immediate implication is that the
matrona's experience of sublimity – her *furor* – is, like the narrator's, a function of the sublime *discordia* – the *furor* – that is the
poem's theme. And this interrelationship is reflected in the specific
contours of the *matrona*'s sublimity. As identified above, a defining feature of the poem's vision of *discordia*, and of the *Bellum
civile* itself, is its endlessness. Endlessness is, likewise, what characterises the *matrona*'s vision of the civil war: *consurgunt partes
iterum* (1.692), she cries as she is whirled once again (*rursus*,
1.693) through the cycle of violence (*nova da mihi cernere litora
ponti / telluremque novam: vidi iam, Phoebe, Philippos*, 1.693–
4).[52] I suggested previously that the endlessness with which Lucan
endows his poem is a function of its sublime immediacy. As we
saw, even as the narrator denies his capacity to speak his theme,
he asserts his poem's success, declaring that we, its readers, will
forever be left *attoniti* (7.212) at its sublime power. Such too is
the effect that the Bacchic *matrona* has on Rome, left *attonitam*
(1.676) at her flight.[53]

Yet endlessness is also what generates the unpresentable 'obscurity' of Homer's Eris (Longinus speaks of what stretches beyond
the bounds of this world, Burke of 'infinity').[54] And, for Lucan,
even as it marks the on-going impact of his poem, endlessness is
paradoxically the very quality that underpins the unpresentability

[50] The echo is amplified by the compression of 1.1–7 (*bella...plus quam
civilia...cognatasque acies...infestisque obvia signis / signa, pares aquilas et pila
minantia pilis*; see Conte 1966/2010; Henderson 1987/2010: 465–6, 487–8) into the
remainder of 1.681–2 (*o Phoebe, doce, quo tela manusque / Romanae miscent acies
bellumque sine hoste est*).
[51] Masters (1992) 143.
[52] See Roche (2009) 379. Lucan here turns to his own poetic use the conventional conceit
by which the battles of Pharsalus and Philippi were conflated with each other (cf. Virg.
Georg. 1.489–90; Manilius 1.908–13; Ov. *Met.* 15.824); cf. Luc. 7.853–4, 9.270–1 and
see Henderson (1987/2010) 488.
[53] Roche (2009) ad loc. The link between the two lines is reinforced by the broader
structural connections plotted by Dick (1963) 42–3 between the series of prodigies,
auguries and prophecy at Luc. 1.524–2.15 and the corresponding series at 7.152–213.
[54] *De sub.* 9.5, 35.3; Burke (1990) 58.

of Rome's *discordia*. As the image of apocalypse at the beginning of Book I reminds us, the civil war is an event of absolute magnitude, too vast in scale and consequence to handle. Like that of the apocalypse, this magnitude, this endlessness, thus imposes on speech, indeed on history (as the narrator cries after Pharsalus, *in totum mundi prosternimur aevum*, 7.640; cf. 7.387–9), a permanent end. Where the endlessness of the *Bellum civile* enables it to reach towards future readers, the endlessness of the civil war that is the poem's subject ultimately overwhelms. So it is that, at the end of the book, the *matrona* collapses, *deserta furore*.

Subtly, then, the *matrona*'s experience of sublimity can be seen to reflect the manner in which the poem itself constructs its theme. Her vision of civil war points at once to the central problem of Lucan's subject and to his attempt to mould a solution to this problem from the problem's own constituents. Endlessness pulls two ways; the civil war continues, at once intractable and persistent. As it touches the paradoxes according to which the *Bellum civile* operates, the sublimity experienced by the *matrona* in response to the sublimity of the civil war speaks directly to Lucan's own efforts to present what lies beyond presentation.

A second representation of the experience of sublimity that Lucan suggests lies behind his poem is to be found in Book 5 in the figure of the Pythian priestess Phemonoe, whom Pompey's follower Appius visits in the hope of discovering his future. Like the *matrona*, Phemonoe carries a powerful metapoetic charge, ruled like the poet by both Apollo and Bacchus (5.73–4)[55] and associated with the *furor* of the poem's subject (5.118, 150, 184).[56] Lucan's account of her possession also reflects Longinus' understanding of the Pythia as a metaphor for the sublimity of artistic inspiration. Let us look again at the Longinian passage: 'zealous imitation of the great prose writers and poets of the past' is one possible way of attaining the sublime, he writes,

[55] Cf. Roche (2009) ad 1.677.
[56] On Phemonoe's metapoetic status, see O'Higgins (1988) 208–17, Masters (1992) 133–49; Morford (1967) 64 notes how the *matrona*'s inspiration foreshadows the Pythia's. See also Dick (1965); Ahl (1976) 121–30.

πολλοὶ γὰρ ἀλλοτρίῳ θεοφοροῦνται πνεύματι τὸν αὐτὸν τρόπον, ὃν καὶ τὴν
Πυθίαν λόγος ἔχει τρίποδι πλησιάζουσαν, ἔνθα ῥῆγμά ἐστι γῆς ἀναπνέον ὥς
φασιν ἀτμὸν ἔνθεον, αὐτόθεν ἐγκύμονα τῆς δαιμονίου καθισταμένην δυνάμεως
παραυτίκα χρησμῳδεῖν κατ᾽ ἐπίπνοιαν· οὕτως ἀπὸ τῆς τῶν ἀρχαίων μεγαλοφυΐας εἰς τὰς τῶν ζηλούντων ἐκείνους ψυχὰς ὡς ἀπὸ ἱερῶν στομίων ἀπόρροιαί
τινες φέρονται[.]

For many are carried away by the inspiration of another, just as the story runs
that the Pythian priestess on approaching the tripod where there is, they say, a
rift in the earth, exhaling divine vapour, thereby becomes impregnated with the
divine power and is at once inspired to utter oracles; so, too, from the natural
genius of those old writers there flows into the hearts of their admirers as it were
an emanation from those holy mouths. *De sub.* 13.2

The parallelism turns upon a double movement of rupture and
transcendence: the prophetess achieves sublime insight by strad-
dling the void (ῥῆγμα); the writer achieves lasting greatness by
opening himself to the influence of his predecessors.[57] Lucan's
account of Phemonoe evidences the same pattern: the 'earth's vast
chasms' (*vastos telluris hiatus*, 5.82) from which she receives
inspiration remind us of the gaping *hiatus* upon which Lucretius
builds sublimity (Lucr. 5.375, 6.584, 6.599 – and also by association of the Longinian διάστημα, *De sub.* 9.4–9); once inside the
Delphic cavern (*vastisque adducta cavernis*, Luc. 5.162), she is
broken by Apollo and transported out of herself (*artus / Phoeba-
dos inrupit Paean, mentemque priorem / expulit atque hominem
toto sibi cedere iussit / pectore*, 5.166–9). Bacchic self-alienation
gives her knowledge of all time past and future (5.177–81), of
the extent of the sea and the sum of the sands (*non modus Oceani,
numerus non derat harenae*, 5.182), a potent image for the vaunted
reach of Lucan's own apocalyptic poem.[58]

---

[57] Lucan's own response to Virgil is another site of the *Bellum civile*'s sublimity: Masters
(1992) 118–33 demonstrates the complex relationship between Lucan's Phemonoe and
Virgil's Sibyl Deiphobe; in Longinian terms, Phemonoe's possession metapoetically
represents the intertextual qualities of the language with which Lucan describes her.
Cf. Hardie (2009a) 109–16 on the intertextual sublimity of Virgil's metapoetic *Fama*
(identified as a 'mathematical' sublimity due to the sheer number of intertexts *Fama*
incorporates). See further Thompson and Bruère (1968/2010) on Lucan's use of Virgil;
compare Lausberg (1985) and Green (1991/2010) on Lucan's use of Homer.

[58] See Masters (1992) 145–7. Note the echo of the *modum* at once enforced and destroyed
by the civil war in the narrator's vision of apocalypse at Luc. 1.82.

In concert, then, with the Bacchic *matrona*, the metapoetic figure of Phemonoe allows us to see the sublimity of the poetic
experience claimed by the Lucanian narrator in relation to the *Bellum civile*'s composition. And, again, this poetic surrogate reveals
the effects of this sublimity on artistic expression. Inspired by the
god, Phemonoe's vision, encompassing in its totalising reach all
the events of the civil war, proves literally, paradoxically, breath-
taking. As Dolores O'Higgins and Jamie Masters have pointed
out, Phemonoe never gives voice to all that she sees:[59] despite its
lengthy build-up, her riddling prophecy to Appius spans a mere
three lines (5.194–6), deceiving him into thinking he will escape
death in the war (5.224–31); 'the rest Apollo stifled and he blocked
her throat' (*cetera suppressit faucesque obstruxit Apollo*, 5.197)
(contrast Appius' desire *finemque expromere rerum*, 5.68, an inversion of the poem's perpetual postponement of 'the end'). Like the
Bacchic *matrona*, Phemonoe thus gestures towards the tension
between speech and silence that the narrator later, at Pharsalus and
at Troy, articulates explicitly (7.552–6, 7.207–13, 9.980–6). This
tension is, we have seen, the driving force behind Lucan's refrac-
tive use of language. Phemonoe dramatises the way this tension
itself stems from the sublime apprehension of civil war's sublimity. The object of Phemonoe's vision, like the object of Lucan's,
is something that the mind may grasp but that beggars expressive
capabilities.

The foregoing reading of the poem's representation of its own
genesis responds to a Kantian analysis of the sublime's impact on,
our powers of reason and imagination. This reading also resembles
Kant's model in its positive ethical colouration: while Phemonoe
and the *matrona* direct our attention to the problem of sublime
speech, Lucan of course ultimately does give voice to his theme
and, in so doing, I have suggested, realises and resists its horror.
It is important, however, to remember the ease with which such
colouration bleeds away. As we have seen, the sublime has no
necessary connection with goodness or redemption. Indeed, one
of the *Bellum civile*'s most extraordinary features is the current

<hr/>

[59] O'Higgins (1988) 214–17, Masters (1992) 147–8.

of complicity that it generates between the whirlwind of Caesarian violence, the narrator and, hence, us as readers. *Pharsalia*, we
remember, is emphatically described as *nostra*: does the narratorial assertion *me teque legent* set up a distinction between Caesar
and the narrator or imply that they are, at some level, the same,
both creators of *bellum civile*?[60] We have seen how in Book I
Lucan literalises in the image of apocalypse the sublimity of the
inconceivable, of the Longinian idea that 'the whole universe is not
enough to satisfy the speculative intelligence of human thought'
(*De sub.* 35.3). Is Lucan's endeavour to present the unpresentable
then to be viewed under the sign of the world-destruction brought
about by Caesar? Thus far I have focused attention upon the positive effects of Longinus' communicational sublime, emphasising
the intensity of engagement it promotes between author and reader.
But if the driving force of the sublime is successful communication, the Nuremberg rallies, for instance, (and Riefenstahl's films
of them) have as great a claim to sublimity as Sappho's Φαίνεταί μοι. In his discussion of Demosthenes' speech against Midias,
Longinus notes how 'the orator does just the same as the aggressor,
he belabours the minds of the jury with blow after blow' (οὐδὲν
ἄλλο διὰ τούτων ὁ ῥήτωρ ἢ ὅπερ ὁ τύπτων ἐργάζεται, τὴν
διάνοιαν τῶν δικαστῶν τῇ ἐπαλλήλῳ πλήττει φορᾷ, *De sub.*
20.2). Longinus' comments on this speech were cited above for
their emphasis on the sublime ἐνάργεια of Demosthenes' words,
on how these words force us fully to confront, and so to condemn,
the unpresentable violence of Midias' actions. But this sublimity
can swing the other way too. As Longinus points out, by enacting
Midias' violence Demosthenes becomes one with Midias – as,
we might say, Lucan's narrator becomes one with Caesar even as
he strives to make us fully aware of the horrific effects of Caesarism (and as, in their shared sublimity, Homer for Longinus
becomes one with Eris: *De sub.* 9.4). Most disturbingly, given
the sublime's tendency to meld subject and object, and given the
Bellum civile's insistence on being received as a sublime work,
this identification easily passes over from the text to us as reading
subjects.

---

[60] Henderson (1987/2010) 457–8; Johnson (1987) 120–1; Ormand (1994/2010) 342.

The Thessalian witch Erictho, a gruesome mirror-image of Phemonoe, ensures that we do not forget this dark side to the sublime.[61] Another figure marked as a potential surrogate for the poet, she unsettlingly reconfigures the sublimity experienced by the Pythian priestess. The basic structural resemblance between the two episodes first signals the connection. As Appius in Book 5, driven by his desire to discover the war's outcome, sought out the Pythian priestess, so in Book 6, on the very eve of Pharsalus, it is anxiety about his fate that impels Pompey's son Sextus to track down Erictho; but where Phemonoe's prophetic power arises through divine possession, Erictho, who is said to exert mastery even over the gods (*omne nefas superi prima iam voce precantis / concedunt carmenque timent audire secundum*, 6.527–8, cf. 6.443–51, 492–9), uses necromancy, forcing a dead soldier's spirit temporarily to re-enter his corpse and reveal the future. As she declares:

> 'tripodas vatesque deorum
> sors obscura decet: certus discedat, ab umbris
> quisquis vera petit duraeque oracula mortis
> fortis adit.'

> 'The tripods and the prophets of the gods
> are graced with obscure answers; he who seeks the truth
> from ghosts and approaches bravely the oracles of relentless death,
> let him leave certain.'   6.770–3

Picking up these initial cues, critics have been quick to identify Erictho's particular metapoetic characteristics.[62] Like the narrator (1.63, 7.553, 9.980), she is described as a *vates* (6.651, cf. 6.628 where the term is applied to the corpse that is to become her zombie); like the narrator in his endeavour to make present again a long-finished conflict, she is able to bend time to her will (as Sextus says, *suo ventura potes devertere cursu*, 6.591, cf. 6.605–10) but is impotent to change critical historical events (*at, simul a*

---

[61] Cf. Schiesaro (2003) 22, 52–3, 120–1, 127–32 on the metapoetic role of Atreus in Seneca's *Thyestes*, who can be seen 'to embody a form of artistic and behavioural sublimity which transcends humanity and attracts the audience beyond and even against the purview of their ethical beliefs' (p. 127).

[62] Martindale (1980) 373–5; O'Higgins (1988) 218–25; Masters (1992) 205–14. See also e.g. Ahl (1976) 130–49; Johnson (1987) 19–33.

prima descendit origine mundi / causarum series, atque omnia fata laborant / si quicquam mutare velis, unoque sub ictu / stat genus humanum, tum, Thessala turba fatemur, / plus Fortuna potest, 6.611–15); like the narrator, she reanimates and gives voice to the dead; just as the narrator can barely express his horror at his own theme, so he views Erictho's *carmina* (6.647, 682, a common word for both poetic song and magical incantation)[63] as *crimina* (6.507).[64]

What has not been previously remarked, however, is the way in which, albeit less obviously than Phemonoe (or the *matrona*), Erictho is also marked with sublimity. Her hellish powers of speech exceed all imagining (*ficti quas nulla licentia monstri / transierit, quarum quidquid non creditur ars est*, 6.436–7; cf. Lucan's incredible description of Marius' murder, *vix erit ulla fides tam saevi criminis*, 2.186); their reach extends to the heavens (*per aetherios... recessus*, 6.445). The cavernous hollow into which she descends to perform her necromancy (*haud procul a Ditis caecis depressa cavernis / in praeceps subsedit humus*, 6.642–3) reminds us of the *hiatus* through which Phemonoe receives inspiration (5.82) as well as the deep grottoes that Seneca mentions among things that may be considered *speciosi ex horrido* (that is to say, in Burkeian terms, sublime).[65] Her ability physically to reverse the norms of nature induces a sickening vertigo: under her spells the sea rises up though the winds are still, waterfalls hang from cliffs, rivers flow uphill, 'mountains dip their peaks' and, instead of towering on high, Olympus looks up at the clouds (6.469–77); such inversions offer a perverted literal counterpart to the radical changes wrought upon (our perception of) the world by the sublimity of Lucretian atomism.[66] Indeed Erictho's defining unnaturalism, the revivification of the soldier's corpse, effects a movement

[63] Masters (1992) 206.   [64] Masters (1992) 210; cf. Ov. *Ars* 134.
[65] Sen. *Ep.* 41.3; see Schiesaro (2003) 127. Cf. Sen. *Thy.* 651–82, *Oed.* 530–47, *Her. O.* 1618–41.
[66] Note too the gigantomachic undertones that the Lucretian sublime shares with Erictho's heaven-harrying powers: the witch can so shake the earth that Olympus is brought low (*summisso vertice montes / explicuere iugum, nubes suspexit Olympus*, 6.476–7) and laid bare for all to see (*tantae molis onus percussum voce recessit / perspectumque dedit circum labentis Olympi*, 6.483–4); Lucretius' gigantomachism is discussed in Chapter 3.

103

from death to life that the sublime also follows (a movement we will later see replayed, though rather differently framed, in the narrator's response to the dead Pompey).[67]

And the sublimity of this metapoetic figure again gives us a clearer understanding of the sublimity of the *Bellum civile*'s own poetry. Where Apollo prevented Phemonoe from speaking more than a few words, Erictho is all too capable of uttering the *nefas* of her *carmina*, of speaking what is unspeakable.[68] In so doing, she unpleasantly twists our perception of the way in which Lucan also gives sublime voice to the *nefas* that is civil *discordia*: in making this *nefas* present Lucan not only bears witness to but also re-enacts, and so becomes complicit with, this *nefas*.[69] To read his words as a monument of resistance is to feel only half their force. Erictho reminds us that the sublimity of the *Bellum civile*, like all experiences of the sublime, cannot be so neatly or comfortably contained.

The Bacchic *matrona* and Phemonoe, on the one hand, and Erictho, on the other, offer miniature sketches of the Lucanian sublime's twin ethical poles. In the next two chapters, through consideration of the *Bellum civile*'s presentation of Caesar and Pompey, I examine these poles in more detail. My contention is that, in aesthetic terms, there exists a strange parity between Caesar as he crosses the Rubicon, fells the Massilian grove and braves the Adriatic storm, and Pompey as he flees Pharsalus and, subsequently, lies dead on the Egytian shore, a 'plaything of the sea' (*ludibrium pelagi*, 8.710). Lucan's presentation of each is achieved according to the same experiential dynamic. Both emerge as sublime objects – paradoxical, excessive, transgressive things that refuse to conform to our normal cognitive categories. But the sublimity is in each case differently directed. Where the aesthetics of Pompey's corpse point towards a morally reassuring experience of loss sublimely recuperated, the aesthetics of Caesarian *motus* suggest something altogether less comfortable, a sublimity grounded in might and

---

[67] Like the murder of Marius Gratidianus, the ghastly incredibility of Erictho's activities identifies her with the grotesque as well as the sublime; compare in particular Luc. 6.540–6 with 2.173–90.

[68] O'Higgins (1988) 217; Masters (1992) 212.   [69] Masters (1992) 7–10.

violence: overwhelmed by Caesar's extraordinary force, we align ourselves with his demonic energy and locate transcendence in destruction. I want to emphasise, however, that the sublimity of Lucan's *poem* cannot be separated from either. The readerly astonishment (*attonitam* 1.676, *attoniti* 7.212) asserted by the narrator is a function of both 'Caesarian' and 'Pompeian' sublimity. And this duality has important implications for our appreciation of the *Bellum civile* as a whole. Existing hermeneutic criticism tends to revolve around the question of whether the poem offers an 'engaged' lament for the lost Republic or 'nihilistic', cynical laughter in the dark, whether Lucan backs Pompey's tarnished cause or is covertly complicit with Caesarian violence. An aesthetic approach to the poem obviates the need to decide. What stimulates Lucan's creative energies, irrespective of ideological implication, is the hit of the sublime.

CHAPTER 3

THE CAESARIAN SUBLIME

Lucan portrays Caesar as a larger-than-life, hyper-kinetic, awe-inspiring source of destruction, a literally superhuman force. In this chapter I focus in particular on his association with and response to objects and phenomena from the natural world that both the ancient and post-classical traditions cite as common sources of sublimity.[1] In so doing, I also analyse the ways in which Lucan reworks the sublimity of Lucretius' *De rerum natura*, shifting its focus from the epistemological to the political and, in the process, bringing out its more troubling ethical implications. Philip Hardie has explored how Virgil figures Aeneas' struggle in imagery and language of vision which recall both Longinus' and Lucretius' emphasis on seeing as a means to sublimity.[2] In particular, he reminds us of the importance of Epicurus' sublime flight of the mind and facing down of *Religio*'s monstrous gaze at Lucr. 1.62–79 as a model for Virgil's narrative.[3] But Aeneas' progress through the epic plot of Epicurus' career begins in terror amid the storm of *Aeneid* 1 and culminates in his enraged, markedly un-Lucretian killing of Turnus at the end of Book 12. Moreover, his victory, and that of Rome, is not over but according to *Religio*. Aeneas, in other words, follows Lucretius' instructions for the achievement of sublimity with only limited success. By contrast, I suggest, Lucan's Caesar rises fully to Lucretius' challenge: fearlessly surmounting all obstacles, like Lucretius' godlike Epicurean, he puts himself on a par with the divine, supplanting the traditional epic gods who are so conspicuously absent from Lucan's poem.[4] In doing so, however, he reveals

---

[1] In the eighteenth century, Caesar himself was commonly listed among such objects: see Kirwan (2005) 2, 17, 41, 43–4, 46.
[2] Hardie (2009b) 153–79.   [3] See also Hardie (1986) 194–200.
[4] On the absence of Lucan's gods, see eg. Le Bonniec (1970); Ahl (1976) 280–305; Johnson (1987) 1–18; Feeney (1991) 250–301; Bartsch (1997) 108–114; Sklenár (2003) 1–12. Hunter (2009) 143–8 argues that Apollonius' *Argonautica* constitutes the type for

106

the sublime's tendency towards tyranny and domination, thereby bringing to the fore a problematic that, although of considerable concern to post-classical theorists, was only hinted at in Lucretius and Virgil.

Like lightning

Famously, Lucan introduces Caesar in Book 1 by comparing him to a thunderbolt in an extended simile:

> qualiter expressum ventis per nubila fulmen
> aetheris inpulsi sonitu mundique fragore
> emicuit rupitque diem populosque paventes
> terruit obliqua praestringens lumina flamma:
> in sua templa furit, nullaque exire vetante   155
> materia magnamque cadens magnamque revertens
> dat stragem late sparsosque recolligit ignes.

> Just so flashes out the thunderbolt shot forth by the winds through clouds,
> accompanied by the crashing of the heavens and sound of shattered ether;
> it splits the sky and terrifies the panicked
> people, searing eyes with slanting flame;
> against its own precincts it rages, and, with nothing solid stopping
> its course, both as it falls and then returns great is the devastation
> dealt far and wide before it gathers again its scattered fires.   1.151–7

The comparison hinges upon Caesar's overwhelming might. As Ahl puts it: 'Nothing can stop him... The power described is superhuman. Caesar is energy incarnate, a Zeus-like being whose attacks wither and destroy all in their way.'[5] It is this

---

Longinus of the non-sublime epic partly on the basis of its reduction of contact between the human and the divine. However, as Hunter concedes, (the absence of) such features should not be given excessive weight in analyses of sublimity. Longinus' account of the sublime is partisan, composed in response to rivals such as Caecilius; it is not the specific instances of sublimity that he cites but his underlying conception of the 'logic' of the sublime, of what sublimity is, that is important. Indeed, what fascinates Longinus is not so much the sublimity of the gods per se as the way in which the experience of the sublime allows us to participate in divinity ourselves (*De sub.* 36.1; cf. 13.2, 16.2, 33.5, 35.2). Caesar offers an unsettling paradigm of precisely such participation.

5   Ahl (1976) 198. See further Aymard (1951) 99–100. Lightning is also used as a way of representing great individuals by Plutarch (*Cato minor* 20) and Quintilian (*Inst.* 8.6.71: a lost hymn by Pindar likened Hercules *non igni nec ventis nec mari, sed fulmini... ut illa minora, hoc par esset*); see Morford (1967) 55.

power that provides lightning, thunderbolts and sudden flashes of light with a well-established pedigree as objects of the sublime. By way of contextualisation, before considering the details of Lucan's simile, I briefly highlight some examples from this tradition.

Longinus uses lightning as an image for literary ὕψος. He introduces the comparison near the start of his treatise: 'a well-timed flash of sublimity shatters everything like a bolt of lightning and reveals the full power of the speaker at a single stroke' (ὕψος δέ που καιρίως ἐξενεχθὲν τά τε πράγματα δίκην σκηπτοῦ πάντα διεφόρησεν καὶ τὴν τοῦ ῥήτορος εὐθὺς ἀθρόαν ἐνεδείξατο δύναμιν, De sub. 1.4). Demosthenes' eloquence provides a recurrent example: he 'out-thunders (καταβροντᾷ), as it were, and outshines (καταφέγγει) orators of every age. You could sooner open your eyes to the descent of a thunderbolt (κεραυνοῖς) than face his repeated outbursts of emotion without blinking' (34.4, cf. 12.4). Longinus' striking citation of the brilliance of Genesis 1:3–9 ('God said, "Let there be light", and there was light', De sub. 9.9), participates in this same line of imagery.

Lightning is used as a natural corollary for sublime speech by Latin critics too.[6] Like Longinus, Cicero praises Demosthenes' fulmina (Att. 15.1a.2, Orat. 234). Singling out the Marathon oath on which Longinus also dwells (Dem. De corona 208; see De sub. 16.2–4, 17.2), Quintilian juxtaposes the way Demosthenes surpasses (superavit) others in 'power, sublimity and force' (vi sublimitate impetu) with the 'lightning bolts and thunderclaps' (fulminibus et caelesti fragori) that mark Pericles' rhetoric (Inst. 12.10.23–4).[7] The lightning-like qualities of Pericles' oratory are also adduced by Pliny (Ep. 1.20.19) and Cicero (Orat. 29). These assessments of Pericles reach back to Aristophanes' lines 'And then in wrath Pericles, that Olympian, did lighten and thunder (ἤστραπτ' ἐβρόντα) and stir up Greece' (Ach. 530–1):[8] as Quintilian argues, the fact that even the poets of Old Comedy admitted the 'unbelievable power' (vim incredibilem) of Pericles' rhetoric

---

[6] See Russell (1964) xxxix and ad De sub. 12.4, 34.4.
[7] Cf. Quint. Inst. 9.2.62, 11.3.168.   [8] Cf. Quint. Inst. 2.16.19.

is proof of its true greatness.[9] Such *vis* is also to be found in Homer:

> summam expressurus in Ulixe facundiam et magnitudinem illi vocis et vim orationis nivibus <hibernis> copia [verborum] atque impetu parem tribuit. cum hoc igitur nemo mortalium contendet, hunc ut deum homines intuebuntur. hanc vim et celeritatem in Pericle miratur Eupolis, hanc fulminibus Aristophanes comparat, haec est vere dicendi facultas.

> When he comes to express the supreme eloquence, in Ulysses, he gives him a mighty voice, and a force of speech 'like a <winter> blizzard' in its volume and violence. So 'no mortal will contend' with him, and 'men will look upon him as a god'. This is the force and speed that Eupolis admires in Pericles and Aristophanes likens to the thunderbolt. This is in truth the power of speech.[10] Quint. *Inst.* 12.10.64–5

To the thunderbolt as an image for mighty speech is here added the winter storm, another potentially sublime natural phenomenon. Again, the comparison centres upon dynamic force and power: like Pericles', Ulysses' speech is irresistible in its *impetus*.

Lightning is also a source of sublimity in Lucretius.[11] A substantial part of Book 6 is devoted to discussion of its physical causes (Lucr. 6.96–422). The analysis displays the same fascination with lightning's overpowering force:

> nunc ea quo pacto gignantur et impete tanto
> fiant, ut possint ictu discludere turris,   240
> disturbare domos, avellere tigna trabesque,
> et monimenta virum commoliri atque ciere,
> exanimare homines, pecudes prosternere passim,
> cetera de genere hoc qua vi facere omnia possint,
> expediam, neque te in promissis plura morabor.   245

> And now in what manner these thunderbolts are produced,
>   and made with so strong a rush
> that they can split open towers with a stroke,
> overturn houses, tear out beams and rafters,

---

[9] Quint. *Inst.* 12.2.22. Quintilian's comments, like those of Cicero and Pliny, are directed in support of Pericles' thunder against the puritanically restrictive criteria of those self-styled 'Attici' who would exclude Pericles from the canon of great orators: see Quint. *Inst.* 12.10.23–4. Cf. Plin. *Ep.* 9.26, 2.5. For further discussion of the stylistic debates between Atticists and Asianists, cf. Cic. *Brut.* 51, 325, *Orat.* 27, 212, 230–1; Tac. *Dial.* 18. See Russell (2001) 190.

[10] Russell's translation (2001).   [11] Hardie (2009a) 81.

> demolish and displace the monuments of great men,
> kill human beings, lay low animals all around,
> and by what force they can do all else of this kind,
> I will expound, and delay you no longer with promises.
>
> Lucr. 6.239–45

vis, impetus, ictus and their cognates recur throughout the discussion in Book 6.[12] Nothing can withstand lightning's fire (*nil omnino obsistere possit*, Lucr. 6.227; cf. 6.331–4: *nec facilest tali naturae obsistere quicquam . . . non igitur multis offensibus in remorando / haesitat, hanc ob rem celeri volat impete labens*): its power exceeds that of the sun (*tanto mobilior vis et dominantior haec est*, 6.238). Lucretius also responds to the scale of the scene in which lightning typically strikes. The size of the thunderclouds is stunning: *scilicet hoc densis fit nubibus et simul alte / extructis aliis alias super impete miro* (6.185–6); he watches as they tower around mountains (*per magnos montis cumulata*, 6.191) and, in an extraordinary conflation of the stationary and the mobile, of solid rock and insubstantial vapour, actually likens them to mountains, propelled through space by the winds (*cum montibus adsimulata / nubila portabunt venti transversa per auras*, 6.189–90).

The classical sensitivity to lightning's sublimity is mirrored in lightning's recurrent enumeration among objects of the natural sublime by eighteenth-century writers. Burke observes that 'lightning is certainly productive of grandeur'[13] while Kant's sublime objects include 'thunder clouds towering up into the heavens, bringing with them flashes of lightning and crashes of thunder'.[14] Again, it is the power of the lightning bolt or flash (Kant's dynamical sublime), and, to a lesser extent, its scale (Kant's mathematical sublime), that thrills. More recent associations of lightning with the sublime, in art as well as nature, can be traced too. Lyotard, for instance, identifies the 'zips' of Barnett Newman's paintings – thin, straight lines that 'strike through' blocks of colour 'in a rectilinear slash' – as lightning-like triggers of sublimity: the zip 'descends

---

[12] *vis*: Lucr. 6.137, 181, 244, 295, 300, 309, 310, 319, 320, 325, 380; *impetus*: Lucr. 6.138, 174, 186, 239; *ictus*: Lucr. 6.294, 311, 323, 313, 316.
[13] Burke (1990) 73.   [14] Kant (2003) 144.

like a thunderbolt... The work rises up... in an instant, but the flash of the instant strikes it like a minimal command: Be.'[15]

Against this background, we can see Lucan's introductory comparison of Caesar with lightning as a programmatic statement of the future dictator's sublimity.[16] The simile is dominated by indicators of violent motion. The first line refers to the ancient belief, endorsed by Lucretius, that lightning was caused by the collision of clouds (or by the raging of wind imprisoned within clouds);[17] it is accompanied by, or equated with, the 'shattering' of the ether and the 'crashing' of the heavens (Luc. 1.152);[18] it 'splits' the sky (153) and wildly 'rages' (155). The culmination of the simile owes a particular debt to Lucretius' articulation of the 'dynamic' sublime. Just as 'nothing can block the path' of Lucretian lightning (*nil omnino obsistere possit*, Lucr. 6.227) so here 'nothing solid can stop the course' of the Caesarian thunderbolt (*nullaque exire vetante / materia*, Luc. 1.155–6); the phrase used by Lucretius earlier in the *De rerum natura* of the sublimely destructive power of wind, *dat... stragem* (Lucr. 1.288), is picked up here and amplified, Lucan twice labelling as *magna* the Caesarian lightning's *strages*.

Caesar's introductory simile establishes sudden, blinding illumination as the sensory, experiential corollary of his transgressive actions and, like a musical theme, the motif recurs throughout the narrative, either as an image of Caesar himself or as a part of the epic's physical world, a literal consequence of the conqueror's actions.[19] Lightning is included, for instance, among the sublime portents that appear after Caesar has crossed the Rubicon:

[15] Lyotard (1991) 82, 86, 88. See further Shaw (2006) 120–2. Lyotard's ascription of positive ethical value to Newman's lightning-like sublimity is in direct contrast to the tyrannical drive of Lucan's lightning-like Caesar.
[16] Cf. Hardie (2009a) 71 on the allusion to the Lucretian thunderbolt within Virgil's sublime description of *Fama*, *Aen.* 4.174–5 (cf. Lucr. 6.177, 340–2).
[17] Lucr. 6.96ff., 173–213, 295ff.; cf. Epicurus, *Letter to Pythocles* 100. See further Getty (1940) ad Luc. 1.151, citing. Ar. *Nub.* 404ff.; Arist. *Met.* 2.9; Ov. *Met.* 1.56, 6.695–6, 11.433–6; Sen. *Nat.* 1.1.6, 1.14.5, 2.22, 2.23.1, *Dial.* 1.13.
[18] Burke (1990) 75 includes the noise of thunder among his sources of sublimity. See further on Luc. 1.237–39 below.
[19] Rosner-Siegel (1983/2010); cf. Morford (1967) 55, Ahl (1976) 157, 173, 184–5, 199, 215.

fulgura fallaci micuerunt crebra sereno,   530
et varias ignis denso dedit aere formas,
nunc iaculum longo, nunc sparso lumine lampas.
emicuit caelo tacitum sine nubibus ullis
fulmen et Arctois rapiens de partibus ignem
percussit Latiare caput.   535

Lightning flashed repeatedly in the deceptive cloudless sky,
its fire presenting different shapes in the dense air,
now, with lengthened light, a spear, now, with light spread out, a torch.
A silent thunderbolt flashed out in the cloudless
heaven and, gathering fire from northern parts,
it struck the head of Latium.   1.530–5

The location of these lines mirrors that of Caesar's introductory
simile: there are just over 150 lines between the above description
of the *fulmen* and the end of the book; we encounter Caesar-as-
thunderbolt 150 lines into the poem. This compositional symme-
try helps to reinforce the association of Caesar with lightning and
thunderbolts, linking the description of the lightning as an omen
of Rome's ruin with the earlier simile describing Caesar himself.
Moreover, these dual lightning images frame the epic's first historical incident, which is also our first sight of Caesar in action –
his crossing of the Rubicon. We will examine this scene fully
below but it is worth noting here how, although the passage lacks
specific lightning imagery, the terrifying suddenness of Caesar's
appearance at Ariminum is likened to the speed of a Parthian
arrow (*ocior . . . missa Parthi post terga sagitta*, 1.230) and is dramatically juxtaposed with the swift arrival of daylight (*ignes /
solis Lucifero fugiebant astra relicto*, 1.231–2). It is precisely the
'extreme velocity of its motion' that Burke, following Longinus,[20]
identifies as an essential source of lightning's sublimity; moreover, he continues, 'a quick transition from light to darkness, or
from darkness to light, has yet a greater effect' in producing the
sublime.[21]

---

[20] The speed of Demosthenes' rhetoric is what makes it like lightning (*De sub.* 12.4).
[21] Burke (1990) 73. The sun's arrival is immediately qualified by emphasis on the gloom
that appropriately enshrouds the first day of the war: *maestam tenuerunt nubile lucem*
(1.235). Moreover, some thirty lines later, dawn apparently breaks for a second time (see
Masters 1992: 3–4): *noctis gelidas lux solverat umbras* (1.260). Burke's appreciation
of obscurity and confusion as sources of sublimity suggests that he would have enjoyed
these Lucanian details.

Later in the poem, during the critical battle of Pharsalus, lightning again heralds Caesar's might. As Pompey's troops prepare for
battle, 'the entire ether blocked their approach' (*totus venientibus
obstitit aether*, 7.153):

> adversasque faces immensoque igne columnas   155
> et trabibus mixtis avidos typhonas aquarum
> detulit atque oculos ingesto fulgure clausit;
> excussit cristas galeis capulosque solutis
> perfudit gladiis ereptaque pila liquavit,
> aetherioque nocens fumavit sulpure ferrum.   160

> it hurled down meteors in their faces and columns of immeasurable
> flame and water-greedy cyclones mixed with fireballs
> and with a rain of lightning made them close their eyes;
> it knocked the crests from helmets, flooded hilts
> with melted swords, dissolved the javelins it snatched,
> and guilty blade smoked with the ether's sulphur.   7.155–60

Where in Book 1 lightning flashed ominously in a clear sky and
struck the temple of Jupiter Latiaris,[22] here, as the armies square
up, thunderbolts actually blind the soldiers, wreck their weapons
and hinder their advance.[23] These portents recall Valerius Max-
imus' description of the lightning hurled by Jupiter against Pompey as he marched out of Dyrrachium to fight Caesar (*egresso a
Dyrrachio adversa agmini eius fulmina iaciens*, V. Max. 1.6.12).[24]
Valerius reads this as an index of Caesar's *gloria* and Pompey's
error. So here, following Pompey's resigned acceptance of his
troops' demand for combat, the lightning points to the imminent
loss of the Republican cause (*advenisse diem qui fatum rebus in
aevum / conderet humanis, et quaeri, Roma quid esset, / illo Marte,
palam est*, Luc. 7.131–3; *non vacat ullos / pro se ferre metus: urbi
Magnoque timetur*, 7.137–8). But Lucan's framing of these portents is more complex than Valerius', for the lightning here acts to

---

[22] For this identification of *Latiare caput*, 1.535, see Getty (1940) ad loc.
[23] The lightning at Luc. 7.155–6 appears in not one but several different forms, emphasising
its strength and force: *fax* but also *columna* (cf. Plin. *Nat.* 11.134; Sen. *Nat.* 8.10.3; Man.
1.841) and *trabs* (cf. Man. 1.841; Sen. *Ep.* 94.56, *Nat.* 7.4.4, 5.2); see Dilke (1960) ad
loc. Similarly the lightning at Luc. 1.527–35 appears as a *lampas* and *iaculum* (with
lampas, cf. Luc. 10.502–3; Man. 1.846; Sen. *Nat.* 1.15.4; Plin. *Nat.* 2.96).
[24] Dilke (1960) ad Luc. 7.155.

impose itself between Pompey's men and Caesar's victory, to prevent battle from being joined: it mangles helmets, melts swords and dashes javelins to the ground. It is not simply a sign of Pompey's *error* but also a cosmological attempt to stop this *error* from going any further and, hence, to prevent Caesar from attaining the *gloria* that Valerius confidently ascribes to him. Where previously lightning has been presented in the *Bellum civile* as the imagistic counterpart to or literal consequence of Caesar's actions, here it works against the force of his onslaught. Of course, as Lucan and we know with the benefit of hindsight, Caesar carried the day; his 'lightning' outshone that of the sky; the apocalyptic force of Caesarian revolution proved mightier than apocalypse itself. In their (all too well-founded) fear that the end of their world is imminent, the citizens of Rome previously begged the gods to wrap the sky in flame and send it hurtling to earth *per fulmina* (2.58) – better that than civil conflict. Here, in Thessaly, this wish comes true, yet still the lightning-bolt that is Caesar proves more powerful.

The lightning that precedes Pharsalus thus complicates our understanding of Caesar as a sublime object and of the way in which he attains this status. Caesar himself becomes lightning-like through an agonistic surpassing of lightning's own power. The *adversae faces* delay Pompey's men and so halt Caesar temporarily but he and history soon surge onward. Confronted with the Thessalian lightning, Caesar asserts the truly blistering capabilities of his own military might. In an earlier episode the Massilians plead neutrality in defence against Caesar, positing a hypothetical gigantomachy as a hyperbolic parallel to Rome's civil war and implicitly casting Caesar in the role of *fulmina*-flinging Jove: *ignarum mortale genus per fulmina tantum / sciret adhuc caelo solum regnare Tonantem* (3.319–20). Caesar's angry response picks up on the sublime associations of this analogy and presses their implications further. He likens himself to natural phenomena such as gales and fires:

> 'ventus ut amittit vires, nisi robore densae
> occurrunt silvae, spatio diffusus inani,
> utque perit magnus nullis obstantibus ignis,

sic hostes mihi desse nocet, damnumque putamus   365
armorum, nisi qui vinci potuere rebellant.'

'As the wind loses strength and is dissipated in empty space
unless the forests thick with timber block its path,
and as a great fire dies without fuel,
so lack of enemies hurts me and we think it a loss
of warfare if those who could be defeated do not fight back.'
3.362–6[25]

Although Caesar does not here conceive of himself explicitly as
a *fulmen* or *fulgur*, using instead the more general term *ignis*, his
stress on his need for an obstacle points towards the dynamic at
work behind his ability to out-lighten lightning.[26] Like Caesar, the
would-be sublime subject must have an object against which to
match himself. It is through this confrontation – Kant's 'momentary inhibition of the vital forces and the immediately following,
and all the more powerful, outpouring of them'[27] – that the sublime
is experienced. *perit magnus nullis obstantibus ignis* ('a great fire
dies without fuel'), declares Caesar; at Pharsalus it is lightning's
ignis that is itself 'in the way' and in comparison with which, paradoxically, Caesarian lightning emerges all the brighter. Moreover,
Caesar's simile turns on the awareness that this 'power-transfer'
is a process that underlies the force of natural phenomena too: the
wind's strength derives from its encounter with 'forests thick with
timber' (*robore densae / . . . silvae*).[28] Lucretius claims the same
of lightning:

mobilitas autem fit fulminis et gravis ictus,
et celeri ferme percurrunt fulmina lapsu,
nubibus ipsa quod omnino prius incita se vis   325
colligit et magnum conamen sumit eundi,
inde ubi non potuit nubes capere inpetis auctum,

[25] Cf. Luc. 2.439ff.: *Caesar in arma furens nullas nisi sanguine fuso / gaudet habere vias, quod non terat hoste vacantis / Hesperiae fines vacuosque inrumpat in agros . . .*
[26] Compare Hunink (1992) ad loc., who identifies in Caesar's desire for obstacles an inversion of the virtuous (Stoic) man's need for experiences that will test him, see e.g. Sen. *Dial.* 1.2.4 (*marcet sine adversario virtus*).
[27] Kant (2003) 128–9.
[28] The scientific truth of these statements is obviously problematic. Lucan alters the 'facts' to suit the context; cf. Luc. 9.449–54 where it is asserted that obstacles deplete the wind's power.

exprimitur vis atque ideo volat impete miro,
ut validis quae de tormentis missa feruntur.

The speed, moreover, and heavy blow of the thunderbolt comes about,
and the bolts usually run with so quick a fall,
because first of all within the clouds a force is always aroused
and collects itself and takes on a mighty energy of movement,
and then, when the cloud can no longer contain the increasing rush,
the force is pressed out and therefore flies with a wonderful rush,
like missiles which are hurled from powerful catapults.

Lucr. 6.323–9

'When the cloud can no longer contain the increasing rush, the force is pressed out': the Caesarian encounter with the thunderbolt effects the 'inhibition' and 'outpouring' of the Kantian sublime, but the thunderbolt is itself a product of this same dynamic of 'containment' and 'expression'. According to this logic, sublimity results from a kind of chain reaction, a system of checks and spurs in which the retardation of dynamic force fuels its onward rush. Caesar is sublime – he is like lightning – because he succeeds in transcending lightning's overwhelming power, a power that is itself the sublime result of lightning's own *magnum conamen*.

In the following sections I explore this agonistic dynamic further, focusing in particular on three episodes – Caesar's crossing of the Rubicon in Book 1, felling of the Massilian grove in Book 3 and survival of the sea storm in Book 5 – in which Caesar's subjective experience of the sublime reinforces his status as a sublime object.

The Rubicon (1.183–265) and beyond

The first line of the poem's historical action plunges us *in medias res*:

iam gelidas Caesar cursu superaverat Alpes
ingentisque animo motus bellumque futurum
ceperat.

Now swiftly Caesar had surmounted the icy Alps
and in his mind conceived immense upheavals,
coming war.   1.183–5

This is the second time, following the lightning simile, we have met Caesar and again he is closely associated with an object of the natural sublime. It was noted in the Introduction how mountains, and particularly the Alps, have frequently been reckoned a source of sublimity. In his *Enquiry*, under the heading 'Vastness', Burke hypothesised that we thrill to 'a rock or mountain of... [great] altitude' because 'a perpendicular has more force in forming the sublime than an inclined plane; and the effects of a rugged and broken surface seem stronger than where it is smooth and polished'.[29] This, in Kantian terms, is the mathematical sublime: where lightning overawes us primarily with its power, 'shapeless mountain masses towering above one another in wild disorder with their pyramids of ice'[30] make us tremble because of their magnitude. Lucan's juxtaposition of the Alps' vastness with the 'immense upheavals' in Caesar's mind (*ingentis animo motus*) assimilates the conqueror to this imposing natural backdrop, encouraging us to read the mountains' mathematical sublimity as a counterpart to the dynamical sublimity of Caesar's lightning-like *motus*. More than this: the logic of the sublime suggests that the 'immense upheavals' experienced by Caesar are directly connected with his having overcome (*superaverat*) the Alps. Longinus lists 'the power of grand conceptions' as 'the first and most powerful' of his sources of the sublime (8.1) and Kant reminds us that the experience of the sublime reveals 'a faculty of the mind which surpasses every standard of sense' and, hence, that it is 'the disposition of the mind... but not the object which is to be called sublime'.[31] The Alps, then, are not simply a counterpart to Caesar's sublimity but are a catalyst for it.[32]

There is a Lucretian–Livian intertextual dimension to Caesar's Alpine crossing that reinforces this impression of sublimity. Lucan carefully frames Caesar's invasion to recall that of Hannibal:[33] the lion to which he compares Caesar at 1.205–12 is marked as Libyan;

---

[29] Burke (1990) 66.   [30] Kant (2003) 139.   [31] Kant (2003) 138, 134.

[32] Feeney (1991) 296 compares 1.183–5 with Ovid's description of Jupiter at *Met.* 1.166 (*ingentes animo et dignas Iove concipit iras*): the parallel gives an early suggestion of Caesar's divinity, developing the implications of his opening lightning simile and anticipating his godlike behaviour at Massilia and during the Adriatic storm.

[33] Ahl (1976) 107–12: 'The mere act of crossing the Alps seems to have conveyed a Hannibal-like image' (p. 109 n. 45). See further Masters (1992) 1 n. 1.

the Ariminians see Caesar's actions as analogous to *Martem Libyes* (1.255); Caesar himself wryly observes:

> non secus ingenti bellorum Roma tumultu
> concutitur, quam si Poenus transcenderit Alpes
> Hannibal...
>
> By warfare's vast commotion Rome is shaken
> just as though the Carthaginian were crossing the Alps,
> Hannibal...   1.303–5

As the proem tells us that the civil war is worse than the disasters wrought by Hannibal (1.30–2), so later we hear that Pharsalus is a defeat worse than Cannae (7.408–9) and that, unlike Caesar, at least Hannibal granted burial to his enemy's dead (7.799–803). Following Goebel's identification of an echo of the words of Livy's Hannibal in Caesar's speech to his men before Pharsalus (7.287–8, cf. Livy 21.43.17),[34] it is suggestive to read the Hannibalic allusions surrounding Caesar's transalpine crossing against the particular account of Hannibal's invasion in Livy 21. Andrew Feldherr has recently shown how Livy presents Hannibal as a military version of the Epicurus described by Lucretius at 1.62–79.[35] As Hardie summarises, 'Hannibal bursts through the *claustra Italiae*, the Alps, having led his troops over an *iter immensum* (Livy 21.29.7) and trackless wastes (cf. Lucr. 1.926 *avia Pieridum peragro loca*), and after showing them that *fama* about the Alps is more terrifying than the reality (Livy 21.30.2–11), by applying to the Alps "a rationalising and humanising perspective"':[36]

itaque Hannibal, postquam ipsi sententia stetit pergere ire atque Italiam petere, advocata contione varie militum versat animos castigando adhortandoque: mirari se quinam pectora semper impavida repens terror invaserit... quid Alpes aliud esse credentes quam montium altitudines? fingerent altiores Pyrenaei iugis: nullas profecto terras caelum contingere nec inexsuperabiles humano generi esse.

After deciding to go ahead with his march and make for Italy as planned, Hannibal called a meeting of the men and roused their spirits with a mixture of criticism and encouragement. He was shocked, he said, that hearts ever fearless could have been subject to a panic attack... The Alps – what else did they think them but high mountains? All right, they might well suppose them higher than the crests

---

[34] Goebel (1981) 87.   [35] Feldherr (2009).   [36] Hardie (2009a) 129.

of the Pyrenees, but certainly no points of the earth reached the sky, or were insurmountable for the human race.[37] Livy 21.30.1–2, 6–7

Despite their immense height, Hannibal encourages his men to see the Alps as mountains like any others, dispelling their fears and so enabling them to make the crossing. It is these same fears that Lucretius' Epicurus conquers, opening up the 'bars of nature's gates' (*naturae... portarum claustra*, Lucr. 1.71, cf. the role of Lucan's Ariminians as *Latii claustra*, Luc. 1.253) to allow the advance of human intelligence and reason: 'forth he marched far beyond the flaming walls of the world, as he traversed the immeasurable universe in thought and imagination' (*extra / processit longe flammantia moenia mundi / atque omne immensum peragravit mente animoque*, Lucr. 1.72–4, cf. *De sub.* 35.3).[38] Moreover, as in Hannibal's confrontation with the Alps, Lucretius conceives Epicurus' achievement in terms of vertical as well as horizontal space. Where previously *Religio* had lowered down *a caeli regionibus* (Lucr. 1.64), thanks to Epicurus it is now humankind that can consider itself equal to the heavens (*nos exaequat victoria caelo*, Lucr. 1.79); so Hannibal knows that it is not the Alps but his own men who are truly able *caelum contingere*. Like Caesar's, Hannibal's physical journey across the Alps is thus a kind of objective correlative to Epicurus' sublime mental leap beyond nature's bounds.

Moreover, like Lucan's image of Caesarian lightning, Livy's account of Hannibal's Alpine crossing transfers the sublime from the realm of Lucretian epistemology into that of war. In doing so, it activates the military allusions already contained within Lucretius' description of Epicurus' 'flight of the mind'. 'A man of Greece was the first that dared to uplift mortal eyes against her, the first to make stand against her' (*primum Graius homo mortalis tollere contra / est oculos ausus primusque obsistere contra*, Lucr. 1.66–7): *Graius homo* is a phrase previously used by Ennius of Pyrrhus (*Ann.* 165 Skutsch), a military commander who, like Hannibal, wanted to invade Italy with elephants (not philosophy);[39] the image of Epicurus 'daring' to look the monster *Religio* in the

---

[37] Yardley's translation (2006).   [38] Cf. Lucr. 2.1044–7, 3.16–17.
[39] Hardie (2009a) 129.

eyes and 'stand against' it recalls the procedures and corresponding descriptive vocabulary of epic single-combat, closely echoing
the terms in which Glaucus reproaches Hector at *Il.* 17.166–7 for
failing to duel with Ajax.[40] Lucan capitalises on these martial
overtones in his presentation of the Caesarian sublime, conjuring
a military commander whose dynamic power surpasses even Hannibal's: where Livy's account of Hannibal's Alpine crossing spans
many paragraphs, Lucan's Caesar accomplishes the feat in a single
line; less even than that – one word, *superaverat* (Luc. 1.183, cf.
nec inexsuperabiles, Livy 21.30.7), is all it takes.[41] Shocking in
their suddenness, Caesar's actions out-sublime not only the Alps
but the mountains' previous conqueror too.

The kinetics of Caesar's first scene are complex, however, for
no sooner have the 'immense upheavals' of his Alpine crossing
and revolutionary plans been recounted than they come to a halt
(note the enjambment followed by the abrupt pause at 184–5,
motus . . . / ceperat. ut ventum est . . .). Arrived on the far bank of
the Rubicon, Caesar sees a ghost, described in terms that identify
it too as a sublime thing:

> ingens visa duci patriae trepidantis imago
> clara per obscuram voltu maestissima noctem,
> turrigero canos effundens vertice crines,
> caesarie lacera nudisque adstare lacertis.

> Clearly to the leader through the murky night appeared
> a mighty image of his country in distress, grief in her face,
> her white hair streaming from her tower-crowned head;
> with tresses torn and shoulders bare she stood before him.
>
> 1.186–9

Like the Alps, this *ingens imago* is a direct challenge to Caesar's
ingentis . . . motus, the agonistic relationship pointed up by the
repetition of the adjective at the start of lines 184 and 186: the

---

[40] ἀλλὰ σύ γ᾽Αἴαντος μεγαλήτορος οὐκ ἐτάλασσας / στήμεναι ἄντα κατ᾽ ὄσσε ἰδὼν δηΐων
ἐν αὐτῇ ('you had not the courage to stand before great-hearted Ajax, facing him eye
to eye in the battle cry of the foe'). On the relation of these lines to Lucr. 1.62–71, see
Conte (1994) 1–3.
[41] Cf. Quint. *Inst.* 12.10.23 on how Demosthenes, Longinus' favourite example of the
sublime rhetorician, *superavit* all other orators.

imago confronts Caesar with new sublimity.[42] There is, moreover, a Burkeian colouring to the description of the *imago* shining *clara per obscuram . . . noctem*, recalling as it does Burke's interest in light that 'overpowers the sense'.[43] Is there also, in the darkness that surrounds the *imago*, a hint of Burke's emphasis on 'obscurity' as a fundamental source of the sublime? Burke, we remember, emphasises the effectiveness of poetic personification as a vehicle for sublime obscurity, citing, for instance, Milton's description of Satan:

> He above the rest
> In shape and gesture proudly eminent
> Stood like a tower; his form had yet not lost
> All her original brightness, nor appeared
> Less than archangel ruin'd, and th' excess
> Of glory obscured . . .
> *Paradise Lost* 1.589–94[44]

The details that prick Burke's imagination – Satan's tower-like stature, his form at once bright and obscured – are not dissimilar to those of Lucan's *patriae imago*, tower-crowned and shining through the darkness (though the image summoned by Lucan is undoubtedly easier to visualise than Milton's).

If the *patriae imago* suggests itself as an object of the sublime, Caesar's reaction to it also conforms closely with Burke's description of fear and pain:

> tum perculit horror
> membra ducis, riguere comae gressumque coercens
> languor in extrema tenuit vestigia ripa.
>
> Then trembling struck
> the leader's limbs, his hair grew stiff, and weakness checked
> his progress, holding his feet at the river's edge.   1.192–4

So, of a man in fear, Burke writes, 'his hair stands on end . . . and the whole fabric totters',[45] an observation that in turn reminds

---

[42] Cf. Maes (2005) on *ingens* at Luc. 1.184 and 186 as a metapoetic reference to Lucan's aspiration that his poem should overgo the *Aeneid*. This insight could be expanded along Bloomian lines, reminding us again of the sublimity that Lucan claims for his poem in relation to its predecessors.

[43] Burke (1990) 73.   [44] Cited by Burke (1990) 57.

[45] Burke (1990) 119.

us of Sappho's sublime subject, wracked by 'shivers', unable to hold herself together (*De sub.* 10.3). As we saw in Chapter 1, however, terror and dissolution do not in themselves constitute the experience of the sublime; sublimity hinges on an additional movement of recuperation, of uplift, a movement in which the subject appropriates the awfulness of the sublime object to himself. Thus Caesar, when he begins to speak, associates the *patriae imago* with his own *gens Iulia* (Luc. 1.197), addressing her not as the Republican *patria* but as the *Roma* of future imperial cult (1.200),[46] before asserting:

> 'en, adsum victor terraque marique
> Caesar, ubique tuus (liceat modo, nunc quoque) miles.
> ille erit ille nocens, qui me tibi fecerit hostem.'

> '– here am I, Caesar, conqueror by land and sea,
> your own soldier everywhere, now too if I am permitted.
> The man who makes me your enemy, it is he will be the guilty one.'

> 1.201–3

Caesar's initial terror in the face of the apparition now transmutes into identification with it: he protests to the *imago* that he is *ubique tuus*, firmly distinguishing himself from those (*ille... ille*) who are responsible for his perceived opposition to Rome (conveyed by the direct juxtaposition of pronouns, *me tibi*). The effectiveness of his rhetoric may be gauged from how easily it is forgotten that the *imago*'s words were not addressed to Caesar personally but to his entire army: *tenditis, fertis, viri, venitis, cives* (1.190–2).[47]

Caesar's identification with the *imago* is compounded by his implicit identification with the other gods addressed in his prayer, its apparent anachronisms anticipating his and Augustus' historical appropriation of the gods of the *res publica*.[48] Two of the deities upon whom he prevails in particular connote sublimity. The

---

[46] The term *Roma* was not used to designate the state during the Republic; under Augustus *Roma* became part of the cult of the emperor. See Feeney (1991) 293–4.

[47] Feeney (1991) 292.

[48] See Grimal (1970) 56–9. Feeney (1991) 292–3 compares Ovid's association of Augustus with Jupiter and Rome's tutelary gods at the end of the *Metamorphoses* (15.857–70).

THE RUBICON (1.183–265) AND BEYOND

invocation of Jupiter Tonans (1.196)[49] proclaims the relationship
later acknowledged by the Massilians (3.319–20); indeed, as we
will see during the Adriatic storm in Book 5, Caesar comes to
view himself in Jupiter's place, an assertion of ego at least partly
warranted by his sublime actions, and presaged by his opening
comparison with lightning, Jupiter's defining accoutrement. The
mention of the 'mysteries of Quirinus, who was carried off to
heaven' (*rapti secreta Quirini*, 1.197) is also suggestive.[50] Getty
ad loc. compares Genesis 5:24, 'And Enoch walked with God: and
he was not; for God took him', a reminder of divine power that
echoes Longinus' citation of Genesis 1:3–9 (*De sub.* 9.9): Quirinus' ascension, like that of Enoch and other religious figures, might
be read as a literal enactment of sublime afflatus, a unique species
of event in which the experience of being divinely 'carried aloft'
(*sublimem raptum*), as Livy phrases it in his account of Quirinus'
ascension (1.16.2), becomes physical as well as spiritual.[51]

Caesar, then, associates himself in his prayer not only with
'*Roma*' and thundering Jupiter but also with a figure famous for his
achievement of a literal sublimity, for his physical transcendence
of the boundary between earth and heaven. Immediately following
this speech, Caesar performs a parallel crossing of boundaries,
reconfiguring Quirinus' vertical sublimity on the horizontal plane:
'Then he broke the barriers of war and through the swollen river
quickly took his standards' (*moras solvit belli tumidumque per
amnem / signa tulit propere*, Luc. 1.204–5). *quo tenditis ultra?*
(1.190), the *imago* had asked, a worried echo of the Longinian and
Lucretian awareness of the human desire to go beyond 'the limits
that confine us' (τοὺς τοῦ περιέχοντος . . . ὅρους, *De sub.* 35.3;

---

[49] Jupiter Tonans only appeared in Rome in 22 BC when Augustus erected a temple to him
in thanks for escaping a lightning strike during the Cantabrian War: Suet. *Aug.* 29; Plin.
Nat. 34.78. See Getty (1940) ad loc.

[50] In 45 BC a statue of Caesar was set up in the temple of Quirinus, bearing the inscription
'To the unconquered god': Cassius Dio 43.45.3. See Getty (1940) ad loc.

[51] Given Burke's emphasis on 'obscurity' as productive of the sublime, our sources'
acknowledgement that the actual facts of Quirinus' ascension are uncertain seems
appropriate: it is not just that Quirinus' person was hidden from the crowd of onlookers
(*conspectum eius contioni abstulerit* as Livy has it, 1.16.1) but that the truth of the story
has itself become obscured (Dion. Hal. 2.56; Plut. *Rom.* 27). Predictably perhaps, the
event was accompanied by thunder and lightning (*cum magno fragore tonitribusque*,
Livy 1.16.1; Getty (1940) ad Luc. 1.197 compares Hor. *Carm.* 3.3.15–16, Ov. *Fast.*
2.495–6, *Met.* 14.806–28).

Lucr. 1.72–4, 3.16–17). Caesar now answers this question with action: his *ingentis... motus*, ignited once more, blast through the delay (*mora*) caused by the *ingens imago*;[52] where previously he hesitated (1.194–5), he now advances rapidly into Italy.[53] The dynamic reflects that of Caesar's swift *superaverat* at the start of the Rubicon episode and its allusion to Hannibal's Lucretian encounter with the Alps in Livy 21. Just as Caesar surmounts the mountains' sublime height, so here he transcends the inhibiting force of the apparition.

This 'momentary inhibition of the vital powers' and the 'immediately following and all the more powerful outpouring of them'[54] is underscored by Caesar's second simile in the poem, this time comparing him to a lion:

> sicut squalentibus arvis   205
> aestiferae Libyes viso leo comminus hoste
> subsedit dubius, totam dum colligit iram;
> mox, ubi se saevae stimulavit verbere caudae
> erexitque iubam et vasto grave murmur hiatu
> infremuit, tum torta levis si lancea Mauri   210
> haereat aut latum subeant venabula pectus,
> per ferrum tanti securus volneris exit.

> Just so in torrid Libya's
> barren fields the lion, on seeing his enemy at hand,
> crouches in hesitation till he has concentrated all his anger;
> next he goads himself with fiercely lashing tail,
> his mane is bristling, from his massive jaws
> deep he roars – then if a lance, hurled by a swift Moor,
> or hunting-spears pierce and stick in his broad chest, ignoring
> such a terrible wound he rushes onward, driving the weapon deeper.
>   1.205–12

Like Caesar before the Rubicon, the lion hesitates before his enemy (*subsedit dubius*, 207) but this merely serves to concentrate his strength prior to leaping into action: once in motion, he carries all

---

[52] On the concept of *mora* in the *Bellum civile*, see Masters (1992) 3–5.
[53] With Caesar's energetic physical reaction to the gloomy *imago* compare Burke (1990) 133 on the supposedly physiological reasons for the sublime effects of 'blackness': 'when the eye lights on one of these vacuities, after having been kept in some degree of tension by the play of the adjacent colours upon it, it suddenly falls into a relaxation; out of which it as suddenly recovers by a *convulsive spring*' (my italics).
[54] Kant (2003) 128–9.

before him.[55] The emphasis on this dynamic marks the simile's development of its two primary models. In the *Iliad*, as he attacks Aeneas, Achilles is likened to a lion who, struck by a spear, 'gathers himself with his mouth wide open . . . and rushes straight on in his fury' (ἑάλη τε χανών . . . δ᾽ ἰθὺς φέρεται μένει, *Il.* 20.168–72); in the *Aeneid*, as he sees the Latins' morale ebbing, Turnus is likened to a Punic lion who when wounded 'at last rouses himself to fight' (*demum movet arma, Aen.* 12.4–8).[56] While slyly aligning Caesar with two of Aeneas' most famous opponents, Lucan's version of the simile removes the detail of the lion's initial wounding and trains attention instead on the restraint and subsequent sublime release of the lion's power.[57]

Besides imaging the sublimity of Caesar's experience at the Rubicon, this simile also reinforces the opening simile's construction of Caesar as himself a sublime object. Longinus' statement that 'genius needs the curb as often as the spur' (δεῖ γὰρ αὐτοῖς ὡς κέντρου πολλάκις, οὕτω δὲ καὶ χαλινοῦ, *De sub.* 2.2) implicitly draws genius as a beast;[58] like lightning, lions (and other fierce animals) have a strong pedigree as objects of the sublime. Lucretius describes in Book 5 how in former times men experimented with lions in warfare:

> et validos partim prae se misere leones   1310
> cum doctoribus armatis saevisque magistris
> qui moderarier his possent vinclisque tenere –
> nequiquam, quoniam permixta caede calentes

---

[55] Masters (1992) 2 n. 5 believes that the lion runs himself through, pointing up how 'Caesar obscurely destroys himself' through civil war. But the simile does not say whether the lion dies; if anything, the adjective *securus* suggests its survival. That said, Masters' reading allows us to see the lion's action as a kind of death leap, mirroring the ambiguous way in which the Caesarian lightning *in sua templa furit* (1.155) – and there is sublimity to this too. As Porter (2007) 274 observes, and as we will see in Chapter 4 in relation to Pompey, 'the sublime is most intensely felt where it most threatens to annihilate subjective identity'.

[56] Also compare Virg. *Aen.* 10.726–8 and Sen. *Oed.* 919–20.

[57] On this simile and its intertexts, see further Schiesaro (2003) 124–6. Cf. also Luc. 1.291–5: fired by Curio's words of encouragement and eager to continue his advance on Rome, Caesar is compared to a racehorse at the starting gates (*quamvis iam carcere clauso / inmineat foribus pronusque repagula laxet*); and Luc. 7.242–9: Caesar's courage wavers and then surges up at Pharsalus as he sees Pompey's men advancing (*formidine mersa / prosilit . . . fiducia*).

[58] Russell (1964) 65; Whitmarsh (2001) 64.

turbabant saevi nullo discrimine turmas,
terrificas capitum quatientes undique cristas,   1315
nec poterant equites fremitu perterrita equorum
pectora mulcere et frenis convertere in hostis.
inritata leae iaciebant corpora saltu
undique, et adversum venientibus ora petebant,
et nec opinantis a tergo deripiebant,   1320
deplexaeque dabant in terram volnere victos,
morsibus adfixae validis atque unguibus uncis.

Some let slip strong lions before them,
with armed trainers and harsh masters
to control them and to hold them in leash;
but in vain, since when heated with the promiscuous slaughter
they ran wild, and threw the squadrons into confusion, friend and foe alike,
on all sides shaking the frightful crests upon their heads,
nor could the riders soothe the spirits of their horses
terrified at the roaring, nor guide them towards the foe with the curb.
The she-lions enraged bounded
this way and that, and leapt straight for the faces of those that met them,
or tore at others unawares from behind,
and clasping them close bore them to the ground helpless from the wound,
holding fast to them with strong jaws and curving claws.   Lucr. 5.1310–22

Commenting on this passage, Conte writes that 'the sublime is
generated by the image of forces that erupt and overwhelm the
impotent spectator's resistance':[59] the ferocious might of the lions
bursts through the *vincla* that would constrain them, wreaking
havoc among friend and foe alike. Burke also discusses the sublimity of wild animals at some length: they are sublime because
their power, in its superiority to our own, does 'not act in conformity to our will':[60]

We have continually about us animals of a strength that is considerable, but not
pernicious. Amongst these we never look for the sublime: it comes upon us in the
gloomy forest, and in the howling wilderness, in the form of the lion, the tiger,
the panther, or rhinoceros.[61]

The power of such beasts is not benign, cannot be tamed and turned
to human use, but rather, as Lucretius' description shows, exceeds
man's capacities of physical control. Lucretius immediately follows his description of lions' sublime violence with an account of

---

[59] Conte (1994) 26.   [60] Burke (1990) 61.   [61] Burke (1990) 60–1.

that of bulls and it is the bull that Burke uses to underscore his point: both the ox and the bull are strong but whereas the idea of an ox, because the animal is 'innocent' and 'extremely serviceable', is 'by no means grand', that of a bull, a highly 'destructive' beast, is 'great, and it has frequently a place in sublime descriptions, and elevating comparisons'.[62] In comparing Caesar to a lion that charges *per ferrum tanti securus volneris* (1.212), Lucan summons this same Lucretian–Burkeian sense of awe at a force that exceeds the onlooker's powers of control.

The sublime connection between the lightning and lion similes that are first applied to Caesar is brought out by comparison with two passages from Ovid's *Metamorphoses*, both of which unite the ferocious violence of wild beasts with imagery of lightning.[63] In *Metamorphoses* 8 the boar sent by Diana to ravage Calydon springs violently at Meleager and his companions 'like fire struck from clashing clouds' (*ut excussis elisi nubibus ignes*, 8.339); thunderbolts flash from its jaws (*fulmen ab ore venit*, 8.289); it rages with lightning's heat (*nec fulmine lenius arsit*, 8.355).[64] In *Metamorphoses* 11, a herdsman uses similar terms to describe how a monstrous wolf has attacked Peleus' cattle: the 'enormous beast' (*belua vasta*) terrifies the neighbourhood, 'howling with piercing clamour' (*fragore gravi strepitans*, 11.365); its bloody and foaming maw is 'thundering' (*fulmineos*, 11.368). Lucan's Caesarian lightning, 'searing eyes with slanting flame' (*obliqua praestringens lumina flamma*, 1.154), seems a conscious echo of the Ovidian wolf, its 'eyes flashing flames of crimson' (*rubra suffusus lumina flamma*, *Met.* 11.368). Lightning and wild beasts here reinforce each other's sublime associations.

As noted above, in Lucan's scene at the Rubicon there is no explicit reference to lightning. However, subtle details sustain the connection with Caesar's first simile. The word *colligit* is used to describe the momentary inhibition of the Caesarian lion as it gathers its strength for the attack (*subsedit dubius, totam dum colligit*

---

[62] Burke (1990) 60. Pompey is compared to a bull at *BC* 2.601–9 but the simile explains his retreat to Brundisium and does not suggest sublimity.

[63] See Getty (1940) ad Luc. 1.154 and 1.533.

[64] The boar is Lucretius' third example, besides the lion and the bull, of an animal whose might engenders the sublime: Lucr. 5.1309, 1326–29.

iram, 1.207). The same verb is used to describe the same swelling of dammed power in Lucretius' explanation of the thunderbolt's speed (*incita se vis / colligit et magnum conamen sumit eundi*, Lucr. 6.325–6). We also find a cognate of the word in Caesar's opening simile, where lightning, 'both as it falls and then returns, deals great devastation far and wide before it gathers again its scattered fires' (*magnamque cadens magnamque revertens / dat stragem late sparsosque recolligit ignes*, Luc. 1.156–7). The sense here is altered, referring to the thunderbolt's 'return' to heaven after striking the earth rather than to its initial mustering of power, but the Lucretian resonance and subsequent echo in the lion simile collectively imbue the verb with connotations of sublimity. Supporting this connection is the ensuing juxtaposition of Caesar's rapid, terrifying descent on the frontier town of Ariminum, 'swifter than . . . the Parthian's arrow shot over his shoulder' (*ocior . . . missa Parthi post terga sagitta*, 1.230), and the dramatic arrival of daylight: *ignes / solis Lucifero fugiebant astra relicto* (1.231–2). Such blinding speed is a defining feature of Caesar-as-thunderbolt, a supranatural power that here seems to exert its force even over the stars of heaven; it is as if the day has broken at Caesar's command. So too, just as here Caesar is swifter, *ocior*, than a Parthian arrow, his subsequent advance from Rome to Brundisium is 'swifter than the flames of heaven, than a tigress with her young' (*ocior . . . caeli flammis et tigride feta*, 5.405), a double comparison that again collocates the sublime speed of lightning and wild animals and emphasises Caesar's superiority to both.

Reinforcing the opening lightning comparison, the lion simile offers a graphic analogy for Caesar's experience at the Rubicon as a sublime subject. In concluding this section, I want to throw this Caesarian subjectivity into relief by considering the very different response he in turn inspires in the Ariminians and Roman populace. The reminders of the sublime that mark their reaction only serve to emphasise their actual distance from it.[65]

The sublime suddenness of Caesar's arrival at Ariminum, coinciding with that of dawn, is accompanied by a piercing military

[65] Contra Alston and Spentzou (2011) 58–9.

fanfare (another of Burke's sources of sublimity):[66] *stridor lituum clangorque tubarum / non pia concinuit cum rauco classica cornu* (1.237–8). The Ariminians are stricken with terror: *celsus medio conspectus in agmine Caesar, / deriguere metu, gelidos pavor occupat artus* (1.245–6). The details of the scene are strikingly reminiscent of Caesar's own reaction to the *patriae imago*: the tower-crowned *ingens imago* (1.188) is here replaced by *celsus Caesar* ('towering Caesar'); where Caesar's hair previously went stiff (*riguere*, 1.193), here the Ariminians themselves 'stiffen' in fear (*deriguere*). But these correspondences only serve to emphasise the difference between Caesar's experience and that of the Ariminians, for while Caesar soon overcomes his fear in a sublime rush of self-assertion, the Ariminians remain paralysed. Caesar proclaims his surpassing of legal and political limits in a few terse, decisive words:

> 'hic ... hic pacem temerataque iura relinquo;
> te, Fortuna, sequor. procul hinc iam foedera sunto;
> credidimus satis his, utendum est iudice bello.'

> > 'Here I abandon peace and desecrated law;
> > Fortune, it is you I follow. Farewell to treaties from now on;
> > I have relied on them for long enough; now war must be our referee.'

> > > 1.225–7

Caesar's self-glorying emphasis on the event of his transgression might be likened to one of the lightning-like 'zips' that divide Newman's paintings, or to the biblical injunction 'Let there be light' which attracts Longinus (*De sub.* 9.9): in each case we are faced with a proclamation of radical division, an assertion of change between two fundamentally different states, focusing attention on the explosively charged moment in which a line of limitation is crossed – with the crucial difference that the sense of creative enlargement evoked by Newman and Genesis is replaced by Lucan with Caesar's will to destruction. The Ariminians' response to Caesar's advent is the very opposite of such sublimity. They do not even dare speak their fear:

---

[66] Burke (1990) 75–6: 'the noise of vast cataracts, raging storms, thunder, or artillery, awakes a great and aweful sensation in the mind ... a sudden beginning, or sudden cessation of sound of any considerable force, has the same power'.

> vox nulla dolori
> credita, sed quantum, volucres cum bruma coercet,
> rura silent, mediusque tacet sine murmure pontus,
> tanta quies.

> no utterance was entrusted
> to their grief, but deep the silence – so when winter checks
> the birds, the fields are hushed, and so mid-sea is mute,
> unmurmuring.   1.258–61

Caesar's sublimity constrains them (*coercet*, 259); they remain frozen in a state of terror, unable – and unwilling – to effect the move into the sublime.

Meanwhile Caesar, in a replay of the lion simile,[67] sweeps sublimely onwards into Italy with the spreading dawn:

> noctis gelidas lux solverat umbras:
> ecce, faces belli dubiaeque in proelia menti
> urguentes addunt stimulos cunctasque pudoris
> rumpunt fata moras.

> Day had dissipated night's chill shadows
> and now the Fates put to his undecided mind the torch of war
> and goads which urge to battle, so breaking
> all the barriers of restraint.   1.261–4

The response of Rome's inhabitants to this advance mirrors and augments that of the Ariminians. Their fear is whipped up by the *fama* of Caesar's progress:

> Caesar, ut inmensae conlecto robore vires
> audendi maiora fidem fecere, per omnem
> spargitur Italiam vicinaque moenia conplet.
> vana quoque ad veros accessit fama timores
> inrupitque animos populi clademque futuram   470
> intulit et velox properantis nuntia belli
> innumeras solvit falsa in praeconia linguas.
>
> . . .
>
> nec qualem meminere vident: maiorque ferusque
> mentibus occurrit victoque inmanior hoste.   480
>
> . . .
>
>   sic quisque pavendo

---

[67] Note in particular the repetitions *dubiaeque* (1.262)/*dubius* (1.207) and *stimulos* (1.263)/*stimulavit* (1.208).

dat vires famae, nulloque auctore malorum   485
quae finxere timent.

Caesar's massive forces with their gathered might
made him confident to venture higher: he extends
through all of Italy; he occupies the nearest towns.
And empty rumour, speedy messenger of quickening
war, augmented genuine fears; it invaded
people's minds with pictures of calamity to come
and unlocked countless tongues to utter false assertions.

. . .

They picture him not as they remember him: in their thoughts
he seems greater, wilder, more pitiless from the conquest of the enemy.

. . .

          So by his panic each
gives strength to rumour, and they fear ungrounded evils
of their own invention.   1.466–86

Here, as often, *fama* functions as an index of sublimity. For Longinus, for instance, it is sublime writing that guarantees immortal
reputation (1.3).[68] In the case of Lucan's Caesar, *fama* arises from
the sublimity of his transgression of Italy's borders: now that he
has brought an army into Italy, he is, surely, capable of anything
(466–7). Lexical echoes of the Rubicon scene underline the connection. Caesar's gathering of his great forces (*inmensae conlecto
robore vires*, 466) reminds us of the Caesarian lion gathering its
strength (*totam... colligit iram*). As earlier Caesar broke through
the waters of the river (*rumpit... fracti fluminis undas*, 1.221–2),
drove his troops forward (*rapit agmina*, 228) and invaded Ariminum (*invadit Ariminum*, 231), shattering the inhabitants' peace
(*rupta quies populi*, 239), so now reports of these actions 'invade'
people's minds (*inrupit... animos populi*, 470); he unleashes war
from its restraints (*moras solvit belli*, 204) and his reputation
loosens innumerable tongues (*innumeras solvit... linguas*, 472);
his *fama* is swift (*velox properantis nuntia belli*, 471), an apt reflection of his own impetuous speed (*inpiger, et torto Balearis verbere
fundae / ocior*, 229–30).

---

[68] Cf. Prop. 3.1.9: *quo me Fama levat terra sublimis.*

131

Hannibal again offers a suggestive counterpart. His attack on Italy is twice mentioned as the subject of *fama* in Livy 21: it is rumoured (*fama est...*) that his father made him swear himself 'an enemy of the people of Rome' (*hostem... populo Romano*, 21.1.4) and, later, that 'in his sleep he saw a youth of divine countenance, who declared that he was sent to Hannibal by Jupiter to lead him into Italy' (*in quiete visum ab eo iuvenem divina specie, qui se ab Iove diceret ducem in Italiam Hannibali missum*, 21.22.6).[69] This apparition can be seen as the opposite of Lucan's *patriae imago*, encouraging rather than attempting to prevent Italy's invasion.[70] Both visions, however, lead to the creation of *fama* through sublime action. In Hannibal's case, this *fama* is a result of his sublime demolition of the Alps' own terrible *fama*: the 'interminable march' (*iter immensum*) across the barrier (*claustra*) of the Alps is for his men a 'thing made terrifying by rumour, particularly for the inexperienced' (*rem fama utique inexpertis horrendam*, Livy 21.29.7) but Hannibal successfully leads them over, just as the *fama deum* does not overawe Lucretius' Epicurus but, rather, 'all the more goaded the eager courage of his soul, so that he should desire, first of all men, to shatter the confining bars of nature's gates' (*magis acrem / inritat animi virtutem, effringere ut arta / naturae primus portarum claustra cupiret*, Lucr. 1.68–71). The *fama* of Lucan's Caesar arises according to the same agonistic movement: by confronting and overcoming the sublimity of the Alps and the Rubicon, Caesar himself attains sublimity.

fama is the product of sublime action and is also, as Hardie has shown with reference to its personification in the *Aeneid*,[71] itself something sublime: with its speed (1.471) and innumerable tongues (1.472), Caesar's *fama*, like its Virgilian predecessor (*malum qua non aliud velocius ullum. / mobilitate viget virisque adquirit eundo*, Aen. 4.174–5; *quot sunt corpore plumae / ... tot*

[69] See Feldherr (2009) and Hardie (2009a) 130.
[70] Compare also Mercury's appearance to Aeneas in a dream at Virg. Aen. 4.556–70, urging him to set sail for Italy: Hardie (2009a) 78–80 teases out the similarities between the sublime presentation of Mercury here and that of *Fama* earlier in *Aeneid* 4.
[71] See Hardie (2009a) 67–135 on Virg. Aen. 4.173–218 and related passages.

132

linguae, totidem ora sonant, Aen. 4.181, 183) exhibits both a dynamic and a mathematical sublimity.[72] As noted previously, Burke also cites Virgil's *Fama* as an example of something sublimely 'obscure': confronted with its muddle of fact and falsehood (*tam ficti pravique tenax quam nuntia veri. / . . . et pariter facta atque infecta canebat, Aen.* 4.188, 190), 'the mind is hurried out of itself, by a croud of great and confused images; which affect because they are crouded and confused'.[73] In Livy's account of Hannibal's transalpine crossing, such confusion arises from the disjunction between the stories told of the Alps and their brute presence. Although *fama* (*qua incerta in maius vero ferri solent*) had taught Hannibal's men what to expect, the reality is even more terrible: 'everything more terrible to look upon than words can tell renewed their fear' (*cetera visu quam dictu foediora, terrorem renovarunt,* Livy 21.32.7). The *fama* of Lucan's Caesar similarly muddies the relation between fiction and reality, making Caesar seem *maior* and *inmanior* (Luc. 1.479–80) than people remember.[74] As Hannibal's men, contemplating the Alps, 'imagine them to be higher than the summits of the Pyrenees' (*fingerent altiores Pyrenaei iugis,* Livy 21.30.6), so Rome's citizens, contemplating Caesar, 'fear whatever they have imagined' (*quae finxere, timent,* Luc. 1.486). Besides the sublime details of its description, Caesar's *fama* thus constitutes a further node in the allusive nexus linking him to the natural sublime of the Alps and to Livy's Lucretian account of Hannibal's sublime Alpine crossing.

Yet the sublime 'obscurity' of Caesar's *fama* provokes in Rome's inhabitants only fear. To paraphrase Burke, they are sent hurrying out of the city in a great and confused crowd but enjoy none of the 'delight' in this confusion that would make it sublime:

---

[72] Like Caesar's exemplar Hannibal, and like the Caesarian lion, Virgil's *Fama* is also Libyan (*A.* 4.173).

[73] Burke (1990) 57.

[74] Gowing (2005) 83–4 notes that these lines are part of a wider Lucanian concern with memory and its unreliability. In Caesar's account, the Italians welcome him as the beneficent hero they remember (*Civ.* 1.15.18). While in Lucan's version the Italians' fears are described as *vana*, the poem in fact implies that they are well founded: Lucan's presentation of Caesar argues that he really *is* more terrible than Romans (and the dictator's own commentaries) remember.

tum, quae tuta petant et quae metuenda relinquant 490
incerti, quo quemque fugae tulit impetus urguent
praecipitem populum, serieque haerentia longa
agmina prorumpunt. credas aut tecta nefandas
corripuisse faces aut iam quatiente ruina
nutantes pendere domos, sic turba per urbem 495
praecipiti lymphata gradu, velut unica rebus
spes foret adflictis patrios excedere muros,
inconsulta ruit. qualis, cum turbidus Auster
reppulit a Libycis inmensum Syrtibus aequor
fractaque veliferi sonuerunt pondera mali, 500
desilit in fluctus deserta puppe magister
navitaque et nondum sparsa conpage carinae
naufragium sibi quisque facit, sic urbe relicta
in bellum fugitur.

Then, uncertain where to go for safety, where to run from danger,
wherever impulse of flights sweeps them on, they [the Senators] drive
the people rushing headlong, breaking out in hordes who stick together
in a long chain. You might suppose that impious fire-brands
had ignited houses, that homes were swaying, tottering,
shaken by imminent collapse: so the throng rushed
through the city heedlessly, frantic with headlong pace,
as if the sole salvation for their battered fortunes
were to leave the ancestral walls. When stormy Auster
has driven back the mighty sea from Libyan Syrtes
and when the broken weight of the mast has crashed down with its sails,
the captain and the crew abandon ship and leap
into the waves, and each, before the vessel's frame is smashed,
creates his own shipwreck – just so, they abandon Rome and
flee towards war. 1.490–504

Ironically, the passage's vocabulary is that of Caesar in action
(*impetus, urguent, praecipitem, prorumpunt, praecipiti, ruit*) but
here the rush is the product of panic not exultation: the Romans'
hasty exodus superficially contrasts with the Ariminians' paralysis but is rooted in the same terror. Tellingly, it is likened to the
reaction of those caught in an earthquake (494–5) or struck by shipwreck (498–503).[75] Both these parallels are often cited as sublime
events but, as Burke emphasises, can only be construed as such by

[75] Cf. the sea storm simile at Luc. 2.454–61: Latium's inhabitants, terrified at Caesar's
advance through Italy, are likened to waves driven in different directions by the winds.

spectators who are sufficiently detached, either mentally or physically: sublime 'delight' arises 'when we have an idea of pain and danger, without being actually in such circumstances'.[76] Lucretius' discussion of the causes of earthquakes (Lucr. 6.535–607) makes them sublime because it views them through the distancing lens of Epicureanism: armed with an understanding of their true causes, the Lucretian reader is no more perturbed than by the trembling of buildings at a passing wagon (Lucr. 6.548–51). Lucretius frames a vision of shipwreck in the same manner in Book 2 of *De rerum natura*, using it as an analogy for a world in which the number of atoms is finite:

> sed quasi naufragiis magnis multisque coortis
> disiectare solet magnum mare transtra cavernas
> antemnas proram malos tonsasque natantis,
> per terrarum omnis oras fluitantia aplustra   555
> ut videantur et indicium mortalibus edant,
> infidi maris insidias virisque dolumque
> ut vitare velint, neve ullo tempore credant,
> subdola cum ridet placidi pellacia ponti.

> But as when many great shipwrecks have come about,
> the high sea is accustomed to toss assunder transoms, ribs,
> yards, prow, masts, and oars all swimming,
> so that the poop-fittings are seen floating
> around all the shores, and provide a warning for mortals,
> that they eschew the treacherous deep, with her snares, her violence
> and her fraud, and never trust her at any time
> when the calm sea shows her false alluring smile.   Lucr. 2.552–9

Again, the sublimity of this vista is related to our distance from it: we first look down upon the scene as if from the heavens (552–4) and then find ourselves gazing out at it from the shore (555). We are not part of the chaos ourselves and so are free to find an Epicurean *divina voluptas... atque horror* (Lucr. 3.28–9) or a Burkeian 'delight' in it. Lucan's fleeing Romans are unable to achieve such detachment. They are not watching from the shore nor gazing down from the heavens but find themselves, metaphorically,

---

[76] Burke (1990) 47.

in the midst of shipwreck; *naufragium sibi quisque facit* (Luc. 1.503).[77]

The Massilian grove (3.399–452)

The sublimity established for Caesar in Book 1 as he crosses the Rubicon and invades Italy is further developed as he lays siege to Massilia in Book 3. Caesar needs wood for war-engines and his attention falls on a nearby grove, sacred to terrible local deities. Its darkness is the first thing to which our attention is drawn:

> lucus erat longo numquam violatus ab aevo,
> obscurum cingens conexis aera ramis
> et gelidas alte summotis solibus umbras.

> A grove there was, never profaned since time remote,
> enclosing with its intertwining branches the dingy air
> and chilly shadows, banishing sunlight far above.

> 3.399–401

Roman descriptions of woodland typically emphasise shade and gloom[78] but Lucan's ecphrasis here goes further. Instead of a *locus amoenus*, we are presented with a *locus horridus*, fore-shadowing the one in which Erictho performs her necromancy:[79] the literal darkness of the grove (words denoting black, one of Lucan's favourite colours,[80] recur at 3.409, 411 and 424) merely heightens the incomprehensible horror of its rites (human sacrifice, 3.405) and unearthly nature (it is a site of earthquakes, its trees burn with fireless flames, 3.417–20). We have already noticed, in connection with Lucan's theme of *discordia*, with the *patriae imago* and with Caesar's *fama*, the emphasis placed by Burke on

[77] Lucan's Roman shipwreck is also the very opposite of the Homeric shipwreck labelled sublime by Longinus (*De sub.* 10.5): where Rome's citizens bring ruin upon themselves (Luc. 1.503–4), Homer's sailors are 'by the breadth of a hand swept out from under the jaws of destruction' (*Il.* 15.628).
[78] E.g. Hor. *Ars* 16–18; Pers. 1.70; Juv. 1.7–8; Virg. *Aen.* 1.165, 7.81–91, 6.237–42, 8.342–58, 9.86–7, 381–3; Ov. *Fast.* 3.295–9, *Am.* 3.1.1–4, 3.13.7–10. Also prose: Livy 21.1.3; Sen. *Ep.* 41.3. See further Hunink (1992) ad loc. and 167.
[79] For discussion of these terms, see Leigh (1999) 172 n. 15.
[80] See Hunink (1992) 171 on Luc. 3.400.

'obscurity' as an important source of the sublime. Burke's analysis resonates strikingly with the present passage too and is worth recalling:

To make any thing very terrible, obscurity seems in general to be necessary. When we know the full extent of any danger, when we can accustom our eyes to it, a great deal of the apprehension vanishes. Every one will be sensible of this, who considers how greatly night adds to our dread, in all cases of danger, and how much the notions of ghosts and goblins, of which none can form clear ideas, affect minds... Almost all the heathen temples were dark... the druids performed all their ceremonies in the bosom of the darkest woods, and in the shade of the oldest and most spreading oaks.[81]

Besides sharing with the Lucanian scene an emphasis on the general quality of obscurity, as well as the specific instance of heathen rites conducted in dark woods, Burke's discussion also grounds the explanation of obscurity's sublime power in the conjunction of terror and incomprehension: 'It is our ignorance of things that causes all our admiration, and chiefly excites our passions. Knowledge and acquaintance make the most striking causes affect but little.'[82] Lucan offers the same observation in his account of the shapeless images of the gods that adorn the grove:

> simulacraque maesta deorum
> arte carent caesisque extant informia truncis.
> ipse situs putrique facit iam robore pallor
> attonitos; non volgatis sacrata figuris
> numina sic metuunt: tantum terroribus addit,
> quos timeant, non nosse, deos.

> The grim and artless
> images of gods stand as shapeless fallen tree-trunks.
> The decay itself and pallor of the timber now rotting
> is astonishing; not so do people fear deities worshipped
> in ordinary forms: so much does ignorance of the gods
> they dread increase their terror.   3.412–17

So too, the malign powers and barbaric rituals associated with the grove are all the more awe-inspiring because only half-guessed at: men and beasts alike fear to approach the place (3.407–8, 422–5); Caesar's own soldiers are 'affected by the place's awesome

---

[81] Burke (1990) 54–5.   [82] Burke (1990) 57.

majesty' (*motique verenda / maiestate loci*, 3.429–30) and shrink
from touching the trees.

Alien, ancient and blanketed in dark, Lucan's grove, like those
of Burke's druids, is a strikingly sublime object. Indeed, the images
of the groves' unknown deities inspire the same sublime emotion –
'astonishment' (3.415) – as Book 1's Bacchic *matrona* (1.676) and
as Lucan's own poem (7.212). Reminding us of the citizens fleeing Caesar's advance, however, Caesar's soldiers and the local
inhabitants, rather than thrilling to the grove's sublimity, shun it in
terror.[83] For a properly sublime response, we must look instead to
the bullish heroics of Caesar himself. The ecphrasis is abruptly followed by the blunt statement 'this wood he orders to fall beneath
the axe's blow' (*hanc iubet inmisso silvam procumbere ferro*,
3.426); when his men hesitate, Caesar himself grasps an axe and
cleaves an oak in two. As at the Rubicon, Caesar converts fear
into mastery, overcoming the inhibitions of his troops (*inplici-
tas magno... torpore*, 3.432) by his own swift, decisive action
(*primus raptam librare bipennem*, 3.433): another sublime display
of restraint and release. Caesar's felling of the grove thus ensures
that it is to him that the episode's sublimity accrues, enacting his
earlier aggressive assertion that, as a gale needs the resistance of
a forest, and as fire needs fuel, so he suffers in the absence of an
enemy (3.364–5).

I discussed this statement above as a response to the Massilians'
implicit association of Caesar with thunderbolt-wielding Jupiter.
Caesar's felling of the grove intensifies his status as a lightning-
like object of the sublime. We are told that the grove has stood
untouched not only by men and beasts but also by lightning:
*nec ventus in illas / incubuit silvas excussaque nubibus atras /
fulgura* (3.408–10). Caesar, by contrast, succeeds in felling it:
he achieves what even lightning cannot, showing himself more
destructive than that sublime object *par excellence* to which he
was first likened. Weighing the anger of their commander against
that of heaven (*expensa superorum et Caesaris ira*, 3.439), it is no

---

[83] The passage is loaded with words connoting fear: *metuunt* (407, 416), *horror* (411),
terroribus (416), *timeant* (417), *pavet* (424), *timet* (425), *tremuere* (429), *verenda* (429),
torpore (432), *pavore* (438). See Hunink (1992) ad 3.404.

surprise that his soldiers soon follow orders: as in the countdown to Pharsalus (7.154–60), the thunderbolts of heaven are no match for the lightning force of Caesar.[84] Another internal detail reinforces the association. In the poem's first book Caesar's lightning simile is juxtaposed with a comparison of Pompey to an oak tree (*quercus sublimis*, 1.135), reminding us of the susceptibility of tall trees to lightning strikes; in the present scene it is not natural lightning but – even more dangerous – the Caesarian thunderbolt that brings 'a towering oak tree' (*aeriam quercum*) crashing to the ground (3.434).[85] That the Pompeian oak is itself *sublimis* suggests again the agonistic principle behind the Caesarian sublime, always achieved in relation to existing sublime objects.[86] Lucretius' use of tree-felling as an analogy to explain why lightning is seen before thunder is heard participates in this same line of association:

> caedere si quem
> ancipiti videas ferro procul arboris auctum,
> ante fit ut cernas ictum quam plaga per auris
> det sonitum; sic fulgorem quoque cernimus ante
> quam tonitrum accipimus, pariter qui mittitur igni
> e simili causa, concursu natus eodem.

> If you should see someone
> at a distance cutting down a well-grown tree with a double-headed axe,
> you see the stroke before its thud sounds
> in your ears; so also we see lightning before
> we hear the thunder, which is produced at the same time
> and by the same cause as the fire and born of the same collision.

Lucr. 6.167–72

A more powerful Lucretian influence can be felt in the connection drawn by Matthew Leigh between Caesar's actions here and those of Epicurus in the *De rerum natura*,[87] a connection which

---

[84] There is also a difference between lightning's power here and at Pharsalus: before the battle it strikes, though ineffectually; here, in sharp contrast to the Caesarian thunderbolt, it is unable even to touch the sacred grove.

[85] Cf. Rosner-Siegel (1983/2010) 198–9. The *caesis... truncis* (3.413) from which the images of the grove's gods are formed also bring Pompey to mind: cf. 1.140, 8.698. Hewn trunks, evoking Pompey's death, famously litter Lucan's poem: 1.685–6, 2.172, 189–90, 6.584, 9.966. See Narducci (1973).

[86] The reasons for the Pompeian oak's status as *sublimis* are complex: see Chapter 4.

[87] See Leigh (1999).

mirrors Livy's construction of Hannibal's Alpine crossing upon a Lucretian model. As we have seen, the Massilian grove is characterised as a place of infernal darkness, a quality closely connected with its religious power. True to his historical reputation,[88] however, Caesar here displays his scorn for *religio* and orders the grove to be cut down, an act 'richly evocative of the agonistic metaphors employed by Lucretius for the triumph of the mind of Epicurus over the superstitious folly of religion. The villainous general and would-be dictator emerges as a paradoxical bringer of the light.'[89] As Leigh emphasises, Epicurus is hymned by Lucretius for showering illumination upon a benighted world: *o tenebris tantis tam clarum extollere lumen / qui primus potuisti inlustrans commoda vitae* (Lucr. 3.1–2).[90] Epicurus' status as *primus* also finds a specific reflection in the way Caesar 'was the first to dare to grab and wield an axe' (*primus raptam librare bipennem / ausus*, 3.433–4).[91] This line forms the dramatic focus of Lucan's episode and, significantly, it also echoes Lucretius' opening summary of Epicurus' foundational achievement: <u>primum</u> *Graius homo mortalis tollere contra / est oculos* <u>ausus primusque</u> *obsistere contra* (Lucr. 1.66–7); in each case we find the same emphasis on the protagonist's pioneering exploits, the same respect for the daring that these exploits required.[92] We saw above in connection with Livy's Hannibal how these lines hinge upon the figuration of the philosopher as a warrior, driven by *virtus*, boldly battling *contra* the oppressive force of superstition 'to shatter the confining bars of nature's gates' (*effringere... arta / naturae... portarum claustra*... Lucr. 1.70–1, note again the adjective *primus* in line 71). As Leigh puts it, Lucan makes the metaphor concrete, reversing its terms: in place of the Lucretian philosopher-as-soldier, Caesar becomes 'the soldier as unwitting philosopher',

---

[88] Leigh (1999) 173 n. 21 and n. 22 cites Suet. *Jul.* 59, 77, 81.4; Cic. *Div.* 1.119, 2.36–7; App. *BC* 2.153.

[89] Leigh (1999) 174. Leigh notes that the association of light and reason is a commonplace going back to Plato's cave (Pl. *Rep.* 514 A ff.).

[90] On the darkness dispelled by Epicurus' discoveries, cf. Lucr. 1.146 (= 2.59–61, 3.391–3, 6.39–41), 2.15, 5.12. See West (1969) 79–93.

[91] Caesar here additionally behaves as 'the good general who leads from the front': Leigh (1999) 174 and see further Leigh (1997) 106 n. 60. Cf. Aeneas at Virg. *Aen.* 6.183–4.

[92] Lucretius also eulogises Epicurus as the philosopher who first saved mankind at 5.9 (*princeps*) and 6.4 (*primae*).

as 'culture-hero'.[93] Common to the Lucretian and Lucanian figures, however, is the success of their military–epistemological endeavours. Like the triumph of Epicurus against the menacing *fama deum* (Lucr. 1.68), Caesar's felling of the grove strikes a bold blow against *religio*.[94]

Although he does not mention the term himself, Leigh's discussion allows us to view Caesar's actions at the Massilian grove through the Lucretian lens of Epicurean sublimity. Burke strengthens the connection: as an example of a sublimely obscure object, alongside dark, druidical woods, he cites 'the terrible picture which Lucretius has drawn of religion, in order to display the magnanimity of his philosophical hero in opposing her'.[95] In his choice of examples Burke thus highlights obstacles that both Caesar and Epicurus overcome. He also cites Ajax's prayer in the *Iliad* to Zeus to dispel the mist from the Greeks and allow them to perish in the daylight (Ζεῦ πάτερ ἀλλὰ σὺ ῥῦσαι ὑπ᾿ ἠέρος υἷας Ἀχαιῶν, / ποίησον δ᾿ αἴθρην, δὸς δ᾿ ὀφθαλμοῖσιν ἰδέσθαι· / ἐν δὲ φάει καὶ ὄλεσσον, *Il.* 17.645–7), a passage noted by Longinus for its sublimity (9.10).[96] The bringing of light to fearful mortals is precisely what Epicurus and Caesar achieve. Confronting and overcoming the darkness of superstition, their exploits offer parallel instances of the sublime.

Thinking of the Lucanian episode in terms of the sublime opposition between darkness and light reveals a further connection with Lucr. 1.62–79. In both passages the opposition is complicated by references to lightning: sublime illumination contrasts not only

---

[93] Leigh (1999) 176. For the literalisation of metaphor as a device typical of Lucan's poetics, see Leigh (1997) 302. On Lucretius' provocative use at 1.62–79 of the martial imagery of the Roman triumph, see Buchheit (1969/2007).

[94] Leigh's argument runs counter to the assertions of Hunink (1992) 176 and ad Luc. 3.405: 'Brutality, primitivism and barbarism are typical of the grove, and these qualities are not so much opposed by Caesar as surpassed . . . he is not bringing culture and civilisation, but merely pursues logistical aims.' Hunink points out that Caesar's behaviour at Pharsalus (e.g. Luc. 7.566–7, 728–30 and, famously, the breakfast on the battlefield at 7.787–99) is no less bloodthirsty than the Gallic practice of human sacrifice. But in casting Caesar as a kind of warped culture-hero, Lucan is not simply adopting but purposefully subverting his Lucretian intertext.

[95] Burke (1990) 157. On Burke's reading of Lucretius' *Religio*, see Hardie (2009a) 93–4.

[96] This passage occurs shortly after Glaucus' criticism of Hector (*Hom. Il.* 17.166–7), the Iliadic intertext behind Epicurus' sublime achievement at Lucr. 1.62–71: Conte (1994) 1–3.

with the gloom of superstition but also with the blinding terror of the thunderbolt.[97] Epicurus, Lucretius tells us, is not cowed by 'thunderbolts nor heaven with menacing roar' (*fulmina nec minitanti / murmure… caelum*, Lucr. 1.68–9). He provides a model for the rationalising approach to thunder and lightning expounded in Book 6, according to which Lucretius' readers are empowered 'to understand the true nature of the thunderbolt, and to see by what power it plays its part' (*igniferi naturam fulminis ipsam / perspicere et qua vi faciat rem quamque videre*, Lucr. 6.379–80) and hence to attain sublimity. Lucan gives this scenario a further twist. This time, it is not the 'culture hero' but a (supra)natural object – the Massilian grove itself – that is impervious to 'thunderbolts shot from black clouds' (*excussa… nubibus atris / fulgura*, 3.409–10) and, as such, is already in the sublime position achieved by Epicurus. Caesar's destruction of the grove takes the sublime relay a stage further, as he proves himself immune from the terrors of something already immune from lightning – and thus shows himself the true subject of a lightning-like sublimity.

Caesar's Lucretian achievements in this episode display the same sublime subjectivity we witnessed at the Rubicon. They exemplify the antagonistic dynamic according to which his sublimity is attained; they are recognisable in terms of the sublime's traditional imagistic repertoire. They also, however, establish Caesarian sublimity's profoundly anti-religious implications. At the end of the episode, the contempt for *religio* that Caesar shares with Lucretius' Epicurus is contrasted with the reactions of local observers to the felling of the grove. The Gauls lament (*gemuere*, 3.445) the destruction of their place of worship. The Massilians, meanwhile, rejoice: 'for who would think that gods are injured without revenge?' (*quis enim laesos inpune putaret / esse deos?*

---

[97] There are further complexities. Lucretius' blazing thunderbolt is closely allied with darkness: *quod tunc per totum concrescunt aera nubes / undique uti tenebras omnis Acherunta reamur / liquisse et magnas caeli complesse cavernas: / usque adeo taetra nimborum nocte coorta / inpendent atrae formidinis ora superne, / cum commoliri tempestas fulmina coeptat* (Lucr. 6.250–5). Lucan plays on the etymological relation between *lux* and *lucus*, a word 'originally denoting an open place in the wood where the light can fall in': Hunink (1992) 170. The paradox is pointed up at the very beginning of the ecphrasis on the Massilian grove: *lucus erat… / obscurum cingens… aera* (Luc. 3.399–400).

3.447–8). The responses of both groups, however, assume that gods exist, gods to whom the grove belongs and who, because of its destruction, have been injured. Accordingly, Caesar will suffer divine vengeance.[98] But this vengeance never comes.[99] One answer to the Massilians' gleeful question would thus be: Caesar. Caesar is able to destroy the grove and get away with it – because, as his act of deforestation has shown, in Lucan's epic there are no gods to exact vengeance in the first place. Leigh argues that Caesar's demonstration of this fact is 'almost in contradiction of his titanic ambitions': 'the hero who reveals the absence or impotence of the gods is one who is frustrated in his fundamental desire to perform the truly grand and charismatic deed of matching himself against those gods.'[100] But, as the poem progresses, Caesar seems less concerned to 'match' himself with the gods than to put himself in their place, asserting his position as their demonic surrogate. This aspect of Caesar's sublimity comes out especially powerfully during his attempted crossing of the Adriatic in Book 5, to which I now turn.

The Adriatic storm (5.504–677)

Storms at sea, like lightning, the Alps and dark woods, are another traditional topos of the sublime. Kant cites the power of 'the

---

[98] Cf. the consequences of Erysichthon's desecration of the grove of Ceres: Ov. *Met.* 8.741–76; Call. *Hymn* 6.31–65. Leigh (1999) 178–185 adduces several parallel instances, both mythological and historical, in which the felling of sacred groves meets with divine retribution: Hom. *Hymn Aph.* 264–72; Hdt. 75–80; Ap. Rhod. *Arg.* 3.468–89; Hyginus, *Fabulae* 132; Cic. *Mil.* 85.

[99] Leigh (1999) 185–94 cites Augustus' engineering works at Lake Avernus in *c.* 37 BC as a historical parallel for those parts of Lucan's Massilian episode that the traditional paradigm of retribution cannot reflect: through deforestation, Augustus, like his ancestor Caesar, turned a *locus horridus* into a *locus amoenus*, in the process refuting superstition about Avernus' inviolability. See Servius ad Virg. *Aen.* 3.442; Strabo, *Geog.* 5.4.5. Augustus' works were ostensibly undertaken in order to create a base for operations against Sextus Pompeius but served additionally as spectacular propaganda: 'The project [was] designed to impress the beholder with the *colossal power* and *awesome "magnitudo animi"* of its creators' (my italics) (Frederiksen (1984) 33). This is the language of the sublime, both dynamic and mathematical. There was even a rumour that Agrippa, who oversaw the works, welcomed the divine wrath that they inspired (Servius ad Virg. *Georg.* 2.162; Cassius Dio 48.50) – an instance of sublime self-assertion worthy of Lucan's Caesar (compare Caesar's view of the Adriatic storm as fitting tribute to his own greatness, Luc. 5.653–6).

[100] Leigh (1999) 168.

boundless ocean set into a rage'.[101] Joseph Addison, writing earlier
in the eighteenth century, declares:

Of all objects that I have ever seen, there is none which affects my imagination
so much as the sea or ocean. I cannot see the heavings of this prodigious bulk
of waters, even in a calm, without a very pleasing astonishment; but when it is
worked up in a tempest, so that the horizon on every side is nothing but foaming
billows and floating mountains, it is impossible to describe the agreeable horror
that rises from such a prospect. A troubled ocean, to a man who sails upon it, is,
I think, the biggest object that he can see in motion, and consequently gives his
imagination one of the highest kinds of pleasure that can arise from greatness.[102]

Addison's reflections on the sublimity of sea storms are prompted,
he says, by personal experience but also by 'the descriptions of
them in ancient poets'. He especially singles out Longinus' quotation of *Iliad* 15.624–8, Homer's comparison between the might
of Hector's onslaught and that of a great storm wave crashing
over a ship at sea (*De sub.* 10.5). Like the 'agreeable horror'
described by Addison, the sublime turn evidenced in these lines, as
Homer's sailors escape death by a mere 'hand's breadth', suggests
a commingled experience of near-annihilation and wild exaltation.
Lucretius also finds an example of sublimity's 'agreeable horror'
(Lucr. 3.28–9), in the peculiar thrill of watching a ship struggling
in stormy seas:

> suave, mari magno turbantibus aequora ventis,
> e terra magnum alterius spectare laborem;
> non quia vexari quemquamst iucunda voluptas,
> sed quibus ipse malis careas quia cernere suave est.

> Pleasant it is, when on the great sea the winds trouble the waters,
> to gaze from shore upon another's tribulation:
> not because any man's troubles are a delectable joy,
> but because to perceive what ills you are free from yourself is pleasant.
>
> Lucr. 2.1–4

Where Addison's sublime subject is the sailor braving the billows,
Lucretius' is the spectator standing safely on the shore, but in each
case sublimity arises from the conversion of the fear occasioned by

---

[101] Kant (2003) 144.
[102] From the *Spectator* no. 489 (1712), cited by Ashfield and de Bolla (1996) 69.

the sea's size and power into a sense of 'delight' (to adopt Burke's term) on the part of the experiencing subject.[103]

How does Caesar's voyage in Book 5 of the *Bellum civile* relate to this way of experiencing the sea? I offer first some considerations of broad influence and context. As well as the topos of the storm in epic and constructions of seafaring as a moral barometer in rhetorical writing,[104] Mark Morford identifies the long tradition of Greek and Roman writing on meteorological phenomena as an important frame for the Lucanian episode. His comprehensive survey of relevant texts within this philosophical–didactic tradition includes Empedocles' *On Nature*, Aristotle's *Meteorologica*, Theophrastus' *Metarsiologica*, Aratus' *Phaenomena*, Manilius' *Astronomicon*, the *Aetna* poem, Epicurus' *Letter to Pythocles*, Posidonius, Seneca's *Natural Questions* and Pliny's *Natural History*.[105] 'It is impossible to say', Morford concludes, 'how far all these writers and the mass of scientific speculation influenced Lucan. [However,] it is abundantly clear that from the time of Lucretius to that of Lucan there flourished among educated Romans what A. D. Nock called "a sense for the wonders of nature" . . . Lucan's storm-scenes owe much to th[is] vigorous spirit of inquiry and sense of wonder.'[106] With the reading of the stars conducted by Amyclas, Caesar's boatman (5.539–59), we can in fact be more specific: the details are derived from Virgil's *Georgics* (1.351–514), which in turn was modelled on Aratus and Theophrastus.[107] It is to this same tradition of meteorological doxography that Porter also looks

---

[103] Cf. Martindale (2005) 189–90 on the nineteenth-century philosopher and aesthetician Victor Cousin's quasi-Kantian reading of Lucretius' lines. Although Lucretius does not treat sea storms specifically in the *De rerum natura*, he makes reference to their force in his discussion of atoms' invisibility (*principio venti vis verberat incita pontum / ingentisque ruit navis et nubila differt*, 1.271–2) and in his explanation of *presteres* or 'water-spouts' (*quam freta circum / fervescunt graviter spirantibus incita flabris, / et quaecumque in eo tum sint deprensa tumultu / navigia in summum veniant vexata periclum*, 6.427–30); storms form part of the poem's sublime texture.

[104] Morford (1967) 20–6, 29–31.   [105] Morford (1967) 26–8.

[106] Morford (1967) 28, citing Nock (1959) 15.

[107] See Matthews (2008) 114–16; Morford (1967) 38–9. Virgil's discussion includes a list of portents predicting Caesar's death (*Georg.* 1.465–97). Although in the Lucanian episode Caesar comes close to dying, the violence of the storm ultimately serves to highlight his sublime, godlike ability to rise above mortal dangers. Compare his avoidance of punishment after felling the Massilian grove but contrast the flashforwards to his murder at Luc. 7.592–6, 7.610–15 and 10.341–4. Martindale (1976) 52 also notes the influence of the Virgilian passage on Luc. 1.552ff.

when searching for possible antecedents to the sublime speculations of Lucretius and Longinus, citing Theophrastus and Aratus,
as well as Crates of Mallos, Pliny's *Natural History*, Varro, Manilius, the *Aetna* poem, and Seneca.[108] Taken together, Morford's
and Porter's suggestions encourage us to place Lucan's storm in
Book 5 within a literary context already alive to the possibility of
the sublime.[109]

Once located within this context, however, Lucan's storm
rapidly whirls beyond all expectations. Although Caesar's voyage is attested in some historical sources, most indicate that
stormy weather prevented him sailing beyond the mouth of the
river Aous;[110] in Lucan's version not only does Caesar brave the
open sea but the weather turns into a tempest of truly cosmic
proportions, more massive and more violent than anything nature
could summon in reality. And not just reality: Lucan's hyperbolic,
paradox-driven description of the tempest also outdoes its epic
models, amplifying the already awesome details of the storms
in the *Odyssey* (5.291–332, 12.403–25), the *Aeneid* (1.34–156,
3.192–208, 5.8–34) and Ovid's *Metamorphoses* (11.474–572), and
combining them with the Stoic imagery of world apocalypse that
recurs throughout the poem.[111]

Monica Matthews' excellent recent commentary allows us fully
to appreciate the extraordinary nature of the episode.[112] As the
storm rises, a dark, Homeric shudder sweeps over the sea (564–
5), but we can already guess this will be no ordinary epic storm:
not only do the swelling winds drive comets (*cadentia . . . sidera*)
off course, they also seem to shake those stars that normally

Porter (2007) 174–5. Cf. Schrijvers (2006) 97–9.
[109] Cf. Hunter (2009) 134 on *De sub.* 10.5: the sea storm was 'perhaps one of the principal
loci for "cosmic poetry", describing the tumult of nature on the grand, sublime scale';
cf. also Hardie (1986) index s.v. 'storm'; Conte (1996) 55–8.
[110] See V. Max. 9.8.2; Plut. *Caes.* 37–8; Suet. *Jul.* 19.58; Flor. *Epit.* 2.13.35–8; App. Luc.
2.52–9; Cassius Dio 41.43–8. The voyage is not mentioned in Caesar's own *Bellum
civile* (cf. Caes. *Civ.* 3.2–26).
[111] The storm in Seneca's *Agamemnon* (465–578) is another important intertext. On
Lucan's 'imagery of cosmic dissolution', see Lapidge (1979/2010) and the discussion of Luc. 1.67–82 in Chapter 2. For a full analysis of the relationship of Lucan's
Adriatic storm to previous epic, see Matthews (2008), esp. 23–5, 132–42, 166–224,
315–18, developing the remarks of Morford (1967) 20–6, 37–44 and Barratt (1979)
164–226.
[112] See Matthews (2008) ad Luc. 5.561–677.

remain fixed in highest heaven (*summis etiam quae fixa tenentur /
astra polis*), thereby threatening the sky's collapse (561–4).
The prospect of universal destruction intensifies once the storm
has broken: *inde ruunt toto concita pericula mundo* (5.597, cf.
mundumque coercens / monstriferos agit unda sinus, 5.619–20).
The sea lifts all its waves onto the rocks (*in scopulos totas erexerat
undas*, 5.600); true to epic form, all winds blow at once (*cunctos
solita de parte ruentis*, 5.610), carrying water from one sea into
another, but the unprecedented, paradoxical result is that the ocean
as a whole remains in place (*sic pelagus mansisse loco*, 5.612,
cf. 5.646–9). Nevertheless, in a hyperbole more extravagant even
than those in Ovid's account of the Flood in *Metamorphoses* 1,
we are told that on this day (*ille dies*, a phrase that, as it evokes
the final cataclysm, looks forward to the *summa dies* of Pharsalus
itself, 7.195) the deep rose so high that mountains were cast to
the ocean's bed (5.615–17).[113] The Flood is in fact adduced as a
comparison for the current storm (5.620–4) but, in another rever-
sal of expectations, instead of the sea reaching the sky, the clouds
descend right to the water (*tum quoque tanta maris moles crevisset
in astra / ni superum rector pressisset nubibus undas*, 5.625–6).
No sooner has this comparison been suggested than the storm's
violence grows even greater: just as it ruptures nature's ordering
boundaries so, as Matthews observes, does it burst the confines of
mythological precedent.[114] Hades seems to invade the upper world,
doubling the night's darkness (*non caeli nox illa fuit*, 5.627–9); air
cracks apart (5.631); amid the world-encompassing devastation
(*tanta mundi . . . ruina*, 5.637) the very structure of the heavens
threatens to collapse (5.632–6). The astral heights and abyssal
depths to which the waves propel Caesar's boat (5.638–53) conclude the passage with a dizzying destabilisation of familiar spatial
perspectives: *nubila tanguntur velis et terra carina* (5.642).[115]

There is considerable potential among all this for sublime experience. As they swell and gape (*cumque tumentes / rursus hiant*

---

[113] See Matthews (2008) ad loc.   [114] Matthews (2008) ad Luc. 5.620–6.

[115] Cheney (2009) 93–4 identifies the sublimity of these lines as the inspiration for the
sublimity of Dido's speech in Marlowe's *Dido, Queen of Carthage* 5.1.243–52 ('I'll
frame me wings of wax like Icarus, / And o'er his ships will soar unto the sun / . . . Look,
sister, look, lovely Aeneas' ships! / See, see, the billows heave him up to heaven').

undae, 5.640–1)[116] the storm's waves become like those evoca-
tions of void in Book 6 of *De rerum natura*, the earthquakes,
volcanic eruptions and lightning-torn clouds identified by Porter
as physical emblems of the awe-inspiring vacuity that drives the
Lucretian sublime. The prospect of the universe's final destruction, so persistently threatened by the Lucanian storm, conjures
this *hiatus* even more powerfully. Indeed, for Lucretius the way
in which natural disasters tear open the world's fabric (*distracta
suum late dispandat hiatum / idque suis confusa velit complere ruinis*, Lucr. 6.599–600, cf. *vis / exagitata foras erumpitur et simul
altam / diffindens terram magnum concinnat hiatum*, Lucr. 6.583–
4) merely prefigures the ultimate ruin of apocalypse, when death
will gape wide for sky and sun, earth and ocean (*patet immani
et vasto respectat hiatu*, Lucr. 5.375).[117] For the appropriately
attuned subject, this is an awesome vision. In Lucretian terms, the
sublimity of the final cataclysm offers an analogue for the sublimity of atomism, wherein the earth, as it appears to us and as
we previously knew it, truly is snatched from beneath our feet,
pitching us, as rationally detached Epicurean observers, towards
the stars: our plunge into the depths paradoxically ensures the stability of our position, metaphorically speaking, 'above' the earth.
But, as Lucretius acknowledges, this prospect can also prove purely
terrifying:

> proinde licet quamvis caelum terramque reantur
> incorrupta fore aeternae mandata saluti;
> et tamen interdum praesens vis ipsa pericli
> subdit et hunc stimulum quadam de parte timoris,
> ne pedibus raptim tellus subtracta feratur   605
> in barathrum, rerumque sequatur prodita summa
> funditus, et fiat mundi confusa ruina.

> Therefore let them believe as they please that earth and sky
> will remain incorruptible, given in trust to life everlasting;
> and yet sometimes the very present force of peril

---

[116] Matthews (2008) ad loc. points out that although 'the gaping of the sea is a common
idea' (e.g. *dehisco* at Virg. *Aen.* 1.106, 5.142; Sen. *Ag.* 499), the verb *hio* is not used in
this context before Lucan.

[117] See Porter (2007) 171. In this sense, Lucan's hyperbolic figuration of Caesar's storm
as world-engulfing cataclysm can be understood as a poetic consequence of the logic
of Lucretius' thinking about sublimity.

applies this goad of fear also from one part or another,
that the earth may be suddenly withdrawn from under their feet, and fall
into the bottomless pit, followed by the whole sum of things utterly
giving way, and then may come the confused ruin of the world.

Lucr. 6.601–7

These lines conclude Lucretius' discussion of earthquakes but the feared disaster, the *mundi confusa ruina* (607), is the same as that heralded by Lucan's storm. As Porter explains, the fear generated by natural disasters 'is in turn based on a deeper metaphysical fear that the world is not quite the way it is commonly known and experienced (as something more or less solid, permanent and secure), a fear which expresses itself psychologically as, one might say, a pervading *horror vacui*'.[118] This 'ultimate and primordial fear', the 'untrained response to the atomistic view of nature', easily precludes sublimity, as Burke and Kant also emphasise.[119] It requires a particular kind of subject, properly schooled, to see the *barathrum* at the heart of nature's violence, and its concomitant physical and mental dangers, as sublime.

The difference between these potential reactions is the difference between Caesar's response to the storm and that of an Aeneas. Caesar makes two speeches during Lucan's storm episode. His first, in response to Amyclas' concerns about the weather, contrasts starkly with the exchange between Aeneas and his helmsman Palinurus as the storm rises in *Aeneid* 5.[120] Caesar's command to Amyclas, 'If you refuse Italy at heaven's command, seek it at mine' (*Italiam si caelo auctore recusas, / me pete*, Luc. 5.579–80), is to be compared with Palinurus' admission of defeat, 'Noble Aeneas, not though Jupiter should warrant his word, could I hope to reach Italy with such a sky' (*magnanime Aenea, non, si mihi Iuppiter auctor / spondeat, hoc sperem Italiam contingere caelo*, Aen. 5.17–18): rather than quailing before the storm's might, Caesar is filled with awareness of his own powers, his peremptory instruction implying that he possesses a command over the elements such as, in Palinurus' view, even Jupiter does not enjoy; he is 'someone never deserted by the gods, someone who is treated ill by fortune

---

[118] Porter (2007) 171–2.   [119] Burke (1990) 36–7; Kant (2003) 144, 152.
[120] See Matthews (2008) on Luc. 5.578–93.

when she comes only after his prayers' (*quem numina numquam /
destituunt, de quo male tunc fortuna meretur / cum post vota venit*,
Luc. 5.581–3).[121]

Caesar's speech also picks up and reconfigures the agonistic language of the Virgilian passage: 'we cannot resist or stem
the gale' (*nec nos obniti contra nec tendere tantum / sufficimus*,
Aen. 5.21–2), admits Palinurus, to which Aeneas assents, 'I see
you striving in vain against the winds. Change the course of our
sailing' (*frustra cerno te tendere contra. / flecte viam velis*, Aen.
5.27–8). The heroes' powers are defeated; they cannot resist the
might of the gale. Caesar, on the other hand, 'confident that for
him all dangers will give way' (*fisus cuncta sibi cessura pericula*,
Luc. 5.577), exhibits a sublime confidence that he *can* overcome
the storm. 'Do not turn your hand' (*ne flecte manum*, 5.588), he
orders Amyclas, flatly contradicting Aeneas' instruction to Palinurus. The Lucanian passage is peppered with similarly com-
bative imperatives:[122] 'Despise the sea's threats, entrust your sail
to the raging wind' (*sperne minas... pelagi ventoque furenti /
trade sinum*, 5.578–9); 'break through the gales' midst' (*medias
perrumpe procellas*, 5.583); Caesar's command to Amyclas to be
'secure' (*secure*, 5.584) recalls the lion to which Caesar is likened
in Book 1, leaping *securus* at his enemy (1.212). Sublimer still,
Caesar sees the storm as a positive gift (*quaerit pelagi caelique
tumultu, / quod praestet Fortuna mihi*, 5.592–3). Like the Rubicon
and the Massilian grove, the storm constitutes a natural barrier, a
mora, to Caesar's progress yet it is this barrier that causes Caesar's
conception of his own supranatural (or, in Kantian terms, 'supersensible') powers to rise and swell.[123] Reminding us of Lucretius'

---

[121] Cf. Luc. 1.349, 5.351–2, 5.698–9, 7.297–8. Matthews (2008) ad loc. notes that Caesar's
words recall Apollo's revelation of identity at Ov. *Met.* 1.514ff.; the hymnic language
common to both passages underlines Caesar's divine self-perception. Matthews also
reminds us that *tutela* (Luc. 5.584), used by Caesar of himself, more usually refers
to divine protection, especially that of Jupiter, and that Caesar's claim *hanc Caesare
pressam / a fluctu defendet onus* (5.585–6) alludes to the traditional weightiness of
divine bodies (cf. 1.56–7).

[122] On the high frequency of imperatives here and throughout Caesar's speeches, see
Helzle (1994/2010) 355–7, 365–7.

[123] So Ahl (1976) 208–9: 'What this incident shows more than anything else is that there
is nothing Caesar cannot somehow construe to his own advantage. Adversity simply
increases his megalomania. He thinks of himself as a cosmic power; he dares to act

figuration of Epicurus' sublime achievement as the rescuing of mankind from stormy seas (*fluctibus e tantis*, Lucr. 5.11), Caesar grandly assures Amyclas that his mere presence will soon still the storm's fury: *nec longa furori / ventorum saevo dabitur mora: proderit undis / ista ratis* (Luc. 5.586–8). In reality this hubris proves spectacularly ill-founded but this in no way impinges on the quality of Caesar's experience. Even as it prevents him from reaching Italy, the *mora* of the storm launches him into the sublime.

Caesar previously proclaimed his fierce delight in, indeed his need for, such obstacles as a warning to the Massilians (3.362–6, cf. 2.439–46). His sublimely antagonistic attitude is powerfully underscored by the narratorial comment introducing his second storm speech: as the storm's violence reaches its zenith, 'now Caesar thinks the perils worthy of his destiny' (*credit iam digna pericula Caesar / fatis esse suis*, 5.653–4). Caesar's conception of his own destiny can only achieve full realisation when faced with *pericula* like the storm. That the storm has now become literally cataclysmic in scale, threatening to obliterate Caesar along with the rest of the world, only causes his egotism to leap higher. 'How mighty is the gods' toil to throw me down, attacking me with sea so great as I sit in a tiny boat!' (*quantusne evertere... / me superis labor est, parva quem puppe sedentem / tam magno petiere mari!* 5.654–6), he exclaims delightedly.[124] Like his earlier replacement of Jupiter's *auctoritas* with his own (5.579–80), Caesar's words here indicate that he sees himself as equal to or even greater than the gods themselves (note the juxtaposition of *me superis*, but with the stress falling on *me* as the first syllable in the line). In his first speech he had confidently asserted his superiority to the *labor* of the storm, belittling it as something that affected the sky and sea but from which he and his boat remained serenely detached (*caeli iste fretique, / non puppis nostrae, labor est*, 5.584–5); in a variation on this idea, he now exults in the *labor* that it

when the forces of nature shrink back (as in the felling of the Druidic grove in *Pharsalia* 3); it therefore follows that he would view his braving of the storm as a contest between himself and the elements.'

[124] Caesar's attitude may be compared with that of the narrator in the proem to the *Aeneid* (*tantaene animis caelestibus irae?*, *Aen.* 1.11; cf. *tantae molis erat Romanam condere gentem*, *Aen.* 1.33): Caesar converts Virgil's wary astonishment into joyful self-aggrandisement.

costs the gods to destroy him, seeing in the physical discrepancy between his *parva... puppe* and the *magno... mari* an indication of his own extraordinary greatness. Death for Caesar thus becomes not a source of fear but a cause for rejoicing. Where in his first speech he asserted both that the storm worked to his advantage and that his presence would calm the waves, here he regards the storm as a force that benefits his own stature and asserts, in turn, that his drowning will confer glory upon the sea (5.656–9) – a dazzlingly confident expression of the power transfer that Hertz locates at the core of sublime experience.[125] A watery grave is to be welcomed, not feared, for it will shroud Caesar's end in sublime uncertainty (*desint mihi busta rogusque, / dum metuar semper terraque expecter ab omni*, 5.670–1).

This all contrasts pointedly with Aeneas' position in *Aeneid* 1. Overwhelmed by the tempest that Aeolus has unleashed – its pitchy sky (*Aen.* 1.88–9), rolling thunder, flashes of lightning (1.90), mountainous waves (1.105, 114) and yawning sea (1.106–7) all typically sublime – Aeneas goes limp with terror, groans loudly and, lamenting the ingloriousness of drowning at sea, wishes Diomedes had killed him instead in heroic combat at Troy (*Aen.* 1.92–101).[126] Terror is also a response to the storm in *Bellum civile* 5: sailors tremble (Luc. 5.639); fear conquers the helmsman's powers (*artis opem vicere metus*, 5.645).[127] These reactions are entirely, literally natural for even nature is in a state of panic (*extimuit natura chaos*, 5.634).[128] But, like the soldiers'

---

[125] Hertz (1978/1985) 6.

[126] Aeneas' reaction re-enacts that of Odysseus in the storm at Hom. *Od.* 5.297–312.

[127] Cf. Ceyx's helmsman at Ov. *Met.* 11.492–3: *ipse pavet nec se, qui sit status, ipse fatetur / scire ratis rector, nec quid iubeatve vetetve.*

[128] Compare the terrified response to impending shipwreck in the simile used to describe the flight from Rome at Luc. 1.498–503: *naufragium sibi quisque facit.* The use of the term *conpages* to describe the frame of the ship-of-state (*nondum sparsa conpage carinae*, 1.502) reflects Book 5's description of the storm-battered heavens (*motaque poli conpage laborant*, 5.633) and locates the simile within the poem's network of images of collapsing structures, reflective of the cataclysmic effects of civil war: cf. 2.487, 3.491, 3.629, 5.119, 5.596, 6.117, 7.857 and, especially, 1.72–4 (*sic, cum conpage soluta / saecula tot mundi suprema coegerit hora, / antiquum repetens iterum chaos...*); see further Matthews (2008) ad 5.596. Where in Book 5 the tempest has already weakened the structure of the heavens, in Book 1 the narrator bitterly observes that the ship is abandoned even though its planks are still intact.

fear of the Massilian grove in Book 3, this only highlights all the more strongly Caesar's ability to transcend affective norms.

The way in which the panic of others throws Caesar's sublimity into relief is encapsulated by the twin connotations of the verb *despicitur* (followed by an effectively dramatic pause as we peer over the edge) at the beginning of 5.639. Lucan likens the view from the crest of a storm wave to that from the top of Cape Leucate:

> quantum Leucadio placidus de vertice pontus
> despicitur, tantum nautae videre trementes
> fluctibus e summis praeceps mare . . .

> As far below as tranquil sea is seen from the Leucadian
> peak, quaking sailors from the wave-top
> saw the sea's sheer drop . . .   5.638–40

'The idea of looking down from a great height', notes Matthews, 'is common in earlier Latin poetry and is associated both with the security of the philosopher or Jupiter . . . and with terror.'[129] Lucan's immediate model here is Ovid's description of the terrifying glimpse of the abyss caught by Ceyx's crew in *Metamorphoses* 11 (*et nunc sublimis veluti de vertice montis / despicere in valles imumque Acheronta videtur*, *Met.* 11.503–4); Ovid also uses *despicere* to describe both Icarus and Phaethon as they glance giddily down from the heavens.[130] However, as Ovid's use of the adjective *sublimis* might remind us, the view from on high need not always induce knee-loosening bouts of vertigo. Ovid's Pythagoras, for instance, describes the delight (*iuvat . . .*, *Met.* 15.147) he takes in looking down from the heavens (*alta astra*, *Met.* 15.147–8) upon erring mankind in order to correct their ways (*palantesque homines passim et rationis egentes / despectare procul trepidosque obitumque timentes*, *Met.* 15.150–1). This philosophical perspective recalls Lucretius' picture of the sublimely detached gaze of the Epicurean: it is, as we have seen, *suave* to watch a tempest-tossed ship from the vantage of the shore (Lucr. 2.1–4),

---

[129] Matthews (2008) ad loc. Also in Homer, e.g. *Il.* 15.146–7; see Porter (2010) 161–2.
[130] [*Icarus*] *territus a summo despexit in aequora caelo* (Ov. *Ars* 2.87); *summo despexit ab aethere terras / infelix Phaethon* (Ov. *Met.* 2.178–9).

> sed nil dulcius est bene quam munita tenere
> edita doctrina sapientum templa serena,
> despicere unde queas alios passimque videre
> errare.

> but nothing is more delightful than to possess lofty
> sanctuaries serene, well fortified by the teachings of the wise,
> whence you may look down upon others and behold them all
> astray.   Lucr. 2.7–10[131]

To be able to 'look down', *despicere*, without fear, is a defining quality of Lucretius' Epicurean atomist. It is from this perspective that atomic truths allow access to the sublime.

Hardie has recently pointed out that *despicere* also occurs in this Lucretian sense in the storm scene in *Aeneid* 1.[132] The tempest has done its worst and the remnants of Aeneas' fleet bob aimlessly on the water: 'Here and there are seen swimmers in the vast abyss, with weapons of men, planks and Trojan treasure amid the waves' (*apparent rari nantes in gurgite vasto, / arma virum tabulaeque et Troia gaza per undas, Aen.* 1.118–19).[133] The lines recall the analogy used by Lucretius to illustrate what would happen if the supply of atoms in the universe were finite (Lucr. 2.547–59, compared above to Lucan's description of the Romans' fleeing Caesar's advance, 1.498–504). In Lucretius' analogy the reader is placed in the role of sublime spectator, looking on from afar. But who occupies this position in the Virgilian scene? Not, as we have seen, Aeneas nor by implication his Trojans, still terror-stricken amid the storm's rage. Neptune, we are told, 'gazing out over the deep, raised his serene face over the water's surface' *alto / prospiciens summa placidum caput extulit unda,*

---

[131] This vantage point is again that of Jupiter and the gods: Fowler (2002) ad loc. Cf. also the *divina voluptas... atque horror* (Lucr. 3.29) that arises as we gaze down into the atomic void beneath our feet: *nec tellus obstat quin omnia dispiciantur, / sub pedibus quaecumque infra per inane geruntur* (Lucr. 3.26–8).

[132] Hardie (2009b) 160–2.

[133] Cf. Alcyone's Lucretian vision of a shipwreck's flotsam at Ov. *Met.* 11.428: *et laceras nuper tabulas in litore vidi.* Alcyone's response is characterised by fear and foreboding rather than sublimity: her beloved Ceyx is about to drown in a storm, the terrifying violence of which paralyses the ship's helmsman (*Met.* 11.492–3) while the rest of the crew weep, go mute with fear, lament their lot or think of their families (11.539–43). Ceyx does not succumb to the general panic but his thoughts, instead of swelling in sublime self-aggrandisement, remain firmly fixed on Alcyone (*Met.* 11.544–6, 562–7).

Aen. 1.127) and, as Hardie notes, *placidum*, a common word in Lucretius, 'might hint momentarily at an Epicurean detached view'; but Jupiter is an even better candidate, 'looking forth from the sky's summit over the sail-winged sea and outspread lands' (*aethere summo / despiciens mare velivolum terrasque iacentis*, *Aen.* 1.223–4): once the storm is over, we discover him to have been 'watching all along (presumably), looking down . . . from his panopticon at the zenith of the heavens' like the wise man of the proem to Book 2 of *De rerum natura*.[134]

These suggestions of sublime subjectivity in *Aeneid* 1 run counter to the position of the poem's protagonist: *despicere* in this instance connotes sublimity rather than terror and is not used of Aeneas. Turning back to the *Bellum civile*, however, we see that Lucan's usage at 5.638–40 spans both affective associations. Petrified, the *nautae* look down from the wave crest upon a 'precipice of water' but the simile itself conjures a more pacific prospect, the *placidus . . . pontus* contrasting with the storm's angry billows and perhaps glancing instead at the *placidum caput* of Virgil's Neptune. In other words, even as Lucan's *despicitur* suggests the wild-eyed gaze of the frightened sailors, reminding us of Phaethon or Icarus, it also points to the sublime perspective enjoyed by Epicurus or Jupiter and achieved here, in the face of impending death, by Caesar.[135] It is the same perspective as Caesar adopts earlier in Book 5 when faced with the mutiny of his men:

> haud magis expertus discrimine Caesar in ullo est,
> quam non e stabili tremulo sed culmine cuncta
> despiceret staretque super titubantia fultus.

> In no crisis did Caesar learn more clearly
> how he looked down on everything from a height which was
> not firm but shaking and how he stood supported on a rocking platform.

> 5.249–51

Caesar's realisation is Lucretian, in the sense that the world suddenly sheds its appearance of stability: solid foundations are in

---

[134] Hardie (2009b) 161–2.
[135] Cf. Caesar's elevated, godlike view at Luc. 3.88: *excelsa de rupe procul iam conspicit urbem.* Feeney (1991) 295 juxtaposes this line with the intimations of Caesarian divinity at 3.98–103 and compares Ov. *Met.* 1.163–76.

fact riddled with gaps and holes; we tremble at the thought that 'the earth may be suddenly withdrawn from under [our] feet, and fall into the bottomless pit, followed by the whole sum of things utterly giving away' (*pedibus raptim tellus subtracta feratur / in barathrum, rerumque sequatur prodita summa / funditus*, Lucr. 6.605–7). But 'it can be a sublime sensation to stand on nothing'[136] and Caesar, rising to the challenge, subdues the mutineers. He does not fear their anger, as many would (*quem non ille ducem potuit terrere tumultus?* Luc. 5.300); quite the contrary, he is eager to test fortune (*fata sed in praeceps solitus demittere Caesar / fortunamque suam per summa pericula gaudens / exercere*, 5.301–3). So amid the dizzying dangers of the storm (*pericula*, 5.577, 653–4), as he teeters on the wave's brink, the ocean floor gaping wide beneath him, Caesar finds cause for exultation. Looking down upon chaos and impending ruin becomes a sublime experience.

The ocean, Aetna and the Nile

As at the Rubicon and the Massilian grove, Caesar's response to the sea storm's sublimity marks his own entry into the sublime. In turn, the storm's sublime, *praeceps* (5.640) violence becomes a reflection of *praeceps* (5.301) Caesar's megalomaniac sublimity.[137] The same agonistic processes underpin each: as the storm threatens to rupture the *concordes... moras* (5.634) of the elements so it is itself a *mora* that Caesar must overcome. Turning back to the near-mutiny of Caesar's troops earlier in the book, we find this association of Caesar and sea storm foreshadowed. In the speech that quells the storm of his soldiers' anger, Caesar likens himself to the ocean:

> Caesaris an cursus vestrae sentire putatis
> damnum posse fugae? veluti, si cuncta minentur
> flumina quos misceant pelago subducere fontes,

---

[136] Porter (2007) 172.
[137] Cf. Morford (1967) 37: 'The storm is symbolic of Caesar's own tempestuous spirit, of Fortune's fluctuations, of the upheaval in the Roman world: through it all, Caesar is master.'

non magis ablatis umquam descenderit aequor,
quam nunc crescit, aquis.

Do you think that Caesar's career can feel
the loss of your flight? It is as if all rivers
threatened to withdraw the streams they mingle with the sea:
with those waters gone, the sea-level would fall
no more than it now rises. 5.335–9

The same picture is drawn by Lucretius as part of his discussion of sublime natural phenomena in Book 6 of *De rerum natura*. Men wonder, he says, why the sea does not grow larger from all the rivers and streams that run into it (*mare mirantur non reddere maius / naturam, quo sit tantus decursus aquarum, / omnia quo veniant ex omni flumina parte*, Lucr. 6.608–10),

tamen ad maris omnia summam
guttai vix instar erunt unius adaugmen;
quo minus est mirum mare non augescere magnum.

yet all compared with the whole mass of the sea
will be scarce equal to the augmentation of one single drop;
which makes it less wonderful that the great sea does not increase.
Lucr. 6.613–15[138]

The thought of this vast quantity of water is sublime. A sum so great that it literally cannot be increased, we see in it a reflection of mankind's own boundless potential. Caesar brings the aggressive, confrontational implications of this idea to the fore, using it as a means of asserting mastery over other men: the immensity of his *cursus* is like that of the limitless ocean and he turns the tide of mutiny with ease. Comparison with an object of the natural sublime here becomes not simply a reflection of Caesar's sublimity, as with the imagery of lightning and wild beasts, but his means of actually achieving sublimity within the action of the poem. Far from succumbing to the mutineers' demands, he has their leaders executed. His Lucretian proclamation diverts the power of their anger so that it accrues to himself, presenting at once an enactment of and an analogy for sublime subjectivity.

---

[138] Cf. Lucr. 1.230–1. On the wondrous size of the sea, see also Sen. *Nat.* 3.4.

Porter observes that in the series of natural phenomena in Book 6 of *De rerum natura* the ocean (608–38) is immediately followed by Mount Aetna (639–702) and the Nile (712–37). These three prodigies are also found as a group in Longinus:

διόπερ τῇ θεωρίᾳ καὶ διανοίᾳ τῆς ἀνθρωπίνης ἐπιβολῆς οὐδ᾽ ὁ σύμπας κόσμος ἀρκεῖ, ἀλλὰ καὶ τοὺς τοῦ περιέχοντος πολλάκις ὅρους ἐκβαίνουσιν αἱ ἐπίνοιαι· καὶ εἴ τις περιβλέψαιτο ἐν κύκλῳ τὸν βίον, ὅσῳ πλέον ἔχει τὸ περιττὸν ἐν πᾶσι καὶ μέγα καὶ καλόν, ταχέως εἴσεται πρὸς ἃ γεγόναμεν. ἔνθεν φυσικῶς πως ἀγό- μενοι μὰ Δί᾽ οὐ τὰ μικρὰ ῥεῖθρα θαυμάζομεν, εἰ καὶ διαυγῆ καὶ χρήσιμα, ἀλλὰ τὸν Νεῖλον καὶ Ἴστρον ἢ Ῥῆνον, πολὺ δ᾽ ἔτι μᾶλλον τὸν Ὠκεανόν, οὐδέ γε τὸ ὑφ᾽ ἡμῶν τουτὶ φλογίον ἀνακαιόμενον, ἐπεὶ καθαρὸν σῴζει τὸ φέγγος, ἐκπλ- ηττόμεθα τῶν οὐρανίων μᾶλλον, καίτοι πολλάκις ἐπισκοτουμένων, οὐδὲ τῶν τῆς Αἴτνης κρατήρων ἀξιοθαυμαστότερον νομίζομεν, ἧς αἱ ἀναχοαὶ πέτρους τε ἐκ βυθοῦ καὶ ὅλους ὄχθους ἀναφέρουσι καὶ ποταμοὺς ἐνίοτε τοῦ γηγενοῦς ἐκείνου καὶ αὐτομάτου προχέουσιν πυρός. ἀλλ᾽ ἐπὶ τῶν τοιούτων ἁπάντων ἐκεῖν᾽ ἂν εἴποιμεν, ὡς εὐπόριστον μὲν ἀνθρώποις τὸ χρειῶδες ἢ καὶ ἀναγκαῖον, θαυμαστὸν δ᾽ ὅμως ἀεὶ τὸ παράδοξον.

Thus the whole universe is not enough to satisfy the speculative intelligence of human thought; our ideas often pass beyond the limits that confine us. Look at life from all sides and see how in all things the extraordinary, the great, the beautiful stand supreme, and you will soon realise what we were born for. So it is by some natural instinct that we admire not the small streams, clear and useful as they are, but the Nile, the Danube, the Rhine and above all the Ocean.[139] The little fire we kindle for ourselves keeps clear and steady, yet we do not therefore regard it with more amazement than the fires of Heaven, which are often darkened, or think it more wonderful than the craters of Aetna in eruption, hurling up rocks and whole hills from their depths and sometimes shooting forth rivers of that earthborn, spontaneous fire. But on all such matters I would only say this, that what is useful or necessary is easily obtained by man; it is always the unusual which wins our wonder. *De sub.* 35.3–5

The thinking underlying the discussions of Lucretius and Longinus is very similar: 'the examples are adduced by Longinus to illus- trate how mankind is drawn to greatness; whence it occurs that "our thoughts often travel beyond the boundaries of our surround- ings." Lucretius is making much the same point. The attraction to natural prodigies is irresistible; wonder comes naturally, as does

---

[139] In purely literary-critical terms, this reads as an overt rejection of the Callimachean aesthetic of the clear, little spring, traditionally privileged over the filthy 'river of Assyria': Callim. *Hymn* 2.105–12, cf. Prop. 3.3; see Russell (1981a) 36.

the desire to transgress the limits of phenomena (Epicurus is a case in point).'[140] Porter notes that the collocation of these phenomena is 'unique in the surviving literature of antiquity' to Longinus and Lucretius; it points, in his view, towards a sublime 'tradition of commonplaces that may now be lost'.[141] If so, it seems possible that Lucan was also drawing on this tradition in his presentation of Caesar, for, besides identifying himself with the ocean, he is subsequently both likened to Aetna and associated with the Nile and its hidden sources.

In Book 10 Caesar finds himself caught in Ptolemy's palace at Alexandria, besieged by Achillas' troops:

> tangunt animos iraeque metusque,
> et timet incursus indignaturque timere.
> sic fremit in parvis fera nobilis abdita claustris
> et frangit rabidos praemorso carcere dentes,
> nec secus in Siculis fureret tua flamma cavernis,
> obstrueret summam siquis tibi, Mulciber, Aetnam.

> Both wrath and dread
> affect his spirit: he fears attack; is angry at his fear.
> Just so a noble beast hidden in a tiny prison
> bites the barrier and breaks his frenzied teeth;
> and no differently would your flame rage in the caves
> of Sicily if Aetna's summit, Mulciber [Vulcan], were blocked.

> 10.443–8

This is only the second time in the poem that Caesar has fallen prey to fear.[142] The first was in the narrative's opening scene, where we saw him *horror*-stricken by the *patriae imago*. There he swiftly managed to overcome his terror and cross the Rubicon but here he remains trapped: the poem ends with him under attack from all sides, unable to see a way out: 'captured by conditions of the place, he is perplexed; and doubtful whether to fear or pray to die' (*captus sorte loci pendet; dubiusque timeret / optaretne mori*, 10.542–3). Caesar's great *cursus* (cf. 5.239–40, 335) is finally halted by the *incursus* (10.444) of an opponent. Yet, if we look more closely, the passage's similes imply that

---

[140] Porter (2007) 173.   [141] Porter (forthcoming).   [142] *pace* Ahl (1976) 225.

he will not be stopped for long. The blockade is another *mora*, merely a 'momentary inhibition of the vital forces', that Caesar will soon surmount. The *fera nobilis* recalls the Lucretian and Burkeian emphasis on wild beasts as representatives of a power that overwhelms all opposition and, more specifically, the lion to which Caesar is likened as he crosses the Rubicon: our memory of the latter's hestitation (*subsedit dubius, totam dum colligit iram*, 1.207) colours the description of Caesar as *dubius* at 10.542.

The image of Mount Aetna amplifies these suggestions. Lucretius responds to the might and size of Aetna's eruptions as a summons to exercise one's mental powers more vigorously: *hisce tibi in rebus latest alteque videndum/ et longe cunctas in partis dispiciendum* (Lucr. 6.647–8, cf. Lucr. 6.673–9); so earlier in the poem we were told that the Sicilian volcano's lightning-like flames (Lucr. 1.722–5) pale in comparison with the dazzling intellectual achievements of the Sicilian-born Empedocles (*praeclarius*, 1.729), whose bright discoveries (*praeclara reperta*, 1.732) have been outshone in turn by the *vivida vis* of Epicurus (1.68–74).[143] Lucan's image of the volcano, emphasising its explosive potential,[144] redirects this agonistic chain back from the intellectual to the physical sphere, showing Caesar as a phenomenon too massive, too forceful for constraint, ever ready to burst through the boundaries of his surroundings.[145] Aetna's eruption, we remember, was one of the portents following Caesar's crossing of the Rubicon:

[143] See Hardie (2009a) 90 on Aetna in Book 1 of *De rerum natura* as 'a symbol of an Empedoclean sublimity' and on its relationship to Virgil's Aetna (*Aen.* 3.570–87), *Fama* (*Aen.* 4.173–90) and Atlas (*Aen.* 4.246–51).

[144] Berti (2000) ad loc.: 'Lucano sposta la sua attenzazione sulla forza esplosiva dell' eruzione.' This emphasis distinguishes Lucan's treatment: poetic comparisons with Aetna regularly focus instead on the volcano's internal heat, as an image, for instance, for the fire of love. See Aymard (1951) 96.

[145] Lucan's image is a hypothetical, mythologising *exemplum fictum*, expressed in the subjunctive and addressed to Mulciber, but the 'Aetna' poem suggests the flow of the volcano's lava could suffer blockage in reality too: *saepe premit fauces magnis exstructa ruinis / congeries clauditque vias* (*Aetna* 374–5). The ensuing eruption is described in terms evocative of Caesar's brilliant dynamism: *post, ubi conticuere, mora velocius urgent: / pellunt oppositi moles ac vincula rumpunt. / quicquid in obliquum est, frangunt iter: acrior ictu / impetus exoritur; magnis operata rapinis / flamma micat, latosque ruens exundat in agros* (*Aetna* 380–4).

> ora ferox Siculae laxavit Mulciber Aetnae
> nec tulit in caelum flammas, sed vertice prono
> ignis in Hesperium cecidit latus.

> Fierce Mulciber unclosed Sicilian Aetna's mouths
> – not skywards shot the fire's flames but eddying sideways
> they fell on Hesperia's flank.   1.545–7

Like that of the wild beast, the recurrence of Aetna's image at the end of the poem, with Caesar in very different circumstances from those in which we first saw him, reminds us that his might remains dangerous.

The sublime thread connecting Caesar's Aetna and ocean similes is highlighted by Lucan's description of the Pythia Phemonoe in Book 5. As we saw in Chapter 2, Lucan, like Longinus (*De sub.* 13.2), identifies the Pythia with the sublime. Moreover, Lucan identifies both Aetna and the ocean as natural correlates for Phemonoe's sublime state:

> hoc ubi virgineo conceptum est pectore numen,
> humanam feriens animam sonat oraque vatis
> solvit, ceu Siculus flammis urguentibus Aetnam
> undat apex.

> When this power is received in [the] virgin's breast
> and strikes her human spirit, it sounds out and unlocks
> the prophetess' mouth, as the Sicilian peak gushes when Aetna
> is pressured by the flames.   5.97–100[146]

>   nec fessa quiescunt
> corda, sed, ut tumidus Boreae post flamina pontus
> rauca gemit, sic muta levant suspiria vatem.

>   Her weary heart
> is not at rest but, as the swollen sea moans hoarsely
> after Boreas' blasts, so silent sighs relieve the prophetess.
>   5.216–18

The metaphorical storm experienced here by Phemonoe anticipates both the metaphorical storm of the Caesarian forces' attempted mutiny and the literal tempest in which Caesar is caught later

---

[146] Lucretius also associates the Pythia indirectly with Aetna: she is mentioned immediately after the description of Aetna in Book 1 of *De rerum natura* as another point of comparison exceeded by Empedocles (Lucr. 1.736–9).

in Book 5;[147] note in particular the reflection of the Delphic chasm's sublime *hiatus* (5.82) in the cataclysmic *hiatus* of the Adriatic storm. The comparison between Phemonoe's experience and Aetna integrates the image of the volcano within this sequence of sublime episodes, recalling its Lucretian–Longinian association with the grandeur of the ocean and allowing us to read its later application to Caesar as part of the same sublime image pattern.[148]

Completing the Lucretian–Longinian triad, Caesar is also closely linked with the Nile. While banqueting with Cleopatra in Book 10, he turns to ask the sage Acoreus about the origins of the great river: *nihil est quod noscere malim / quam fluvii causas per saecula tanta latentis / ignotumque caput* (10.189–191). As obscurity and uncertainty fascinated Burke, so the secrecy that shrouds the Nile's source here pricks Caesar's restless ego. For all the length and apparent learning of his response (10.194–331), Acoreus only emphasises this unknowability.[149] He claims that the Nile rises near the equator (*medio . . . ab axe*, 10.287) but this, it transpires, is the limit imposed on his knowledge by the god who rules the river's waters (10.286). The source's precise location remains hidden (*subdita Nili / ora latent*, 10.213–14; *vincit adhuc natura latendi*, 10.271), making the Nile a thing of universal wonder (*mirari*, cf. θαυμαστόν, *De sub.* 35.5):

> arcanum natura caput non prodidit ulli,
> nec licuit populis parvum te, Nile, videre,
> amovitque sinus et gentes maluit ortus
> mirari quam nosse tuos.

> Nature has revealed your hidden head to none, has not allowed
> the people to see you in your infancy, Nile, has made remote

---

[147] Morford (1967) 37–8, 60; Barratt (1979) ad 5.216–18; Masters (1992) 143.
[148] Thus, where Phemonoe was identified in my previous chapter as a figure for the sublimity of the poet in his resistance to Caesarism, she also functions as a correlate for Caesar's own sublimity: the sublimity of the *Bellum civile* cannot be disentangled from that of its demonic protagonist.
[149] The confident intimations of sublime enlightenment with which Acoreus begins his disquisition (*'fas mihi magnorum, Caesar, secreta parentum / edere ad hoc aevi populis ignota profanis . . . '*, 10.194–8) promise more than they deliver. Housman (1927) 334–7 brands Luc. 10.210–18 'ungrammatical nonsense' and offers an explanation of the passage's confusions, both grammatical and astronomical. With Acoreus' account, compare Sen. *Nat.* 4.1–2 and Plin. *Nat.* 5.56–7.

your hiding-places and preferred the amazement of the peoples
to their knowledge of your origins.   10.295–8

The sublimity thus suggested by the obscurity of the Nile's origin
is compounded by the power of its flow, reminding us of the 'lofty
waterfall on a mighty river' that Kant mentions as an example of
the sublime in nature:[150]

> sed, cum lapsus abrupta viarum
> excepere tuos et praecipites cataractae
> ac nusquam vetitis ullas obsistere cautes
> indignaris aquis, spuma tunc astra lacessis,
> cuncta fremunt undis, ac multo murmure montis
> spumeus invitis canescit fluctibus amnis.

> But when sheer paths
> and plunging cataracts have met your flow
> and you take offence that any rocks bar your flood, which is
> forbidden nowhere, then with your foam you challenge the stars,
> everything is roaring with your waters, and, as the mountain rumbles
> loud, your foaming stream grows white with waves unwilling.

10.317–22

In its figuration of restraint and release, the passage looks forward to the comparison later in Book 10 of Caesar with Aetna
and a wild beast: both Caesar and the Nile chafe at their con-
finement (*indignaris*, 320; *indignatur*, 444); the rocky obstruction
of the water's path (*obsistere*, 319) finds its counterpart in the
blockage of Aetna's summit (*obstrueret*, 448); the river's roar
(*fremunt*, 321), resounding around the mountains, is echoed by
that of the imprisoned animal (*fremit*, 445).[151] Like Caesar himself (5.301), and like the Adriatic storm (5.640), the waterfall is
something sublimely *praeceps* (10.318). Intolerant of all imped-
iments to its flow, its reach extends even to the stars in heaven
(10.320).

---

[150] Kant (2003) 144. Kant ibid. also lists 'volcanoes with their all-destroying violence'
and 'the boundless ocean set into a rage'.
[151] Two of Lucretius' four explanations for the Nile's summer flooding also adduce processes of blockage and swelling: Etesian (northerly) winds *contra fluvium flantes
remorantur et, undas / cogentes sursus, replent coguntque manere* (Lucr. 6.717–18);
*est quoque uti possit magnus congestus harenae / fluctibus adversis oppilare ostia
contra...* (Lucr. 6.724–8). Cf. Luc. 10.244–7.

It is this sublimity to which Caesar is drawn. Indeed, he regards the navigation of the Nile as an undertaking more compellingly sublime than any he has attempted before, a challenge for which he would willingly abandon even the conquest of Rome: *spes sit mihi certa videndi / Niliacos fontes, bellum civile relinquam* (10.191–2). Previous attempts to find the Nile's source made by rulers such as Cambyses, Sesostris and Alexander are described by Acoreus as expeditions to the very limits of the world (*per ultima terrae / Aethiopum*, 10.273–4; *mundique extrema*, 10.276). To succeed where these rulers failed would require travelling beyond these farthest boundaries – a journey resembling that of the sublime Lucretian–Longinian subject beyond the *moenia mundi* (Lucr. 1.73, 3.16; *De sub.* 35.3). The narrator's savage criticism of Alexander at the beginning of Book 10 underscores this connection between Nilotic exploration and boundary transgression:[152] Alexander's desire to drink from the Nile's spring (Luc. 10.40) is the most extreme example of the insatiability that propels him over normal geographical limits (*non illi flamma nec undae / nec sterilis Libye nec Syrticus obstitit Hammon*, 10.37–8).[153] This insatiability is, of course, something Alexander shares with Caesar and, like Caesar, Alexander is compared to a *fulmen* (10.34).[154] Caesar's desire to conquer the Nile may likewise be read as an index of his sublime desire to go beyond the given.[155]

---

[152] Cf. Schiesaro (2003) 218–19 on Luc. 10.184–7: 'In his desire to reveal the inner secrets of nature, Caesar momentarily turns into a cultural hero of sorts, redolent in many respects of Lucretius' portrayal of Epicurus, who pushed himself to the edge of the world in order to comprehend the regulatory mechanisms of all things, and even more of Alexander the Great, the ruler who embodied a profound link between the thirst for knowledge and the thirst to conquer.'

[153] Matthews (2008) ad 5.477. On Alexander's role in the poem as a Caesarian exemplar, see further Zwierlein (1986/2010) 417–21; Eigler (2005); Rossi (2005) 239, 244; Tesoriero (2005) 205.

[154] Ahl (1976) 224–5 argues that Caesar appears 'cautious and conservative' next to Alexander: where Alexander 'even drank from the source of the Nile', Caesar 'will not gamble with the unknown'. But the narrator expressly tells us that Alexander's death prevented him from reaching the source of the Nile (Luc. 10.40–2) and it is precisely the unknown that piques Caesar's interest.

[155] Cf. Kirwan (2005) 40, 44, 46, who notes how Alexander's sublimity was acknowledged in the eighteenth century as a counterpart to Caesar's. Consonant with his criticism of Alexander, the Lucanian narrator displays an attitude diametrically opposite from Caesar's to the Nile: following Pompey's death, he bitterly remembers the Sibyl's warning that no Roman should even go near the mouth of the Nile (Luc. 8.823–6).

'This world is not enough'

This chapter has thus far considered the ways in which Caesar is
represented as a subject of sublime experience and, consequently,
as himself a sublime object. I want to end by emphasising how,
in representing Caesar as sublime, Lucan realises the potential for
sublimity to result in tyranny and oppression. Lucretius' beneficent
Epicurean sublime offers an instructive point of comparison and
contrast.

The drive to surmount earthly limits, highlighted by Longinus in
his discussion of the sublimity of Aetna, the ocean and the Nile, and
associated by Lucretius with the sublime achievements of Epicurus, marks Caesar's behaviour throughout the *Bellum civile*. During
the episode of the mutiny in Book 5, the extra-terrestrial nature of
Caesar's ambitions is stated explicitly. Caesar has returned from
operations in Spain, ready to march onwards into a 'new world'
(*victrices aquilas alium laturus in orbem*, 5.238). His men's refusal
to go any further is couched in the same global terms. They have
marched and died all over the world (*totoque exercitus orbe / te
vincente perit*, 5.266–7): 'What limit is sought for warfare? What
is enough, if Rome is too little?' (*finis quis quaeritur armis? / quid
satis est, si Roma parum est?* 5.273–4). Caesar's response cun-
ningly throws the soldiers' accusations back at them – he asserts
that their ungratefulness for the victories they have won means
they are truly the ones for whom 'this world is not enough' (*hic
non sufficit orbis*, 5.356, cf. οὐδ᾽ ὁ σύμπας κόσμος ἀρκεῖ, *De sub.*
35.3) – but the fact that Caesar successfully quashes the uprising
and takes his army on to Greece only proves the soldiers' point.
Their perspective is confirmed at the end of the poem as the narrator reflects upon the irony that the man for whom even 'the Roman
world's expanse is not enough' (*Romani spatium non sufficit orbis*,
10.456) is now trapped inside the Alexandrian palace (*spem vitae
in limine clauso / ponit*, 10.459–60).

For Lucretius, the sublime flight beyond the *moenia mundi* is a
fundamentally positive act. It is an epistemological and moral victory that brings true freedom to mankind, a 'free projection of the
mind' (*animi iactus liber*, Lucr. 2.1047) that shatters the 'confining bars of nature's gates' (*arta naturae portarum claustra*, Lucr.

1.70–1) and undoes the bonds imposed by *Religio*; 'death's terrors then leave your heart unpossessed and free from care' (*mortisque timores / tum vacuum pectus linquunt curaque solutum*, Lucr. 2.45–6).[156] In stark contrast, Caesar's agonistic refusal of limitation, his sublime denial that this world is enough, *non sufficit orbis*, brings about not intellectual enlightenment but the moral horror of civil war. It is his ambition to extend this conflict to the ends of the Roman world and beyond that sparks his soldiers' mutinous anger. For the narrator the conflict is an abomination that should have never even been (cf. Luc. 1.21–3); he hopes, ironically and in vain, that the mutiny might bring it to an end (*finem civili faciat discordia bello*, Luc. 5.299; *liceat scelerum tibi ponere finem*, 5.314). Caesar's ultimate crime is thus the diametrical opposite of Epicurus' achievement: by creating absolute freedom for himself, Caesar becomes an insuperable obstacle to the freedom of the rest of Rome; as the narrator laments, after Pharsalus freedom and Caesar will be arraigned against each other in perpetual conflict: *par quod semper habemus, / libertas et Caesar* (7.695–6).

The claims on divinity exercised by Caesar and Epicurus reflect the ethical distance between their respective sublimes. Longinus notes that while 'other qualities prove their possessors men, sublimity lifts them near the mighty mind of god' (τὸ δ ὕψος ἐγγὺς αἴρει μεγαλοφροσύνης θεοῦ, *De sub.* 36.1). Epicurus offers one demonstration of this: in passing beyond the limits of earthly phenomena, triumphing over superstition and falsehood and revealing 'the gods in their majesty and their peaceful abodes' (*divum numen sedesque quietae*, Lucr. 3.18) as they truly are, he enables his fellow humans to enjoy a godlike existence, free from all the fears and vices that hitherto enslaved them: 'nothing hinders our living a life worthy of gods' (*nil impediat dignam dis degere vitam*, Lucr. 3.322).[157] These superhuman achievements make Epicurus most godlike of all: *deus ille fuit, deus* Lucr. 5.8), insists Lucretius and again, a few lines later:

---

[156] Cf. Hardie (2009c) 182.

[157] This is not just Lucretian praise. Epicurus himself makes the same claim, e.g. *Ep. ad Men.* 135 ('you shall live as a god among men'); see Rouse (1992) ad loc.

> nonne decebit
> hunc hominem numero divom dignarier esse?
> cum bene praesertim multa ac divinitus ipsis
> immortalibu' de divis dare dicta suerit
> atque omnem rerum naturam pandere dictis.

> Will it not be proper
> that he be held worthy to be counted in the number of the gods?
> Especially since he was accustomed to discourse often
> in good and godlike fashion about the immortal gods themselves,
> and to disclose in his discourse all the nature of things.

> Lucr. 5.50–4

The divinity attendant upon Epicurus' sublimity is thus located at the heart of the philanthropic project of revealing *rerum natura*. This divinity is something to aspire towards and deserves the greatest praise. And, crucially, it is won with words not violence: Epicurus 'has vanquished all and cast these things forth from the mind by words, not by swords' (*cuncta subegerit ex animoque / expulerit dictis, non armis*, Lucr. 5.49–50).

By contrast, *arma* are precisely what Caesar uses to achieve sublimity. As we have seen, however, this does not prevent him from assuming equality with the gods. Quite the opposite: at the Rubicon he identifies himself with the *patriae imago* (or, as he addresses her, *Roma*) as well as Jupiter, Quirinus and the other deities historically coopted by the Julio-Claudian house (Luc. 1.195–203); at the Massilian grove his anger outweighs that of the gods (3.439) and his felling of the trees escapes divine punishment (3.447–8); amid the Adriatic storm he substitutes his own authority over the elements for that of heaven (5.579–86), derides the *labor* it costs the gods to destroy him (5.654–6) and looks down, Jupiter-like, upon the sea's turmoil (5.639). But where the godlike status of Lucretius' Epicurus arises from his philanthropic discoveries and unshakeable mental calm, these Caesarian assertions of divinity are the product of homicidal megalomania. The comparison of Caesar at Pharsalus to Mars and Bellona, supplying *arma – gladios ac tela* – and urging on the slaughter, makes Lucan's perspective quite clear:

hic Caesar, rabies populis stimulusque furorum,
nequa parte sui pereat scelus, agmina circum
it vagus atque ignes animis flagrantibus addit.

. . .

quacumque vagatur,
sanguineum veluti quatiens Bellona flagellum
Bistonas aut Mavors agitans si verbere saevo
Palladia stimulet turbatos aegide currus,   570
nox ingens scelerum est

. . .

ipse manu subicit gladios ac tela ministrat.

Here Caesar, maddening the people and goading them to frenzy,
goes ranging round the troops, adding fires to spirits already blazing:
wickedness must not be missing in any section of his army.

. . .

Wherever he goes round –
like Bellona brandishing her blood-stained lash
or like Mars, rousing the Bistonians, if with savage whips
he goads his steeds maddened by Pallas' Aegis –
there is a vast night of wickedness

. . .

In person he supplies fresh swords, hands them weapons.

7.557–74[158]

As Epicurus' sublime godlikeness is predicated on his victory
over traditional *religio*, so Caesar's self-proclaimed divinity fills
the gap left in the poem by Lucan's removal of the traditional epic
panoply of gods. Some lines before the comparison with Mars
and Bellona Lucan cynically articulates the relation between the
two themes:

sunt nobis nulla profecto   445
numina: cum caeco rapiantur saecula casu,
mentimur regnare Iovem. spectabit ab alto
aethere Thessalicas, teneat cum fulmina, caedes?
scilicet ipse petet Pholoen, petet ignibus Oeten
inmeritaeque nemus Rhodopes pinusque Mimantis,   450
Cassius hoc potius feriet caput? . . .
. . . mortalia nulli
sunt curata deo. cladis tamen huius habemus   455

---

[158] Feeney (1991) 296 notes that *ipse manu* is also used of divine intervention at Virg.
Aen. 7.143, 621 and compares Stat. *Theb.* 7.738, 752, 753, 759.

vindictam, quantam terris dare numina fas est:
bella pares superis facient civilia divos,
fulminibus manes radiisque ornabit et astris
inque deum templis iurabit Roma per umbras.

> Without a doubt, we have no
> deities: since human life is swept along by blind chance,
> we lie that Jupiter is king. Will he watch Thessalian
> bloodshed from the lofty ether even though he holds his thunderbolts?
> Will Jupiter, then, aim his fires at Pholoë, at Oeta,
> at the grove of innocent Rhodope, at the pines of Mimas,
> and let Cassius strike this head? . . .
>
> . . . Human
> affairs are cared for by no deity. Yet we have revenge
> for this disaster, as much as gods may give to mortals:
> the civil wars will create divinities equal to those above;
> with thunderbolts and rays and stars Rome will adorn
> the dead and in the temples of the gods will swear by ghosts.

7.445–59[159]

The narrator complains that Jupiter's lightning is nowhere to be seen. Of course, lightning *did* earlier attempt to halt the crime of Pharsalus (7.155–60), but it was not hurled by Jupiter. Moreover, it had no effect: the Caesarian lightning that had blasted the Pompeian oak (1.135–57), the Massilian grove (3.408–10, 434), and indeed the temple of Jupiter Latiaris (1.535), proved more powerful and battle was joined. Lucan thus inverts the Massilians' claim that, following conflict in heaven, 'mortal-kind, ignorant of the gods' affairs, only by his thunderbolts would know the Thunderer still ruled alone in heaven' (*ignarum mortale genus per fulmina tantum / sciret adhuc caelo solum regnare Tonantem*, 3.319–20): like the absence of divine punishment for Caesar's desecration of the Massilian grove (cf. 3.447–8), the absence at Pharsalus of Jupiter's thunderbolt argues that 'we lie that Jupiter is king' (*mentimur regnare Iovem*); it is the Caesarian lightning that tells us who really rules. This denial of Jupiter's power closely echoes a passage in Lucretius' discussion of lightning:

---

[159] See Bartsch (1997) 111 for attentive discussion of this passage's complexities and contradictions.

quod si Iuppiter atque alii fulgentia divi
terrifico quatiunt sonitu caelestia templa
et iaciunt ignem quo cuiquest cumque voluntas,
cur quibus incautum scelus aversabile cumquest   390
non faciunt icti flammas ut fulguris halent
pectore perfixo, documen mortalibus acre,
et potius nulla sibi turpi conscius in re
volvitur in flammas innoxius inque peditur
turbine caelesti subito correptus et igni?   395

But if Jupiter and other gods shake the shining
regions of heaven with appalling din,
if they cast fire whither it may be the will of each one,
why do they not see to it that those who have not refrained
    from some abominable crime
shall be struck and breathe out sulphurous flames
from breast pierced through, a sharp lesson to mankind?
Why rather does one with no base guilt on his conscience
roll in flames all innocent, suddenly involved
in a tornado from heaven and taken off by fire?

Lucr. 6.387–95

Like Lucan's narrator, Lucretius adduces the fact that wrongdoers
escape being struck by lightning as proof against belief in Jupiter's
traditional existence. Such knowledge is a boon: the true understanding of lightning's causes that Lucretius offers instead is what
allows the receptive reader to attain sublimity and hence godlikeness, free from superstitious fear of such phenomena. In Lucan,
by contrast, the failure of Jupiter's thunderbolt, and the divinity
attained by Caesar in Jupiter's place, are a cause for anger and
despair.[160] Caesar's ousting of Jupiter sets a grim precedent: as the
narrator predicts in his prayer to Nero at the start of Book 1, 'every
deity will yield to you, to your decision nature will leave which god
you wish to be, where to set your kingdom in the universe' (*tibi
numine ab omni / cedetur, iurisque tui natura relinquet / quis deus*

---

[160] Cf. Luc. 4.110–20 (*sic, o summe parens mundi, sic, sorte secunda / aequorei rector,
facias, Neptune tridentis, / et tu perpetuis inpendas aera nimbis . . .*), 5.620–6 (*sic
rector Olympi / cuspide fraterna lassatum in saecula fulmen / adiuvit . . .*): these two
reminiscences of the Flood, an occasion when Jupiter did direct his elemental weapons
against criminal humanity, only accentuate the sense of shock at the absence of divine
punishment for Pharsalus.

esse velis, ubi regnum ponere mundi, 1.50–2).[161] That the Caesars'
replacement of the gods might be construed as revenge (*vindictam*,
7.456) for Jupiter's failure is very cold consolation indeed.[162]

Yet Lucretius is not blind to the potentially problematic implications of his sublime. His reader, he is aware, may regard his
atomistic arguments against the world's immortality and divine
origin as impious

> proptereaque putes ritu par esse Gigantum
> pendere eos poenas inmani pro scelere omnis
> qui ratione sua disturbent moenia mundi.

> and should therefore believe it right that, like the Giants,
> all they should suffer punishment for a monstrous crime,
> who with their reasoning shake the walls of the world.
>
> Lucr. 5.117–19

The sublime advance beyond the *moenia mundi* (Lucr. 1.73, 3.16),
the act of liberation that we have been told bestows divinity, might
appear to the sceptic disturbingly similar to the mythological transgression of the Giants' assault on heaven; indeed, we saw at the
beginning of Chapter 2 how it may appear to presage the world's
apocalypse (Lucr. 1.1102–10). No sooner has Lucretius acknowledged this view, however, than he brusquely dismisses it as superstitious nonsense, *religione refrenatus* (Lucr. 5.114). Longinus,
on the other hand, is well aware that the sublime can be gigantomachic. He applauds the 'daring' of Homer's description of the
Giants' ascent (*De sub.* 8.2):

> Ὄσσαν ἐπ' Οὐλύμπῳ μέμασαν θέμεν· αὐτὰρ ἐπ' Ὄσσῃ
> Πήλιον εἰνοσίφυλλον, ἵν' οὐρανὸς ἄμβατος εἴη.

> Ossa then up on Olympus they strove to set, then upon Ossa
> Pelion, ashiver with leaves, to build them a ladder to Heaven.
>
> Od. 11.315–16

---

[161] The exact tone and significance of the prayer are notoriously ambiguous: see Grimal
(1960/2010); Due (1962) 93–102; Thompson (1964); Jenkinson (1974); Ahl (1976)
47–9; Johnson (1987) 121–2; Dewar (1994); O'Hara (2007) 131–42; Roche (2009)
7–10.

[162] Cold and also nonsensical: see Due (1962) 101–2; cf. Le Bonniec (1970) 200.

Longinus allusively suggests the connection between the transgression of earthly boundaries and gigantomachy again a few paragraphs later, where the horizon-straddling leap of the divine horses described at *Il.* 5.770–2 (*De sub.* 9.5) is juxtaposed with Homer's Battle of the Gods, a (gigantomachic?) piling together of *Il.* 21.388 and 20.61–5 that centres on the gigantomachic image of 'the whole universe sundered (διάστασιν) and turned upside down' (*De sub.* 9.6).[163]

Gigantomachy also provides Lucan with a frame for Caesar's sublime actions, though his narrator does not share Longinus' enthusiasm for the spectacle. Rather, Lucan uses gigantomachy to drive home the sublime's negative potential, taking up and magnifying that critical perspective which Lucretius was so swift to dismiss: where traditionally the impious Giants fail to storm heaven's gates, Caesar, like Epicurus, manages to install himself in Jupiter's place.[164] The prayer to Nero introduces the motif:

> quod si non aliam venturo fata Neroni
> invenere viam magnoque aeterna parantur
> regna deis caelumque suo servire Tonanti   35
> non nisi saevorum potuit post bella gigantum,
> iam nihil, o superi, querimur; scelera ipsa nefasque
> hac mercede placent.

> But if the Fates could find no other way
> for Nero's coming, if eternal kingdoms are purchased
> by the gods at great cost, if heaven could serve its Thunderer
> only after wars with ferocious Giants,
> then we have no complaint, O gods; for this reward we accept
> even these crimes and guilt.   1.33–8

---

[163] See Porter (forthcoming). Hardie (1986) 85 moves from the sublimity of the Giants' endeavours to that of the text that recounts them: 'The struggle of the gods for supremacy against monstrous divine or demonic opponents, as manifested in the stories of the wars with the Titans, the Giants and Typhoeus, is . . . a recurrent subject for writers or artists seeking a grand or sublime topic. As such, it occupied a literary summit next to that held by the sublimities of natural philosophy'; cf. Innes (1979) and see further Hardie (1986) 85–156.

[164] On Lucan's inversion of the myth, see Henderson (1987/2010) 471, Feeney (1991) 297; on the frequency of gigantomachic imagery throughout the poem, see Mayer (1981) ad 8.551.

Like Caesar in the Massilians' speech (3.15–20),[165] Nero is ostensibly aligned here with Jupiter yet it is the Giants whom he really resembles: as the prayer goes on to insinuate (1.53–9), Nero's apotheosis is something that will disturb, not maintain, the order of the heavens.[166] The prayer's construction of the Giants' war against Jupiter as a precursor to Rome's struggles is reflected in later allusions to Thessaly ('Phlegra'), the location of the civil war's climactic battle, as the place from which the Giants mounted their assault on heaven:[167] the excursus on the snakes of Libya reminds us that the attacking Giants, petrified by Pallas' Gorgon-bearing aegis, had 'Phlegraean' snakes as legs (9.655–8); Earth is described as merciful to heaven because she did not raise her son Antaeus, a Giant to rival her other offspring, on the Phlegraean fields (4.593–7); the account of Thessaly itself in the run-up to Pharsalus begins by mentioning that the area is bounded by Ossa, Pelion and Olympus (6.333–42) and concludes, pointedly, by remembering these mountains' gigantomachic history:[168]

> inpius hinc prolem superis inmisit Aloeus,
> inseruit celsis prope se cum Pelion astris
> sideribusque vias incurrens abstulit Ossa.

> From here the wicked Aloeus launched his sons against the gods,
> when Pelion nearly thrust himself among the lofty stars
> and Ossa, by encroaching on the constellations, stopped their course.

6.410–12

And it is Caesar who acts the Giants' role. At Brundisium, in an attempt to prevent Pompey's escape, he hurls rocks into the sea

---

[165] But note Luc. 3.455–7, where Caesar, giant-like, piles up a star-reaching *agger*; cf. the echo at 3.459–61 of the myth that earthly tremors were caused by Giants trapped beneath mountains. See Masters (1992) 39–40.
[166] Hinds (1988) 26–9; Feeney (1991) 299–300.
[167] At least on one interpretation: the Phlegran gigantomachy was also located variously in Macedonia and Campania. See Braund (1992) 332 s.v. 'Phlegra'.
[168] Masters (1992) 154–5, 176. Masters explains Lucan's confusion of the locations of Ossa and Pelion at 6.333–6 as 'programmatic of what is to come – a geographical catalogue that will overturn the knowns of geography' (p. 154); hence the confusion and the catalogue themselves become gigantomachic (and, we might add, sublime), 'the result of a deliberate policy of doing violence to the order of the world' (p. 177). With Luc. 6.410–12 compare *Od.* 11.305–20, the Iliadic passage quoted by Longinus at *De sub.* 8.2, and Luc. 6.389–90. The Thessalian witch Erictho also has the Giants on her mind: Luc. 6.665.

(*molibus undas / obstruit et latum deiectis rupibus aequor*, 2.661–
2) but the water proves so deep that it would submerge even fallen
mountains (2.663–8).[169] At Dyrrachium he again tries to block
in Pompey, bringing 'huge boulders, blocks torn from quarries'
(*ingentis cautes avolsaque saxa metallis*, 6.34) and breaking up
mountains to build siege-works (*franguntur montes, planumque
per ardua Caesar ducit opus*, 6.38–9), a feat of engineering that
defies *natura* (6.59), but Pompey again forces a way through
(6.118ff. – and this time, moreover, Pompey inflicts major damage
on the Caesarians, 6.133–4, 315).[170] But the tide turns, and the
gigantomachic context presses closest, at Pharsalus. Sharpening
their weapons for battle, the Pompeians are likened to the gods at
Phlegra; it is Caesar and his troops, we understand, who are the
Giants:

> si liceat superis hominum conferre labores,
> non aliter Phlegra rabidos tollente gigantas   145
> Martius incaluit Siculis incudibus ensis
> et rubuit flammis iterum Neptunia cuspis
> spiculaque extenso Paean Pythone recoxit,
> Pallas Gorgoneos diffudit in aegida crines,
> Pallenaea Iovi mutavit fulmina Cyclops.   150

> If I may compare men's labours with the gods,
> not otherwise when Phlegra reared the raging Giants
> did the sword of Mars grow hot upon Sicilian anvils
> and Neptune's trident redden in the flames a second time
> and Paean forge again his arrows after stretching out in death the Python,
> did Pallas spread the Gorgon's locks across her Aegis,
> did Cyclops make Pallenaean thunderbolts anew for Jupiter.   7.144–50

labores here recalls Caesar's description of the Adriatic storm as
an effort (*labor*, 5.655) on the part of the gods to destroy him.[171]
But as Caesar surmounted that *labor*, so here at Pharsalus he

[169] Cf. Luc. 5.615–17: *a quotiens frustra pulsatos aequore montis / obruit ille dies!* Like
the Adriatic storm, Brundisium constitutes another *mora* that Caesar must surmount.
Note in this context the comparison of Phemonoe, whose sublimity anticipates the
Adriatic storm but also allusively associates her with Caesar, to the volcanoes Inarime
and Aetna, traditionally imagined as imprisoned Giants (Luc. 5.97–101), cf. Hom.
Il. 2.783; Virg. *Aen.* 3.578, Ov. *Met.* 5.321; see O'Higgins (1988) 212.
[170] On the gigantomachic imagery of this passage, see further Saylor (1978).
[171] So Matthews (2008) ad 5.654–6: 'Caesar is a test for the gods in the same way as the
Giants once were.'

finally breaks with gigantomachic tradition, defeating Pompey and sealing his (and his successors') claim on divinity. The horror of the Caesarian sublime is the horror of a gigantic victory over heaven.[172]

Lucan's exploitation of the motif of gigantomachy, then, brings to the surface an aspect of the sublime that Lucretius attempts to suppress. And there is a further detail in *De rerum natura* that echoes uncomfortably in Lucan and that I want finally to highlight. Shortly after his quotation of Homer's Battle of the Gods, Longinus holds up as an instance of sublimity the Iliadic lines, τρέμε δ' οὔρεα μακρὰ καὶ ὕλη, καὶ κορυφαὶ Τρώων τε πόλις καὶ νῆες Ἀχαιῶν, and ποσσὶν ὑπ' ἀθανάτοισι Ποσειδάωνος ἰόντος (*Il.* 13.18, 20.60 and 13.19; *De sub.* 9.8): mountains and woods, great cities and ships, all tremble beneath Poseidon's mighty footstep. Lucretius inverts the picture: in *De rerum natura* the 'trampling' is done by Epicurus, beneath whose feet superstition lies vanquished (*religio pedibus subiecta vicissim / obteritur, nos exaequat victoria caelo*, Lucr. 1.78–9), and by the atomist, for whom the world lies revealed underfoot (*sub pedibus quaecumque infra per inane geruntur*, Lucr. 3.27).[173] Like the motif of gigantomachy, such imagery (and indeed the very fact that its Lucretian usage has an Iliadic precedent) alerts us to the aggression latent within the agonism of the sublime. As Conte has it, the sublime enables us to 'put [our fears] under our feet . . . as triumphant generals do'.[174]

The violent, political implications of this Epicurean trampling become overt in the account of anti-monarchical revolution in Book 5 of *De rerum natura*:

---

[172] Compare the gigantomachic allusions that mark the sublimity of Statius' hero Capaneus in the *Thebaid*; true to the mythological model, however, Capaneus' challenge to the gods fails. See Leigh (2006).

[173] Cf. Lucr. 6.605 (*pedibus raptim tellus subtracta*), noted above in the context of Lucan's Adriatic storm; also Lucr. 1.1106 (*terraque se pedibus raptim subducat*), part of Lucretius' vision of the apocalyptic consequences of the mind's sublime flight beyond the *moenia mundi* (Lucr. 1.1102–10). The image of the subterranean infinities that extend beneath our feet finds a Presocratic precedent in a fragment of Xenophanes, γαίης μὲν τόδε πεῖρας ἄνω παρὰ ποσσὶν ὁρᾶται / ἠέρι προσπλάζον, τὸ κάτω δ' ἐς ἄπειρον ἱκνεῖται (B28 = Achilles, *Isag.* 4.34.11 Maas); see Porter (2010) 159–60.

[174] Conte (1994) 33. So also Porter (2007) 179: 'The thrill and awe that a sublime subject feels before nature is for Lucretius perhaps less one of admiration than of domination.'

ergo regibus occisis subversa iacebat
pristina maiestas soliorum et sceptra superba,
et capitis summi praeclarum insigne cruentum
<u>sub pedibus</u> vulgi magnum lugebat honorem;
nam cupide conculcatur nimis ante metutum.   1140
res itaque ad summam faecem turbasque redibat,
imperium sibi cum ac summatum quisque petebat.

Kings therefore were slain; the ancient majesty
of thrones and proud sceptres lay overthrown in the dust;
the illustrious badge of the topmost head, bloodstained ·
beneath the feet of the mob, bewailed the loss of its high honour;
for men are eager to tread underfoot what they have once too much feared.
So things came to the uttermost dregs of confusion,
when each man for himself sought dominion and exaltation.

Lucr. 5.1136–42

The overthrow of the kings, like Epicurus' victory over *Religio*,[175]
leads eventually to the establishment of Republican *libertas* and
the rule of law (5.1143–4). Lucretius, however, does not appear
wholly enthusiastic about the process: if the rule of kings was arro-
gant and harsh (*superba*), the revolt of the *vulgus* is characterised
by bloodshed (1138) and self-seeking chaos (1141–2). As Burke
unhappily discovered after revolution had broken out in France,
the sublime can look very different in the mountains and on the
battlefield.

Once again, Lucan argues that Lucretius' half-spoken anxieties
are well founded. Leaving the carnage of Pharsalus, Caesar makes
for Troy, that 'memorable name' (*nomen memorabile*, 9.964),[176]

---

[175] Cf. Lucr. 2.1091 (*dominis superbis*), 5.87 = 6.63 (*dominos acris*): see Hardie (2009c)
182, who also compares Cic. *Tusc.* 1.48 on those who *liberatos ... se per eum* [sc.
Epicurum] *dicunt gravissimis dominis*.

[176] Tesoriero (2005) 210 n. 28 on 9.964 and 9.973 usefully summarises recent critical
responses to the word *nomen* in the *Bellum civile*: 'On the emptiness of the *nomina*
here, see Ahl (1976) 215, where he notes a reminiscence of Pompey: *Magni nominis
umbra*, 218; also Ormand (1994) 52 [see p. 342 in Tesoriero 2010]. Henderson (1987)
141–51 [see pp. 466–83 in Tesoriero 2010] discusses the importance of *nomen* in
Lucan, especially the *nomen Caesar* as the name of power; he sees epic as a means to
give power to a name. Bartsch (1997) 133–5 sees in these empty *nomina* the potential
for interpretation, the possibility that meaning can be created, especially by poets.
Lucan has already hinted at the "flexibility" of the *nomen* in this passage, 9.956: it
provides a foretaste of what Caesar, inspired by the poet's interjection (980–6), will do
for Troy: give his own *nomina* to places.' See also Feeney (1986/2010).

and tours its ruins. 'No stone is without a story' (*nullum est sine nomine saxum*, 9.973), reiterates the narrator, wryly, but Caesar

> inscius in sicco serpentem pulvere rivum
> transierat, qui Xanthus erat. securus in alto   975
> gramine ponebat gressus: Phryx incola manes
> Hectoreos calcare vetat.

> unwittingly had crossed a stream creeping
> in dry dust – this was Xanthus. Oblivious, he placed
> his footsteps in the deep grass: the Phrygian local tells him
> not to tread upon the shade of Hector.   9.974–7

Caesar's ignorance of what he is seeing causes him practically to trample (*calcare*, 979, cf. *conculcatur*, Lucr. 5.1140) over Hector's grave. As Zwierlein has pointed out, *calcare* is Caesar's characteristic action:[177] less than a hundred lines later, we are reminded how at Pharsalus Caesar 'trampled on the Senate's limbs with face unmoved' (*duro membra senatus / calcarat voltu*, 9.1043–4); before the battle Caesar himself declared, 'I seem to look at streams of blood and kings trampled on together and the Senate's mangled body' (*videor fluvios spectare cruoris / calcatosque simul reges sparsumque senatus / corpus*, 7.292–4).[178] The narrator makes the effects of this trampling painfully clear: 'for all the world's eternity we are prostrated. Every age which will suffer slavery is conquered by these swords' (*in totum mundi prosternimur aevum. / vincitur his gladiis omnis quae serviet aetas*, 7.640–1). Where in Lucretius it is the insignia of kings, *domini*, that are trodden under foot, in Lucan the same action sets a *dominum* (7.646) in place. Troy presents an ominous picture of what Rome under this *dominus* will become: Caesar's trampling of the ruins of Rome's ancestor-city is at one with his trampling and ruination of Rome itself.[179] In Book 6 there is a fleeting suggestion that these actions

---

[177] Zwierlein (1986/2010) 422.

[178] The narrator's attitude following Pompey's murder is shown to be the very reverse of Caesar's: anxious that Pompey's tomb is so ruinous, his *nomen* so inconspicuous, that the visiting traveller will miss both unless they are pointed out (Luc. 8.820–2), he wishes that Pompey's corpse had simply been left unburied; that way, there would be no danger of visitors accidentally trampling his remains (*erremus populi cinerumque tuorum, / Magne, metu nullas Nili calcemus harenas*, 8.804–5).

[179] See e.g. Ahl (1976) 209–22; Zwierlein (1986/2010) 422–30; Ormand (1994/2010) 340–2; Edwards (1996) 64–5; Bartsch (1997) 131–49; Rossi (2001); Tesoriero (2005).

will rebound upon Caesar, as Erictho's zombie instructs Pompey's son Sextus, 'Make haste to die ... and trample on the shades of the gods of Rome' (*properate mori ... / et Romanorum manes calcate deorum*, 6.807–9). Thus Rome would exact revenge for Pharsalus upon the deified Caesar(s)[180] (cf. the deification of Caesar and his successors as ironic 'revenge' for Jupiter's failure to stop the battle at 7.455–9). But this vision is conjured through the necromancy of the hellish Erictho, is delivered to a self-serving coward and requires the death of Caesar's enemies for its fulfilment. It is with good reason that, amid the desolation of Troy-Rome, like the lion to which he is compared at the Rubicon (1.212), Caesar remains sublimely *securus* (9.975).[181]

For Lucan, the freedom bestowed by Caesar's sublime *cursus*, his casting of the world beneath his feet, is by definition the destruction of the freedom of his fellow Romans. It is this ambivalence between freedom and domination that casts a shadow, albeit fleetingly, over Lucretius' sublime. By locating sublimity in the realm of military conquest instead of intellectual discovery, Lucan lengthens this shadow considerably. This does not alter the nature of Lucretius' investment in the sublime, but it does point up its partiality, forcing us to look hard at the slippery, double-edged character of the freedoms that sublimity bestows. As the *sub pedibus* motif suggests, in the experience of the sublime liberation and tyranny are unsettlingly mingled.

---

[180] Ahl (1976) 145–6; Johnson (1987) 32; O'Higgins (1988) 219–21.

[181] Note how the phrase *securus in alto* leaves Caesar momentarily suspended at the end of 9.975 – as though on high in Lucretius' *templa serena* – before we and he come back down to earth with *gramine*; thanks again to Philip Hardie for this observation. On the further implications of *securus* here, see Rossi (2001) 317, who suggests that the adjective denotes Caesar's contempt for Troy's ruins, and Tesoriero (2005) 209 n. 25, who argues *contra* Rossi that it is an indication of Caesar's 'aimlessness'.

CHAPTER 4

THE POMPEIAN SUBLIME

I turn in this chapter from the Caesarian sublime and its associated effects of tyranny and domination to consider an alternative type of sublimity, markedly different in its ethical colouring and bound up not with the overwhelming impact of natural phenomena or human violence but with a particular way of experiencing the past. This 'Pompeian' sublime may not possess the immediate visibility and force of the Caesarian; as the poem moves through and beyond Pharsalus, however, it progressively reveals itself as a mode of sublimity in which Lucan's poem is equally firmly rooted. We will see, moreover, that repeated textual correspondences and echoes bring this sublimity into direct contact and opposition with that of Caesar. In order to trace its emergence I focus attention upon the first-person interventions of the poem's narrator. I concentrate in particular on two sections: the narratorial apostrophes as battle is joined and ended at Pharsalus in Book 7, and the narrator's lament over Pompey's corpse and makeshift burial at the climax of Book 8. As a preliminary, I offer an outline of two of the most suggestive discussions of what a sublime experience of the past might look like, one ancient, one modern, and consider the relation between them.

The historical sublime

Longinus and Ankersmit

The *Peri hupsous*, we have seen, foreshadows the later association of lightning and sublimity, so dramatically incarnated by Caesar. But it also provides a model for the historical sublime that forms a counter-weight in the *Bellum civile* to Caesarian might. The shape and operation of this alternative Longinian sublimity have been sketched by critics, including, most illuminatingly, Porter. To

179

recap from Chapter 1: Longinus' quotation from Genesis aside, Longinus cites no text later than the fourth century BC; he stresses the memorial function of reading great literature,[1] extolling the inspirational power of 'the great prose writers and poets of the past' (*De sub.* 13.2) and drawing our attention to the way a text's powers of visualisation (φαντασία) can in turn bring that text to life;[2] this reimagining of the past is reflected in the recurrent movement of loss and restitution that marks those texts to which Longinus is drawn (Sappho's Φαίνεταί μοι being perhaps the most striking example, *De sub.* 10.2–3); and this movement is in turn enacted by the *Peri hupsous* itself, as it breaks up the literature of the past into fetishised fragments and then integrates these fragments to produce (a text of) sublimity.[3] Thus, in Porter's words, 'for Longinus, the museal past is not permanently frozen; it is mobilised in the reproductive imagination of its readers . . . the sublime is . . . an exponentially heightened form of remembrance: it is the vivid presentation of the past in the latter's most memorable aspects'.[4] The sublimity of the *Peri hupsous* creates an idealised image of the Greece that was and enables this past to be experienced once again as a thing of the present. Hence Longinus' assertion: 'it is our nature to be elevated and exalted by true sublimity. Filled with joy and pride, we come to believe we have created what we have only heard' (*De sub.* 7.2).

This reading of Longinus' interest in sublimity as a means of relating past to present resonates strikingly with Ankersmit's recent work *Sublime Historical Experience* (2005). Ankersmit's study seeks to investigate how and why historical consciousness arises. Bypassing traditional historical issues of truth ('What happened?') and representation ('Who is telling us what happened, and how?'), he focuses attention on the 'tertium quid' of historical experience – specifically, on the question of a historical subject's awareness of there having been a past at all.[5] The model

---

[1] *De sub.* 4.7, 9.3, 13.2–14.3, 36.2, 44.1, 44.9.   [2] *De sub.* 7.3, 15.1–12.

[3] This process governs both the treatise as a whole and the construction of individual quotations, e.g. the conflations of verses from the *Iliad* at *De sub.* 9.6 and 9.8, and the selective quotation from Plato, *Timaeus* 65C–85E at *De sub.* 32.5.

[4] Porter (2001) 78–9.

[5] Cf. Porter (2006a) 19 on the question of what it is, or rather what it was, to have a past.

of experience that he constructs to answer this question exhibits the structure of the sublime. Our consciousness of the existence of the past, Ankersmit argues, comes into being 'by a movement comprising at the same time the *discovery* and the *recovery* of the past':

> Historical experience involves, in the first place, a Gestalt-switch from a timeless present into a world consisting of things past and present. This gives us the discovery of the past as a reality that has somehow 'broken off' from a timeless present. This is 'the moment of loss'. But at the same time historical experience aims at a recovery of the past by transcending again the barriers between past and present. And this could be characterised as 'the moment of desire or love' ... [T]hese complementary movements of the discovery (loss) and the recovery of the past (love) ... constitute together the realm of historical experience. Past and present are related to each other as man and wife in Plato's myth of the origin of the sexes ... *The sublimity of historical experience originates from this paradoxical union of the feelings of loss and love, that is, of the combination of pain and pleasure in how we relate to the past.*[6]

The Burkeian combination of pain and pleasure, or, in Kant's terminology, the dual inhibition and expansion of one's 'vital forces',[7] here results not from an encounter with the awesome power of lightning or the fearsome might of the lion, but from an experience of the past, from a glimpse – at once devastating and exhilarating – of the difference between 'what is' and 'what was': 'sublime historical experience,' as Ankersmit observes, 'is the experience of a past breaking away from the present'.[8]

Ankersmit's construction of the sublime within the space between past and present strongly resembles the form of sublimity that Porter's reading reveals in Longinus: both theorists identify sublimity with a particular 'experience of the past'.[9] Yet,

---

[6] Ankersmit (2005) 9.

[7] Ankersmit (2005) 335 relates his theory to both Kant and Burke: 'the same momentary disruption of our normal cognitive apparatus' underpins each model.

[8] Ankersmit (2005) 265.

[9] Ankersmit (2005) 318. Porter (forthcoming) uses the same phrase as a heading in a section on the *Peri hupsous*. The two theorists also find common ground in Stephen Greenblatt's discourse of experience: Porter (forthcoming) suggests that Greenblatt's terms of 'resonance and wonder' 'capture quite nicely Longinus' theory of the sublime' (see Greenblatt 1990: Chapter 9 heading); as a parallel to his model of the sublime, Ankersmit (2005) 360 cites Greenblatt's observation that 'to experience Renaissance culture is to feel what it is like to form our own identity, and we are at once more rooted

while he acknowledges Burke and Kant, Ankersmit does not mention Longinus. This perhaps should not surprise: the historical implications of Longinus' discourse emerge only obliquely and gradually and, Porter's reading aside, have not been widely recognised. The similarities between the two models, however, make it profitable to read them side by side. Longinus offers a more specific precedent than either Burke or Kant for Ankersmit's sublime. He allows us to see that Ankersmit's sublime is not simply a localised post-modern offshoot of the concept's eighteenth-century formulations but instead has firm roots within the concept's history. At the same time, Ankersmit provides a helpful means of expanding and clarifying the logic behind the Longinian sensibility: by explicitly identifying the category of the sublime with his model of historical consciousness, he shows us how the dynamic that fascinates Longinus works, augmenting through methodical exposition his predecessor's practice of allusion and associative exemplification.

There is a further reason, specific to my present inquiry, that makes Ankersmit a valuable supplement to Longinus, for the manner in which he expands upon Longinian thinking brings us into immediate contact with the preoccupations of the *Bellum civile*. The impact of violently transformative historical events is central to Ankersmit's argument. Situations of radical social or political upheaval are what engenders the sublime's 'paradoxical union of feelings', the awareness of having moved from one order of existence into another. Ankersmit considers such violent upheavals under the rubric of trauma. Like 'terror' in the Burkeian (and Kantian) model, trauma denotes an experience upon which the sublime is predicated and yet which it also transcends. Thus, 'the past is... born from the historian's traumatic experience of having entered a new world and from the awareness of irreparably having lost a previous world forever'.[10] Lucan's theme of civil war and the consequent shift from Republic to Principate is, I suggest, a powerful example of the kind of historical transformation

and more estranged by the experience' (see Greenblatt 1980: 175). Cf. Sedley (2005) 4–8, who identifies sublimity as a defining feature of New Historicism's, and specifically Greenblatt's, sceptical refusal to limit meaning to either text or context.
[10] Ankersmit (2005) 265.

in which Ankersmit is interested. Moreover, the Lucanian narrator's response to his subject matter well exemplifies the connection Ankersmit draws between trauma and sublimity. In order to see how this is so, and how Ankersmit expands upon the logic of Longinus, we will need to spend a little longer examining Ankersmit's sublime and the role of trauma within it. I hope that the correspondences I subsequently draw between the thought and phraseology of the *Bellum civile* and the terms of Ankersmit's analysis will confirm the value of the theoretical footwork.

Trauma and the historical sublime

Ankersmit's suggestion that there is 'a great deal of overlap' between trauma and the sublime reflects recent critical interest in the points of correspondence between the two concepts:[11] 'In both we have to make do with an experience of the world that is too terrible to fit within the matrix of how we "normally" experience it.'[12] Significantly, however, Ankersmit distinguishes between two types of trauma. The first, although painful and terrible, nevertheless admits the possibility of narrativisation, closure and hence reconciliation with the subject's identity, though these processes may prove extremely difficult and take considerable time. Such might be the kind of trauma inflicted on an individual by an experience of severe physical or mental violence; such is generally a private trauma. But in the second, more extreme, type this integration of experience and identity is not possible. The traumatic event is literally 'too terrible', resulting in the complete and irreparable loss of the subject's former, pre-traumatic identity. Here, Ankersmit writes, 'any reconciliation of a former and a new identity is categorically out of the question – and this also means that no room is left for a mechanism that might give us the redemption from trauma'. Consequently, and crucially, 'the new identity is mainly constituted by the trauma of the loss of [the] former identity – precisely *this* is its main content'.[13] We become 'what we are no

---

[11] See e.g. the essays in Ray (2005): 'these engagements with contemporary art and politics work to demystify and reorient the sublime through a dialectical treatment that opens it to history and links it to the psychoanalytic category of trauma' (p. 5).
[12] Ankersmit (2005) 334.   [13] Ankersmit (2005) 324.

longer',[14] our past and present separated by an unbridgeable gulf. It is on this second kind of trauma that Ankersmit focuses. The scale and power of such traumatic events means that they typically engulf entire societies. They are public events, although their traumatic effects will necessarily be manifested in individuals. Ankersmit's favoured example is the coincidence of the French and Industrial Revolutions on the threshold between the eighteenth and nineteenth centuries, and the responses to 'these two paramount progenitors of modernity' of writers such as Alexis de Tocqueville, Joseph von Eichendorff and Walter Benjamin.[15]

Two aspects of this second type of trauma require emphasis. The paradoxical position of the post-traumatic subject reconfigures conventional wisdom about the relationship between identity and memory. Ordinarily we will say that our identity is based on our ability to remember who we are, that our identity is rooted in our past. Following a traumatic event of the particular kind in which Ankersmit is interested, however, the past – the pre-traumatic past – emerges as something permanently removed from our present identity, something from which our identity has been violently up-rooted. It is a past that no longer defines who we are. In such circumstances we might say that it is, strangely, forgetting rather than remembering that underpins identity. It is our forgetting of the past, our disassociation of ourselves from it, that comes to define who we are. Yet, at the same time, it is the very awareness of this radical disengagement from the past that continues to define the post-traumatic self. Identity remains connected to the past in

---

[14] Ankersmit (2005) 318, cf. 333.
[15] Ankersmit (2005) 143. Contrary to LaCapra (1994), Ankersmit denies that the Holocaust constitutes an example of insuperable trauma: it would be 'a moral infamy if the Holocaust would have unleashed a historical trauma, as I understand this notion, for this would suggest that we had accepted Hitler's legacy somehow' (pp. 351–2). This seems misguided. The refusal to accept Hitler's legacy has not expunged the Holocaust from collective consciousness or permitted it to find adequate narrativisation; rather the reverse. Together with Hiroshima, the Nazi genocide constituted the most extraordinary rupture within the twentieth century. It has a strong claim to be considered the kind of inassimilable trauma that prompts sublime experience. See Ray (2005) 33–49 ('Joseph Beuys and the "After-Auschwitz" Sublime'). (It is worth noting, however, that Ray's concept of a post-Kantian, post-WWII sublime is geared not towards conservative nostalgia, as Ankersmit's is, but towards revolutionary 'mourning': 'the sublime . . . will now be the name of an event in which ethics, politics and aesthetics intersect, and in which mourning meets the project of transformation' (p. 9).)

the sense that the loss of this past continues to be remembered. We are thus presented with a deeply paradoxical situation, in which identity both is and is not a function of memory and the past. We are faced, as Ankersmit puts it, with the task of 'not forgetting – or remembering – to forget': 'one has discarded . . . [the] past from one's identity, and in this sense one has forgotten it. But one has not forgotten *that* one has forgotten it, for that one has forgotten precisely *this* is constitutive of the new identity.'[16]

Conversely, it is in this dissociation of past from present identity that the past emerges into objective existence. What was previously our identity is now transformed into something distinct from ourselves. No longer a state of being, something that can be lived, this identity instead becomes an object of knowledge, something about which we can learn. Again, this shift in status hinges upon a paradox, for it is only once this identity has been lost that we become truly aware of it. Where previously, we might say, it proved transparent and elusive, the self in which we were always tangled up, now with distance it becomes tangible and opaque.[17] And it is because of this paradox that any post-traumatic awareness of the past remains fraught with tension. Ankersmit describes the predicament – the jabbing awareness of an identity that has been lost and is never to return – as 'the pain of Prometheus'. The nearer this awareness comes to completion, the more it accentuates the differences between then and now, pushing the past ever further away:

The historical search for our former identity is motivated by the desire to become this identity again; but each time part of the past identity has, in fact, been recaptured, a new dimension has (unintentionally) been added to the difference between a former and our present identity . . . In this way the Promethean pain and our wish to assuage this pain keep each other going in a permanent *perpetuum mobile* – and there will be no room for either the temporary calm of repression or for the dissolution of trauma.[18]

---

[16] Ankersmit (2005) 333; cf. ibid. 318–21, 333–4, 339–40.
[17] Ankersmit (2005) 350: 'a previous identity . . . [can] take on its opacity only from the perspective of a new identity, which, in its turn, is invisible to us because of its essential transparency. Identity is like our shadow: always outside our grasp and never coinciding with ourselves.'
[18] Ankersmit (2005) 328–9.

In some cases, telling the right story about a traumatic event will enable the gap between past and present, which this event has opened up, to be closed, thereby resealing a temporarily sundered identity and so preventing the emergence of a distinct and discrete pre-traumatic self. But the 'Promethean' situation envisaged by Ankersmit is different, for here the narration of trauma, the construction of history and the concomitant attempt to 'recapture' the past must all be performed from the perspective of a present that has floated free of any previous existence; the pursuit of the past through knowledge and narrative will hence only ever succeed in emphasising the past's distance. At the same time, however, it is because of this very distance that the past achieves body and substance as a distinct entity.[19]

Ankersmit understands sublime experience in terms analogous to this formulation of irredeemable traumatic experience. We are overwhelmed by the power or immensity of the sublime object. Like the object of traumatic experience, it proves too much for our normal cognitive faculties – we cannot get over it. In both cases we encounter something beyond our powers of comprehension. Moreover, as with trauma, the experience of the sublime leads to an uncanny doubling of identity. So shattering is the experience that it causes a break between the 'everyday' identity we previously inhabited and the newly heightened sense of self that sublimity bestows. In turn, the contours of this 'everyday' identity achieve a hitherto unperceived, and potentially unsettling, vividness and clarity. Ankersmit frames this shift in terms of a 'dialectics of directness and indirectness' familiar also from studies of trauma.[20] On the one hand, the sublime or traumatic event renders indirect what were previously direct processes of perception; that is, the mental frameworks through which we perceive the world, and which normally remain invisible to us, suddenly, from the altered perspective of the post-traumatic or sublime subject, become strangely apparent. At the same time, however, this very enlargement of vision – the sudden awareness of the real

---

[19] Cf. DeLillo (1997) 11: 'Longing on a large scale is what makes history'; ibid. 803: 'This is the world's wistful implication – a desire for something lost or fled or otherwise out of reach.'

[20] Ankersmit (2005) 344 and, in particular, 335-7.

'indirectness' of our normal perceptions – endows reality itself, of which our previous perceptual frameworks are now a part, with a startlingly new directness. The experience is one of derealisation or depersonalisation: a subject loses a familiar reality or, rather, rediscovers reality from a new perspective. Hence emerges a split in identity, comparable to that of the traumatised subject discussed above:

> Sublime experience is . . . the kind of experience inviting or necessitating us to discard or to dissociate a former self from the self that we are after having had the sublime experience in question. Sublime experience then is the kind of experience forcing us to abandon the position in which we still coincide with ourselves and to exchange this for a position where we relate to ourselves in the most literal sense of the word, hence, as if we were *two* persons instead of just *one*. This . . . is how identity, (traumatic) dissociation, and the epistemological paradoxes of sublime experience all hang together.[21]

But there is also a crucial difference between the sublime and trauma. Where the reorientation of identity imposed by trauma is fundamentally negative, characterised by pain and grief, that produced by the sublime, though also spurred by loss, additionally promotes a movement of subjective restitution. If the derealisation experienced by the traumatised subject nauseates and disorients, for the sublime subject it becomes a source of exhilaration. It promotes what Arthur Danto, analysing the same processes of self-dissociation, called the 'transfiguration of the commonplace', a phrase connoting not breakdown and permanent erasure but redemption and rebirth.[22] The dissociation specific to the sublime carries with it an implicitly positive charge: where the identity of the post-traumatic subject is wholly defined by loss, sublimity leads to both the destabilisation *and* the reassertion of identity, to the simultaneous evacuation and intensification of reality.

This brings us back to the *Peri hupsous*. Among Longinus' examples of sublimity Sappho's Φαίνεταί μοι, briefly discussed in Chapter I, stands out as a particularly powerful illustration of Ankersmit's theme: enumerating the parts of her body like distinct

---

[21] Ankersmit (2005) 347.
[22] Danto (1983) 206: 'my beliefs . . . are invisible to me until something makes them visible and I can see them from the outside'. Although Danto does not deploy the concept of the sublime, his thinking bears strongly on Ankersmit's; see Ankersmit (2005) 345–50.

objects, the speaker experiences a moment of numbing depersonalisation which yet allows her to achieve a new kind of wholeness,
figured in the act of poetic composition; as Longinus exclaims, 'Do
you not admire the way in which *she brings everything together –
mind and body, hearing and tongue, eyes and skin? She seems to
have lost them all, and to be looking for them as though they were
external to her*' (*De sub.* 10.3).[23] And, as we have seen, in the *Peri
hupsous* Sappho herself becomes a fragmented instantiation of
the past, the dynamic of her poem reproduced through Longinus'
own writing practice. As Porter notes, the power of both Sappho's
poem and Longinus' framing of it turns upon a movement of destitution: 'in elevating Sappho into a figure for sublime production
generally, Longinus simultaneously produces an image of Greek
literature as a body that has been dismembered and reunited into
scintillating literary fragments'.[24] Violent loss, figured by Sappho
and in Longinus' commentary as bodily trauma, is in each case the
precondition for a new kind of wholeness. And this, moreover, is a
dialectic analogous to the movement of the sublime adumbrated by
the other theorists whose assistance I have previously enlisted: in
the Lucretian paradigm it is atomism's vertiginous force, its radical destabilisation of our customary perspectives on the world, that
paradoxically enlarges our sense of our own capabilities and of our
position within the universe; Burkeian terror is tinged with tranquillity, the Kantian power of reason elevates us above the object
before which our powers of cognition collapse. The sublime, in
other words, may be regarded as a particular version of traumatic
experience, one in which loss is made good. For Ankersmit, as
for Longinus, this traumatic experience presents itself most powerfully when we turn to contemplate a vanished past. Through
such contemplation, the past not only emerges via traumatic loss
as a distinct object but is also momentarily revivified; desolation
mutates into a sense of grandeur and elevation.

---

[23] This is Porter's (forthcoming) translation (my italics). Ankersmit's own illustration is
taken from John Banville's novel *Eclipse* (2000), in which the protagonist suddenly
finds an entirely 'commonplace' scene 'transfigured', a derealising effect that leads him
to perceive himself as an objective part of his surroundings: ' it was *I* that was happening
here' (*Eclipse*, p. 33). Like the speaker of Sappho's poem, Banville's character attests a
sublime sense of self-dissociation.

[24] Porter (forthcoming).

Sites of the historical sublime

Radical trauma, then, is not to be identified with the sublime. But the two types of experience do display important structural resemblances. In this sense, we might think of trauma (like Burkeian terror) as providing certain conditions of possibility for the sublime. Ankersmit's emphasis on trauma alerts us to a specific kind of situation out of which sublime experience may arise. In particular, his analysis helps us see how, like the natural phenomena that fascinated Lucretius and Kant, revolutionary historical events can act as triggers for sublime experience. In Ankersmit's example, the French and Industrial Revolutions were events that 'created an insurmountable barrier between past and present that could impossibly be denied or undone anymore – and this barrier became the clearly delineated face the past had turned toward us. The past had become, for the first time in history, an almost tangible reality.'[25] Ankersmit emphasises the unique nature of these twin revolutions, arguing that the changes experienced by the Western world between 1789 and 1815 were 'wholly unparalleled in all the history of mankind', but his model could theoretically be applied to any radical rupture between a past and present order of existence. He describes his study as a 'research programme' designed to encourage 'the identification and investigation of these sublime experiences of rupture', citing as examples the 'trauma of the Civil War' in the US South and 'the two dramatic caesuras of 1917 and 1989' in Russia.[26] Following this lead, I suggest in this chapter that the Roman civil war provides us with another such incident of rupture and that the Lucanian narrator's response to this traumatic event exemplifies a form of what Ankersmit would call 'sublime historical experience'.

Boundary violation, suicide and the sundered self

I begin my analysis by considering how throughout the poem the trauma of the civil war is presented in terms, also adopted

[25] Ankersmit (2005) 143. Cf. Blix (2008) 1 for similar observations about how the French Revolution reconfigured temporality.
[26] Ankersmit (2005) 13.

by Ankersmit, of sundered identity and, more specifically and graphically, of suicide.

The civil war that Lucan recounts heralded Rome's transformation from Republic to Principate. Shadi Bartsch's eloquent summation of the poem's attitude towards these epoch-defining events well captures what was at stake:

Lucan's view of civil war relies on the notion that such conflict is best characterised as the violation of the most important boundaries that constituted human society at Rome before the fall of the Republic: the boundaries that separated Italy from its provinces and regions further afield; that distinguished family members from strangers and friends from enemies, citizens from aliens and patriots from traitors; that gave meaning to ethical terms such as virtue and evil, heroism and cowardice; that made possible the old social rankings of the Republic, in which senators and slaves stood on either side of an all but impassable gulf . . . For Lucan, Pompey's loss against Caesar at Pharsalus in 48 BC would cause the demolition of yet another boundary, that which separated the Republic from dictatorship, principate, and empire; and as he looks back from his own time in the 60s AD he has clearly in mind (whether for the purposes of history or propaganda) the inversions that loss engendered: ex-slaves in office, foreigners as Romans, the senatorial body, both physically and institutionally, compelled to self-slaughter by imperial paranoia and greed.'[27]

This characterisation of Lucan's (or rather, the Lucanian narrator's) retrospective gaze marks the historical sensibility of the *Bellum civile* as the very kind in which Ankersmit is interested. In the narrator's view, the civil war opened up a gulf within history: the rupture of the boundary that delineated Rome's Republican identity produced, paradoxically, an 'insurmountable barrier between past and present'.

The sundering of identity suffered by the metaphorical body of the Roman state, its division into Republic and Principate, is reflected in the violence repeatedly inflicted upon and by the *Bellum civile*'s human subjects.[28] Adapting Julia Kristeva's notion of the abject,[29] Bartsch persuasively argues for this obsession with the violation of bodily boundaries as an expression of deep-seated

[27] Bartsch (1997) 14.
[28] The bibliography on this theme is extensive: see in particular Henderson (1987/2010), esp. 441–2, 482–3; Masters (1992) 1–5, 64, 72; Bartsch (1997) 10–47; Dinter (2005). Cf. Most (1992).
[29] See Kristeva (1982).

anxieties surrounding subjectivity, anxieties provoked by and reflecting the collapse of the 'body' of the Republic: the *Bellum civile*'s fascination with bodily mutilation manifests an 'interest in everything that "threatens the subject with the impossibility of the self" by attacking the very categories that make up "self"'.[30] In particular, Bartsch points out how under the force of this attack subjects are reconfigured as objects. As exemplified in the murder of Marius Gratidianus (Luc. 2.173–90), discussed in Chapter 2, bodies are reduced to body parts, human selfhood is replaced by spilled guts and severed limbs.

This concern with the transgression of the boundary between subject and object (or, to put it the other way around, the erection of a division between subject and object within a previously integral identity) brings us closer again to Ankersmit's discourse of trauma and to the Longinian sense of the past. The connection is underscored by Lucan and Ankersmit's shared use of suicide as a metaphor for their concerns. As Ankersmit observes, the suicidal subject, in killing himself, turns upon his own body as upon an alien object; incidents of traumatic historical rupture effect a comparable cleaving of identity, as a society's former self is objectified and killed off. 'Moving to a new and different world really *is* and also *requires* an act of violence, in fact nothing less than an act of suicide.'[31] However, where the suicide of an individual by definition terminates that individual's existence, this metaphorical, societal suicide paradoxically ensures that the terminated identity continues to subsist as the new identity's shadow-image: 'the kind of cultural suicide which takes place in historical transitions ... [has] the character of the exchange of a former identity for a new one[;] such transitions can properly be described as seeing the former self as if it were the self of somebody else'.[32] This societal suicide, then, is not fatal but instead wrenches wide a gap between a culture's present and its past; this gap, this loss of identity, is what brings the sense of a past into being.

Lucan's theme of civil conflict, of Rome at war with itself, at once victorious aggressor and defeated victim, makes suicide an

---

[30] Bartsch (1997) 22.   [31] Ankersmit (2005) 343.
[32] Ankersmit 344. Cf. Alston and Spentzou (2011) 56–7 on the relation between the abject and the sublime.

obviously attractive metaphor.[33] The motif is established in the
poem's very first verses:

> bella per Emathios plus quam civilia campos
> iusque datum sceleri canimus, populumque potentem
> in sua victrici conversum viscera dextra.

> Of wars across Emathian plains, worse than civil wars,
> and of legality conferred on crime we sing, and of a mighty people
> attacking its own guts with victorious sword-hand.　　　　1.1–3

A few lines later, the narrator reflects that, if Rome truly could
not staunch her bloodlust (*si tantus amor belli tibi*, 1.21), she
should have first waged war against the rest of the world before
turning weapons upon herself (*tum . . . / in te verte manus*, 1.21–3);
it is self-inflicted wounds that cut the deepest (*alta sedent civilis
volnera dextrae*, 1.32). Right from the beginning, then, Lucan
signals to us that, as Martindale puts it, this poem is to be read
'under the sign of self-slaughter, both individual and collective'.[34]
As the suicide, in turning upon himself, becomes his own enemy,
so Rome's soldiery, instead of attacking those lying beyond the
empire's borders, march against each other. Bartsch spells out
the logic underlying the equation: 'Lucan's image of civil war as
a senseless manifestation of self-slaughter' reflects how 'suicide
and the act of self-sacrifice are paradigmatic cases of the melding
of subject and object, since the murderer and the victim, the priest
and the offering, are one and the same'.[35] In the case of the Roman
civil war, this 'melding' of subject and object is also a rupturing of
the state's identity. It is in Rome's suicide that the abyssal division
between Republic and Principate opens up.

The metaphor is reinforced by repeated instances of actual suicide within the epic. The sea battle at Massilia in Book 3 becomes
a bizarre litany of self-willed death: combatants grapple with each
other, gladly drowning themselves in the attempt to drown their
enemy (*inplicitis gaudent subsidere membris / mergentesque mori*,
3.695–6); blinded by a bullet and already near his end, Tyrrhenus
fights on, eager to be killed in the place of comrades who are still

---

[33] See Hill (2004) 213–36.　　[34] Martindale (1993) 480.　　[35] Bartsch (1997) 24.

fit for battle (*ingentem militis usum / hoc habet ex magna defunctum parte cadaver: / viventis feriere loco*, 3.719–21); crazed with grief, the father of the fatally wounded Argus refuses to outlive his son and, to make doubly sure of his own death, first falls on his sword and then hurls himself into the sea (*letum praecedere nati / festinantem animam morti non credidit uni*, 3.750–1).[36] Scaeva takes this appetite for self-destruction to new lengths during his *aristeia* at Dyrrachium in Book 6.[37] Introduced as a soldier who attained the rank of centurion through shedding much (of his own) blood (*sanguine multo*, 6.145), he exhorts his men to offer up their lives for Caesar (*terga datis morti? cumulo vos desse virorum / non pudet et bustis interque cadavera quaeri?* 6.153–4) before himself leaping headlong into the Pompeians' midst, sustaining blows from all sides (6.189–90, 194–5, 202–6) and only finally collapsing when pierced in the eye by an arrow; as he does so, he manages one final kill, proclaiming his *amor mortis* to the last (6.245–6).[38] And there is the poem's most extraordinary scene of suicide, that of Vulteius' Opitergian soldiers in Book 4. Trapped on a raft by the Pompeians, the entire troop perishes in an orgy of self-slaughter: *pariter sternuntque caduntque / volnere letali, nec quemquam dextra fefellit / cum feriat moriente manu* (4.558–60).[39]

These episodes offer a literal illustration of the idea of civil war as suicide. Additionally, as commentators have observed, the language in which they are described regularly enacts the confusion of subject–object relations that suicide exemplifies.[40] In the case of the Opitergians, for instance, it is not weapons that attack flesh;

[36] See Bartsch (1997) 16–17, 24, 28, 38, 54; Leigh (1997) 246–58.
[37] On this episode, see in particular Leigh (1997) 158–90. Also Ahl (1976) 117–19; Henderson (1987/2010) 441–45; Johnson (1987) 57–60; Hardie (1993) 68–9; Bartsch (1997) 24, 52, 54; Sklenár (2003) 45–58.
[38] Scaeva's reappearance in the final lines of the extant poem (10.543–6) perhaps implies that he did not die at Dyrrachium after all. But it is uncertain how literally we are to take Caesar's 'looking back' at this point (*respexit*, 10.543) at his star centurion: is Caesar simply remembering Scaeva's efforts? Scaeva's actions in Book 6 can clearly be regarded as suicidal even if, despite all the odds, he managed to survive: Hill (2004) 215–16, for instance, considers the scene one of the poem's major instances of suicide and notes its commonly recognised analogies with the Vulteius episode.
[39] See Ahl (1976) 119–21; Saylor (1990); Bartsch (1997) 24, 56; Leigh (1997) 182–3, 218–19.
[40] Bartsch (1997) 23–9; Hill (2004) 217.

chests and throats do the killing themselves: *nec volnus adactis / debetur gladiis: percussum est pectore ferrum / et iuguli pressere manum* (4.560–2). When addressing his men, Scaeva idealises this very scenario: *confringite tela / pectoris inpulsu iugulisque retundite ferrum* (6.160–1). Even Marius Gratidianus, though executed by Sullan partisans, becomes in linguistic terms the author of his own death: described as a *victima*, he remains the subject of his sentence, offering 'a sacrifice unspeakable', *non fanda piacula*, (that is, himself) to the ghost of Catulus (2.174–6). Lucan's syntax repeatedly performs for us the disjunctive effects on subjectivity of the trauma of civil war.

Also noted by critics is the way in which these suicides subvert traditional Roman ideas of noble, self-willed death, offering instead an uncomfortable 'identification of ethical exemplarity with self-destructive frenzy'.[41] This destabilisation of ethical norms again emphasises the dissociative effects of civil strife: amid the traumatic rupturing of Roman identity, terms such as *virtus* no longer coincide with themselves (as Ankersmit might put it). In the Massilian sea battle, for example, Argus' father is described as a martial *exemplum* for his fellow Massilians but, in the same breath, his ability to act as a *miles* is denied (3.730) and instead of the *virtus* one would expect of such an *exemplum*, he exhibits only a mad, all-consuming desire to die before his son. The disintegration of the normative terms of *virtus*-based exemplarity is even more apparent in the reaction of Scaeva's men to his actions at Dyrrachium. He is lauded as an *exemplum* of true *virtus*: *ac velut inclusum perfosso in pectore numen / et vivam magnae speciem Virtutis adorant* (6.253–4). But the narratorial comment that concludes Scaeva's *aristeia* offers a very different perspective. Scaeva, we are told, would be

> felix hoc nomine famae,
> si tibi durus Hiber aut si tibi terga dedisset
> Cantaber exiguis aut longis Teutonus armis.
> non tu bellorum spoliis ornare Tonantis   260

---

[41] Hill (2004) 217. See further Roller (2001) 17–63.

templa potes, non tu laetis ululare triumphis.
infelix, quanta dominum virtute parasti!

> happy in this claim to fame
> had robust Iberians or Cantabrians with tiny weapons
> or Teutones with lengthy weapons fled from you.
> But you cannot adorn the Thunderer's temple
> with spoils of war, you cannot yell in happy triumphs.
> Unhappy man! with such enormous valour you bought a master!

6.257–62

Scaeva's *virtus* is all for nothing: it has been exercised not against barbarians but fellow citizens, in support not of Rome's dominance over her enemies but of her own subservience to Caesar. Such *virtus* is in fact no *virtus* at all. As Scaeva himself says, it is 'love of death' (*mortis amor*, 6.246) that motivates his actions. Elsewhere in the poem, this is a quality ascribed to barbarian peoples such as those whom the narrator wishes Scaeva had been fighting: the Druids are said to have spirits *capaces mortis* (1.461–2); the *indomitos populos* of Spain are *mortis amore feros* (4.147); the man born amid the snows of the North is characterised as a *mortis amator* (8.364). Scaeva's actions, in other words, far from showing him to be the quintessence of Roman *virtus*, present him as a barbarian, an enemy of Rome. His suicidal behaviour demonstrates a radical alienation from his own Roman identity.

The suicide of the Opitergians is framed so as to exhibit the same disjunction.[42] Vulteius urges upon his men the glory of suicide, asserting that their deaths will function as a traditional *exemplum* of Stoic *virtus* (*nescio quod nostris magnum et memorabile fatis / exemplum, Fortuna, paras*, 4.496–7):

> 'vita brevis nulli superest, qui tempus in illa
> quaerendae sibi mortis habet; nec gloria leti
> inferior, iuvenes, admoto occurrere fato.   480
> omnibus incerto venturae tempore vitae
> par animi laus est et, quos speraveris, annos
> perdere et extremae momentum abrumpere lucis,

---

[42] See Eldred (2002); Hill (2004) 219–21.

accersas dum fata manu: non cogitur ullus
velle mori.'   485

'Life which remains is short for no one who finds in it the time
to seek death for himself; and the glory of death is not
diminished, men, by advancing to meet a fate close at hand.
Since the period of life to come is uncertain for everyone,
praise of courage is equal whether you reject years
you hoped for or cut short a moment of life's end,
so long as by your own hand you invite the Fates: no one is forced
to wish to die.'   4.478–85

The narrator takes a rather different view. An event comparable to
the mutual slaughter of the Spartoi of Thebes and Phasis (4.549–
56), the Opitergian suicide is characterised not as an act of *gloria*
but of fratricidal *furor* (4.540, 562–5). Moreover, we are told that
'to escape slavery by one's own hand is not an arduous act of val-
our' (*non ardua virtus / servitium fugisse manu*, 4.576–7). In such
a situation meeting death in fact calls for less *virtus* than inflicting
it (*minimumque in morte virorum / mors virtutis habet*, 4.557–8):
pietas becomes the ability to execute a comrade with a single stroke
of the sword (*pietas ferientibus una / non repetisse fuit*, 4.565–6).
As in the case of Scaeva and of Argus' father, traditional Roman
values here find themselves perverted. Terms such as *virtus* and
pietas, like *Roma* itself, no longer signify what they once did. The
identity of their referents has been ruptured: between the poem's
protagonists and the narrator there emerges a radical discrepancy
in how these terms are understood. The Opitergians' actions will
thus indeed become an *exemplum* (*nullam maiore locuta est / ore
ratem totum discurrens Fama per orbem*, 4.573–4) but not of the
kind Vulteius intends, their bid for *virtus* and fame emerging as
synecdoche for the moral horror that characterises the entire civil
war: *totumque in partibus unis / bellorum fecere nefas* (4.548–
9). This *nefas* is that of brothers killing brothers, fathers sons,
comrades fellow comrades. It is the *nefas* of identities riven by
trauma, of subjects that were previously one becoming the alienated objects of their own gaze. *iam latis viscera lapsa / semianimes
traxere foris* (4.566–7): dragging their splayed innards across the
deck, the half-dead Opitergians come to stand for the ruptured,
abject, self-alienated body of Rome itself.

Pharsalus

If the actions of Vulteius and his men, like those of Scaeva and the berserk combatants at Massilia, enact the suicidal trauma of the civil war in miniature, it is Caesar's victory over Pompey at Pharsalus that elicits from the narrator the fullest and most ago-nised expression of this trauma's magnitude and irreversibility.[43] I will focus in particular on two passages in which the narrator pauses to reflect on the battle's significance. The traumatic sunder-ing of Roman identity, implicit in the themes of abjection, suicide and fratricide considered above, here receives direct and explicit expression. Marking the beginning and end of the battle's main nar-rative, these passages frame Pharsalus as an occasion when Rome's identity underwent a seismic shift, when its Republican self was finally lost and, hence, as the pivotal moment when Romans first came to see themselves, along the lines of Ankersmit's model, as 'other people'. At the same time, within the frame of this realisa-tion, we can discern the initial steps taken by the narrator towards the sublimity that emerges fully in his subsequent response to Pompey's tomb.

The first apostrophe begins just as battle is being joined:

> ergo utrimque pari procurrunt agmina motu   385
> irarum; metus hos regni, spes excitat illos.
> hae facient dextrae quidquid non expleat aetas
> [ulla nec humanum reparet genus omnibus annis]
> ut vacet a ferro. gentes Mars iste futuras
> obruet et populos aevi venientis in orbem   390
> erepto natale feret. tunc omne Latinum
> fabula nomen erit; Gabios Veiosque Coramque
> pulvere vix tectae poterunt monstrare ruinae
> Albanosque lares Laurentinosque penates,
> rus vacuum, quod non habitet nisi nocte coacta   395
> invitus questusque Numam iussisse senator.
> non aetas haec carpsit edax monimentaque rerum
> putria destituit: crimen civile videmus
> tot vacuas urbes. generis quo turba redacta est
> humani! toto populi qui nascimur orbe   400

---

[43] Strangely, this climactic moment has not so far attracted the level of critical attention afforded to other parts of the poem.

nec muros inplere viris nec possumus agros:
urbs nos una capit. vincto fossore coluntur
Hesperiae segetes, stat tectis putris avitis
in nullos ruitura domus, nulloque frequentem
cive suo Romam sed mundi faece repletam   405
cladis eo dedimus, ne tanto in corpore bellum
iam possit civile geri. Pharsalia tanti
causa mali.

So from both sides the troops run forward with equal impetus
of anger: fear of tyranny arouses these, those the hope.
These sword-hands will achieve things that no future age
can make good nor humankind repair in all the years,
though it be free from warfare. That fight will crush
the future races, and it will rob of birth and sweep away
the people of the generation entering the world. Then all
the Latin name will be a fable: Gabii, Veii, Cora
hardly will be indicated by their dust-covered ruins,
the hearths of Alba and the house-gods of Laurentum,
an empty country which no senator inhabits except unwillingly
on night ordained, complaining of the decree of Numa.
It is not devouring time which has eroded and abandoned in decay
these memorials of the past: it is the crime of civil war we see,
so many empty cities. To what has the multitude of humankind
been reduced! We peoples born in all the world
are not enough to fill with men the town-walls and fields;
a single city holds us all. The cornlands of Hesperia are worked
by chained labourer, the house with its ancestral roof decaying
stands, about to fall on no one; and Rome, crowded
by no citizen of her own but filled with the dregs of the world,
we have consigned to such a depth of ruin that in a body so immense
civil war cannot now be waged. The cause of such a great catastrophe
is Pharsalia.   7.385–408

Charging towards each other, the two armies are suddenly left suspended as the narrator pulls back to consider the future implications of the imminent carnage. Its effects, he declares, will never be
undone (387–9). Pharsalus will be an event that will 'overwhelm'
(*obruet*, 390) not only Pompey and the battle's combatants but
future Romans too. A great swathe of Rome's young men will die
in the fighting, men who would have fathered the next generation of
citizens. After Pharsalus, claims the narrator, there will be barely
enough Romans to fill the city itself (400–2, 404–5), let alone

to populate Italy's other towns or till its fields (395, 399, 402–
3). As he later laments, it will be Rome's erstwhile subjects –
Galatians, Syrians, Cappadocians, Gauls, Iberians, Armenians,
Cilicians – who will constitute the Roman people: *post civilia
bella / hic populus Romanus erit* (7.542–3): bluntly, Rome will be
'filled with the dregs of the world' (*mundi faece repletam*, 405);
the city as it was will cease to exist. Rome will no longer be Rome.
The trauma of Pharsalus, and of the civil war as a whole, will rob
it of its identity.

What is more, for the narrator, it is precisely the loss of this
identity by which Rome's new, post-Pharsalian self is to be defined.
He couches his lament for Rome's demise in terms of the death
of its citizens and the concomitant collapse of buildings, human
habitats and physical civilisation. The Italy of his own day appears
a kind of post-apocalyptic wasteland, all but devoid of life. The
passage looks back to the very beginning of the epic:

> at nunc semirutis pendent quod moenia tectis
> urbibus Italiae lapsisque ingentia muris   25
> saxa iacent nulloque domus custode tenentur
> rarus et antiquis habitator in urbibus errat,
> horrida quod dumis multosque inarata per annos
> Hesperia est desuntque manus poscentibus arvis.

> But now the walls are tumbling in the towns of Italy,
> the houses half-destroyed, and, the defences collapsed,
> the huge stones lie; no guardian occupies the homes
> and in the ancient cities wanders only an occasional inhabitant;
> Hesperia bristles now with thorns, unploughed
> through many a year, lacking the hands for fields which demand them.

> 1.24–9

at nunc (24): from its beginning the poem focuses our attention
on the present-day consequences of the civil war. The narratorial
intervention at Pharsalus urges the same perspective, first by casting our minds forward from the battle, predicting what Italy will
look like in the years to come (*tunc*, 7.391), then through direct
present-tense claims about the situation of the narrator and his contemporaries (*populi qui nascimur*, 7.400). But which Italy do lines
7.391ff. in fact describe – that of the Caesars or that which was lost
with the Republic? Ahl sees here a reflection of the rural realities

of the imperial period[44] but we need not be constrained to read so literally. The narrator is mesmerised by ruin not (only) because that is what he sees around him but because these tumbling walls, deserted houses and bramble-ridden fields offer a metaphorical picture of Rome's former, Republican identity after Caesar has burst across the sky. So far as the narrator is concerned, contemporary Rome may as well be a vagabond slum, its neighbouring fields and cities crumbling into the dust. Lucanian Rome is lying in ruins because that is the state of the Republic and the Republic is the only Rome that truly counts. Imperial Rome can only be comprehended by the narrator as the ruin of what Rome was. Its identity is entirely 'constituted by the trauma of the loss of [its] former identity'. It is 'what it is no longer'.

As we have seen in our discussion of Ankersmit, this traumatic predicament also prompts a specific structure of remembrance in relation to the lost identity. Pharsalus marked the death of the Republic and the emergence of a new, distinct (un)Roman self. In this sense, post-Pharsalians like our narrator have forgotten the Republic: it is no longer part of who they are. The ruination of the Republic and the narrator's attendant anguish at one level represent this forgetting: as Ankersmit observes, 'the historical transformations occasioning this variant of forgetfulness are always accompanied by feelings of a profound and irreparable loss, of cultural despair and of hopeless disorientation'.[45] But, as it continues, the narrator's apostrophe complicates the scenario:

> cedant feralia nomina Cannae
> et damnata diu Romanis Allia fastis.
> tempora signavit leviorum Roma malorum,   410
> hunc voluit nescire diem.

> The fatal names of Cannae and Allia,
> long cursed in the Roman calendar, must yield their place.
> The dates of lighter disasters Rome has marked;
> this day she wanted to ignore.   7.408–11

---

[44] Ahl (1976) 216–17, citing App. *BC* 1.7, Lucr. 2.1144–74, Hor. *Ep.* 1.11.7–8, Prop. 4.1.33–4, 4.10.27–30, Cic. *Planc.* 23, Strabo 5.3.2: 'at worst, what Lucan says is only an exaggeration'.

[45] Ankersmit (2005) 324.

Caesar's victory at Pharsalus is a catastrophe of such magnitude that it will displace other notorious defeats from the Roman calendar. Battles such as Cannae and Allia, fought against mere barbarians (Hannibal and the Gauls respectively) rather than between Romans, pale in comparison. Despite, or rather because, of this, while commemorating lesser disasters, Rome has attempted to forget the horror of Pharsalus. Yet it has found itself incapable of so doing. As the narrator hopelessly demands in the closing lines of the book, 'what length of time will be enough for distant ages to forget and to forgive you for the losses of the war?' (*quod sufficit aevum / inmemor ut donet belli tibi damna vetustas?* 7.849–50). The *damnum*, the loss, is too great to be simply forgotten. It is a permanent, ghastly latency, an absence that forever attests the death of the Rome that was. While Rome's former identity is lost and, hence, forgotten, the fact of this loss will thus always be remembered. *hunc voluit nescire diem*: Rome had to remind itself to forget Pharsalus, condemned 'not to forget to forget'. The radical nature of the trauma, even as it abruptly severs past from present, paradoxically ensures that this past is retained.

Further: it is in the very disappearance of this past that this past emerges into objective existence. There is an intimation of this idea in the complaint 'then all the Latin name will be a fable' (*tunc omne Latinum / fabula nomen erit*, 7.391–2). Instead of something live and real, the Latin name will ossify into a mere *fabula*, a story. It will become derealised, losing the presence and meaning it once had.[46] At the same time, it is precisely through this reconstitution as *fabula* that the *Latinum nomen* becomes an identifiable entity, something that can be narrated and described, a discursive object.[47] The germ of this paradox can also be detected amid the ruins of the Republic's towns. Covered with dust, they will barely (*vix*, 7.393) succeed in marking where these towns once were. Gabii, Veii and Cora, Alba and Laurentum will lose their former reality,

---

[46] The line contains an unsettling echo of the prophecy of Virgil's Anchises regarding the future cities of the Latin League (*haec tum nomina erunt, nunc sunt sine nomine terrae*, Virg. *Aen.* 6.776): Leigh (1997) 87–8. See Ahl (1976) 218 on Lucan's use of the word *nomen* to connote a 'name without substance' or 'an appellation that belies the true nature of the thing'.

[47] Cf. Bartsch (1997) 131–7.

becoming dissociated even from their own paltry remains (Italy's towns are the object of the sentence, *ruinae* its subject). But these ruins do not totally fail in their signifying function. They may only just succeed in indicating their former identities but succeed they still do. Indeed, as we saw, for the narrator this successful signification – the lost past witnessed by these ruins – continues to define the Italy of his own day, thereby endowing the derealised Italy of the Republic with a new kind of presence.

The idea that an identity's loss precipitates this identity's full manifestation finds its most powerful expression in the next section of the narrator's interjection:

<blockquote>
pro tristia fata!
aera pestiferum tractu morbosque fluentis
insanamque famem permissasque ignibus urbes
moeniaque in praeceps laturos plena tremores
hi possunt explere viri, quos undique traxit   415
in miseram Fortuna necem, dum munera longi
explicat eripiens aevi, populosque ducesque
constituit campis, per quos tibi, Roma, ruenti
ostendat, quam magna cadas.
</blockquote>

<blockquote>
O bitter Fates!
Air noxious to inhale, putrefying diseases,
maddening famine, cities given up to fires,
quakes which bring the walls of crowded cities tumbling –
all can be made good by these men who are dragged from
everywhere to a pitiable death by Fortune: as she deploys
and takes away the offerings of long ages, she stations on the plains
the peoples and the generals through whom to show you in your fall,
Rome, how mighty was your fall.   7.411–19
</blockquote>

Contrasting with, and intensified by, the preceding abrupt exclamation (*pro tristia fata!* 411), this single, enormously long sentence drives home the enormous scale of Rome's loss at Pharsalus. Disease, famine, a city's sack or an earthquake could not cause such devastation. Pharsalus, more violent still, its death toll even greater, is worse than all such disasters. But, perversely, Lucan makes this point by stating that the (soon to be) dead of Pharsalus could in fact make good these lesser losses. The damage done by such events, the literal and metaphorical abysses that they wrench open, could be redeemed, 'filled up' (*explere*, picking up *moenia... plena*,

414), by those who died at Pharsalus – that is, if these dead were still living. A strange, grotesque kind of redemption, then, one that serves in fact to point all the more powerfully the depth of Rome's loss. Famine may be *insanam* (413) but civil war is the ultimate madness, *furor*.[48] And yet the ascription of active agency (*possunt*, 415) to Pharsalus' dead *viri* sets in motion a train of thought in which what has been lost achieves a hitherto unperceived tangibility, becoming for the first time truly visible. For it is through these *viri*, arrayed on the battlefield, that Fortuna shows Rome what Rome was: *populosque ducesque / constituit campis, per quos tibi, Roma, ruenti / ostendat, quam magna cadas* (417–19). Earlier in the book the narrator makes a similar observation about the effects of Pharsalus on Roman identity: *advenisse diem qui fatum rebus in aevum / conderet humanis, et quaeri, Roma quid esset, / illo Marte, palam est* (7.131–3). This is a battle that will decide what Rome will be. Lines 417–19 present the logical consequence of this historical rupture: in acquiring a new identity, Rome finds itself alienated from its former self; it experiences its collapse as if it were that of somebody else. The trauma of Pharsalus thus both permanently erases Rome's Republican self and, paradoxically, endows this self with a materiality it never previously possessed. The assonance and juxtaposition at the beginning of 417 of the verbs *explicat* and *eripiens* underscores the point. As the Lucanian narrator sees it, it is in snatching away Rome's gifts that Fortuna displays them at their most dazzling. And this implies that it is more than just the materiality of its former identity that Rome suddenly sees: for the narrator, it is also in collapse that Rome's real greatness emerges (*quam magna cadas*). Dissociation of identity, and the attendant derealisation of experience, leads to a paradoxically amplified awareness of reality, that is to say, of Rome's glory.

We are edging here towards the sublime. The sudden revelation of Rome's *munera* and magnitude is a gesture in the direction of transcendence. It begins to establish the sublime's peculiar double movement, whereby defeat appears as, indeed becomes, triumph and greatness manifests itself amid disaster. Longinus

---

[48] Cf. Luc. 1.8, 681, 7.95.

cites Demosthenes' response to Athens' defeat at Chaeronea and the city's consequent loss of freedom as an example of sublimity (Dem. *De corona* 208; *De sub.* 16.2–4): in eliding the battle with that fought at Marathon ('it cannot be that you [who strove for the freedom of Greece] were wrong; no, by those who risked their lives at Marathon'), as well as with those at Salamis, Artemisium and Plataea, Demosthenes imbues the occasion when Philip destroyed Athens' freedom forever with the same status as former occasions when this freedom was heroically and famously defended. Apostrophising the dead of Marathon, 'deifying' them as Longinus puts it (ἀποστροφὴν ἐγὼ καλῶ, τοὺς μὲν προγόνους ἀποθεώσας, *De sub.* 16.2), and thereby giving the heroic past they represent new and everlasting life, Demosthenes paradoxically manages to turn Chaeronea and *its* dead into a reminder of Athenian greatness. But it is only because of Athens' defeat that this adjuration becomes sublime; Longinus excludes from sublimity a similar oath uttered by Eupolis (said to have influenced Demosthenes) on the grounds that it was addressed to Athens while the city was still 'in prosperity and needing no consolation' (*De sub.* 16.3–4).[49] As Hertz emphasises, 'Demosthenes' audience is estranged from itself by a military defeat that is the equivalent of Sappho's near-death, and it is precisely this defeat that underwrites Demosthenes' fiction.'[50] Hence Porter, on the same passage: 'The sublime may be associated with ideals of heroism and freedom, but these are sublime only when they are imperilled, when they are imagined as potential, or simply when they are no more... If ideologies have emotions bound up with them, then sublimity would be the emotion of this particular ideological feeling – of the greatness of what it is to be Greek on the verge of the attainment or loss of this greatness.'[51] So we might say, as battle is joined at Pharsalus, Lucan's narrator is swept up by the awareness of the greatness of what it is to be Roman on the verge of this greatness' destruction. It is through the dead of Pharsalus that Rome's greatness shines forth.

---

[49] Eupolis, *Demes* fr. 106 Kassel–Austin: οὐ γὰρ μὰ τὴν Μαραθῶνι τὴν ἐμὴν μάχην / χαίρων τις αὐτῶν τοὐμὸν ἀλγυνεῖ κέαρ.

[50] Hertz (1978/1985) 14.   [51] Porter (2001) 82; cf. Porter (2006b) 350.

Moreover, the Rome that Pharsalus conjures up for the narrator itself displays characteristics regularly associated with objects of the sublime:

> quae latius orbem
> possedit, citius per prospera fata cucurrit? 420
> omne tibi bellum gentis dedit, omnibus annis
> te geminum Titan procedere vidit in axem;
> haud multum terrae spatium restabat Eoae,
> ut tibi nox, tibi tota dies, tibi curreret aether,
> omniaque errantes stellae Romana viderent. 425

> What city held a wider sway
> over the world or advanced more swiftly through prosperity?
> Every war gave you nations, every year
> Titan saw you advance towards twin poles
> so that – because not much space of the eastern land remained –
> for you the night, for you the entire day, for you the ether sped,
> and everything the wandering stars saw was Roman. 7.419–25

Picking up the *tibi* of 7.418, the repeated personal pronouns (*tibi... te... tibi... tibi... tibi*) continue to point Rome's awareness of what it was. A state bigger (*latius*) and more powerful (*citius*) than any other (419–20), victorious in all its wars, its sway extending over almost the entire world (*omne... omnibus*, 421; *omniaque*, 425; cf. 423), this is a Rome that enthrals the observer with both its size and might. And not just the human observer: the whole cosmos marvels at Rome's magnificence (422, 424–5). Indeed, as Rome engulfs the globe, night and day seeming to turn for it alone, it becomes itself a part of the universe's fabric, something to be numbered alongside the sun and stars. The universe was of course for Kant a paradigmatic example of a sublime object because of its 'absolute magnitude', its refusal to be constrained by comparisons and, hence, by human comprehension. Lucan's narrator does not elevate Rome quite so high; Rome is only conceptualised as a significant part of the universe, not equated with the universe itself. Yet this invocation of the heavenly bodies, like the rhetorical question at 419–20, effectively thrusts Rome beyond all earthly comparisons. In terrestrial terms, Rome's greatness is indeed absolute, sublime.

This assertion of incomparability brings us back to the way in which Pharsalus is presented. As Rome was a state unparalleled in size and might, so Pharsalus, the battle that caused its collapse, remains a disaster without equal. One way of conceptualising this parallelism sees Pharsalus' unique status as a function of that of Rome. It is because the unrivalled might of Republican Rome was finally overwhelmed at Pharsalus that the battle was such a singular event. But, following the logic of the power-transfer that Hertz identifies within the sublime, we can reverse the flow of causation and observe that it is also because of the unprecedented, incomprehensible scale of the destruction at Pharsalus that, for the narrator, Republican Rome in turn becomes a sublime thing. The series of catastrophic events adduced by the narrator in order to highlight Pharsalus' unique status (7.412–14) culminates with an earthquake, one of those Lucretian phenomena (Lucr. 6.535–607) whose singular power the sublime subject manages at once to resist and to appropriate. The narrator's experience of Pharsalus repeats and magnifies this achievement. It is because the devastation wrought by the battle exceeds all comparison that Rome's greatness comes to exceed all comparison. In the narrator's own words: the dead of Pharsalus outnumber those of all other disasters (*hi possunt explere viri*, 7.415) and it is as a direct result of these dead (*quos*, 415, *per quos*, 418) that the incomparable scale of Rome's greatness is made manifest (*quam magna cadas*, 419).

Yet this sublimity is short-lived. Rome's greatness can only block out the rupture inflicted by Caesar's victory for the very briefest of moments before the poem's affective balance tilts back towards the pain of defeat. Demosthenes' oath after Chaeronea makes his listeners 'feel as proud of the war with Philip as of their victories at Marathon and Salamis'; 'carried away' by the 'transcendent sublimity and emotion' (ὑπερβάλλον ὕψος καὶ πάθος) of his words, they no longer regard Chaeronea as a disaster (*De sub.* 16.2–3). For the Lucanian narrator, by contrast, Pharsalus remains a catastrophe, the battle that ruined Rome, *tanti causa / mali* (7.407–8). At 7.419 it is *cadas* not *magna* that receives emphasis as the last word of the sentence: the previous concatenation of clauses slowly tumbles towards this rhythmic low. And, after the bright epiphany of Rome's greatness, it is to Rome's downfall that the narrator's attention now reverts: *sed retro tua fata tulit par omnibus annis / Emathiae funesta dies* (426–7). That heavy opening monosyllable abruptly punctures the sublimity of the preceding lines. In a single day Pharsalus halts and undoes Rome's mighty advance *per prospera fata* (420). The sublime experience of what Rome was gives way to the traumatised awareness that this identity has been permanently destroyed. Worse than this, in fact, for the *libertas* that was previously essential to Roman selfhood will now be enjoyed instead by Rome's enemies in Germany, Scythia and beyond the Tigris:

> fugiens civile nefas redituraque numquam
> libertas ultra Tigrim Rhenumque recessit
> ac, totiens nobis iugulo quaesita, vagatur
> Germanum Scythicumque bonum, nec respicit ultra   435
> Ausoniam, vellem populis incognita nostris.

> Liberty, in flight from the crime of civil warfare, has withdrawn
> beyond Tigris and Rhine, never to return,
> and wanders on, after so many murderous attacks,
> a blessing on Germany and Scythia, no longer mindful
> of Ausonia – how I wish our people had never known her!

> 7.432–6

A still more painful twist of the knife: Rome will not simply lose its identity but will effectively exchange it with those barbarian peoples against whom Rome formerly defined itself. There could be no greater sign of collapse. Scaeva's *mortis amor*, we remember, marked his misrecognition of barbarian values for Roman; here the narrator truly recognises an erstwhile, and quintessential, Roman attribute as belonging to barbarians. And this shift will be permanent: Rome's *libertas* is never coming back (*redituraque numquam*, 432, *nec respicit ultra*, 435). After Pharsalus Rome will never be the same again, its Republican self lost forever.

This pessimism is reinforced by the embittered apostrophe that marks the end of the main account of the battle (7.617–46). The narrator provides a generalised overview of the battle's defining characteristics, describing the fighting in terms of fratricide and abjection familiar from the examples discussed earlier: amid a flurry of *viscera* and *vitalia*, wounds assume active agency (*volnus / exierit*, 619–20), a sword is thrust from a dying man's throat by his final breath (621–2), a soldier 'stands firm' as his limbs fall around him (*steterit dum membra cadunt*, 623), blood 'splits' the air (*perruperit*) as it arcs from severed veins (625); one man strikes his brother's breast, another lacerates his father's face (626–7, 628–9).[52] In each case, however, the narrator professes himself unable to identify victim or aggressor. He is prevented from detailing individual deaths (*singula fata sequentem*, 618) or indicating who did what to whom:[53] the repeated indirect questions of the sentence spanning 7.617–30 go unanswered. He explains: 'when the world is dying I feel shame to spend my tears on the innumerable deaths' (*inpendisse pudet lacrimas in funere mundi / mortibus innumeris*, 617–18):

> mors nulla querella   630
> digna sua est, nullosque hominum lugere vacamus.
> non istas habuit pugnae Pharsalia partes,
> quas aliae clades: illic per fata virorum,
> per populos hic Roma perit; quod militis illic,
> mors hic gentis erat; sanguis ibi fluxit Achaeus,   635
> Ponticus, Assyrius; cunctos haerere cruores
> Romanus campisque vetat consistere torrens.

> No death deserves
> its own lament; we have no space to grieve for individuals.
> Pharsalia did not have those elements of battle
> which other calamities had: there, Rome was ruined by the destinies
> of warriors, here by entire peoples; a soldier's death there
> was here a nation's death; here streamed Achaean blood,
> Pontic and Assyrian – all that gore is stopped from sticking
> and congealing on the plain by a torrent of Roman gore.   7.630–7

The scale of the carnage makes it unseemly to single out and mourn specific soldiers. A series of sharp contrasts emphasises that the losses incurred lacked all precedent (*non istas . . . quas, illic . . . hic*,

---

[52] Cf. Luc. 7.180–3, 320–5, 463–6, 762–3, 775–6.

[53] The preceding account of the death of Domitius Ahenobarbus (7.599–616), Nero's ancestor, is one (historically attested: App. *BC* 2.82; Tac. *Ann.* 4.44.5; Suet. *Nero* 2.3; cf. Caes. *Civ.* 3.99.5) exception to this inability. For discussion of Lucan's handling of the scene and its political implications, see Lounsbury (1975); Ahl (1976) 47–54; Masters (1994). Domitius' earlier pardon by Caesar at Corfinium (2.478–525) elicits from the narrator a classic statement of the denatured ethical norms that obtain in a post-Republican world: *poenarum extremum civi, quod castra secutus / sit patriae Magnumque ducem totumque senatum, / ignosci* (2.519–21).

Achaeus, Ponticus, Assyrius . . . Romanus): worse even than Pompey's prediction (*quot regna iacebunt! / sanguine Romano quam
turbidus ibit Enipeus!* 7.115–16), this was a battle in which entire
peoples perished (633–5) – and the number of Roman dead out-
numbered all (635–7). Once again, the incomparable nature of
Pharsalus overwhelms (cf. 7.412–15).

But from this exceptional, truly cataclysmic status we can also
infer a more radical rationale behind the narrator's inhibition. The
identification of individuals is not possible because, as the language of abjection and fratricide reminds us, Pharsalus destroyed
Roman identity. It is not just that individual deaths blur and fade
amid the general slaughter but that this slaughter ensured the end
of an entire order of existence, 'the death of a whole world' (*funere
mundi*, 617). With this loss, the loss of Rome's old and true self,
vanished the narrator's ability to identify actual Romans. The apostrophe continues:

> maius ab hac acie quam quod sua saecula ferrent
> volnus habent populi; plus est quam vita salusque
> quod perit: in totum mundi prosternimur aevum.   640
> vincitur his gladiis omnis quae serviet aetas.
> proxima quid suboles aut quid meruere nepotes
> in regnum nasci? pavide num gessimus arma
> teximus aut iugulos? alieni poena timoris
> in nostra cervice sedet. post proelia natis   645
> si dominum, Fortuna, dabas, et bella dedisses.

> From this battle the peoples receive a mightier wound
> than their own time could bear; more was lost than life
> and safety: for all the world's eternity we are prostrated.
> Every age which will suffer slavery is conquered by these swords.
> How did the next generation and the next deserve
> to be born into tyranny? Did we wield these weapons or shield
> our throats in fear and trembling? The punishment of others' fear
> sits heavy on our necks. If, Fortune, you intended to give a master
> to those born after battle, you should have also given us a chance to fight.
> 7.638–46

In terms even more explicit than those of his earlier apostrophe, the narrator spells out what Pharsalus means: a new Caesarian world, defined not by *libertas* but servitude (641) and the
rule of a *dominus* (643, 646), engulfing the narrator's own day

(*prosternimur, gessimus, nostra*, cf. 7.389–91, 400–2) and stretching on for eternity (*totum aevum, omnis aetas*, cf. 7.387–9, 432–6). This permanent loss of *libertas*, this *funus mundi*, is why Pharsalus means more (*maius, plus*; cf. *bella... plus quam civilia*, 1.1) even than its horrendous death toll (639–40). The turning point of the civil war, the event that severed Republic from Principate, a gaping wound that will never heal: it is around this battle that the narrator's historical consciousness springs, his awareness that a new world has dawned and that, with it, an old world has vanished forever.

The narratorial apostrophes that frame Pharsalus powerfully articulate the experience of a previously stable identity splitting in two. Indeed, I want to suggest that they together provide a paradigmatic illustration of Ankersmit's theorisation of the subjective effects of a traumatic rupture in the fabric of history. Moreover, the first apostrophe shows this trauma shifting into sublimity, the alienation of an identity becoming the ground for its transfiguration. We will encounter this structure of feeling again, developed and sustained, in the narrator's portrayal of Pompey. At Pharsalus, however, as the second apostrophe reminds us, sublimity subsides back into the brute reality of sheer loss. It remains hobbled, unable to soar free. Trauma reasserts its pull. The man caught in an earthquake may fail to maintain the mental distance necessary to sense the sublime, and so here, faced with the still more terrible trauma of Pharsalus, the narrator ultimately remains too deeply wounded by the Republic's death to transcend it.

Pompey

The inconsistencies in the portrayal of Pompey have long been remarked.[54] As Masters and Bartsch have both in different ways shown, the key discrepancy lies between his representation at the

[54] See, for example, Marti (1945); Due (1962) 106; Brisset (1964) 114; Lintott (1971/2010) 260–5; Ahl (1976) 150–89; Narducci (1979) 125–30; Rosner-Siegel (1983/2010) 191–200; Martindale (1984/2010) 278–9. Bartsch (1997) 76, 85–90 offers a valuable summary of the main critical positions: Lucan was simply incompetent and failed to make of Pompey a consistent and plausible character; Pompey is modelled as a Stoic *proficiens* and changes as he gains wisdom; Pompey's inconsistencies are a realistic reflection of flawed humanity; the deterioration in Lucan's relationship with Nero prompted the increasingly favourable characterisation of Caesar's Republican rival.

level of the poem's action and at the level of narratorial comment: while the events of the poem show him to be vacillating and weak, the narrator paints him in increasingly favourable colours.[55] Within this disjunction, I suggest, we can discern the beginnings of sublimity. I examine three key passages: the comparison with the oak tree with which the narrator introduces Pompey in Book 1; the portrait of Pompey in Book 7 following Pharsalus; and the narrator's apostrophe over Pompey's tomb, or lack thereof, in Book 8.

The oak tree (1.135–43)

stat magni nominis umbra,   135
qualis frugifero quercus sublimis in agro
exuvias veteris populi sacrataque gestans
dona ducum nec iam validis radicibus haerens
pondere fixa suo est, nudosque per aera ramos
effundens trunco, non frondibus, efficit umbram,   140
et quamvis primo nutet casura sub Euro,
tot circum silvae firmo se robore tollant,
sola tamen colitur.

He stands, the shadow of a great name;
like in a fruitful field a lofty oak,
bearing the people's spoils of old and generals'
hallowed dedications; clinging with roots no longer strong,
by its own weight it stands firm, and spreading naked branches
through the air, it makes shade with trunk, not foliage;
and though it totters, ready to fall beneath the first Eurus,
though all around so many trees upraise themselves with sturdy trunks,
yet it alone is venerated.   1.135–43

The comparison of Caesar with a lightning bolt, discussed in Chapter 3, is located immediately after this passage (1.151–7). The immediacy of the juxtaposition invites us to infer that as tall trees are often blasted by lightning so Pompey will be struck down by

---

[55] Masters (1994); Bartsch (1997) 73–130. Both readings regard the narrator's stance as fundamentally compromised but where Masters argues that it represents a '*reductio ad absurdum* of politically committed writing' (p. 168), Bartsch characterises it as a Rortyite enactment of 'ideology in cold blood'. Other readings that see the inconsistencies in Pompey's portrayal as part of a purposeful artistic strategy include Feeney (1986/2010); Johnson (1987) 67–100; Ormand (1994/2010) 330–8; cf. O'Hara (2007) 131–42.

Caesar,[56] while *trunco* also glances towards Pompey's decapitated
corpse as it lies on the shore of Egypt (*truncus*, 8.698, cf. 1.685–
6, 2.189).[57] These premonitions of doom are compounded by the
simile's allusive identification of Pompey with Republican Rome.
At Pharsalus the narrator laments that, after the battle, the Latin
name will become a fable (*omne Latinum / fabula nomen erit*,
7.391–2); here Pompey is described as a *magni nominis umbra*
(135). Anticipating Rome's fate, Magnus has become dissociated
from himself, the mere shadow of his traditional epithet. He is the
(dis)embodiment of the empty Republican ideal to which Cato later
declares allegiance: *tuumque / nomen, Libertas, et inanem prose-
quar umbram* (2.302–3; cf. 9.202–6: Pompey's *nomen* represents
for Cato the *fides ficta libertatis*). Like Rome, Pompey is defined
by what he is no longer. Both are ruins of their former selves. As
Italy's dwellings totter on the brink of collapse (*ruitura*, 7.404),
so Pompey's oak is ready to fall (*casura*, 141); its roots bereft
of vitality (*nec iam validis radicibus*, 138), it resembles Rome's
rotten houses and decayed walls (*tectis putris avitis /... domus*,
7.403–4, *semirutis... moenia tectis*, 1.24).

Yet for all this the Pompeian oak, and by implication the lost
Republic that Pompey champions, rises *sublimis* (136), a sublime
thing. Pompey's alienation from his *magnum nomen*, the death of
the Magnus that was, does not mean that this greatness has vanished. Though weak and tottering, the oak continues to be adorned
with offerings (*exuvias... sacrataque... dona*, 137–8); it alone
is honoured while stronger neighbouring trees are ignored (*sola
tamen colitur*, 143). It is this tension, this vision of stature amid
decrepitude, that makes the oak sublime. This way of seeing was
achieved momentarily by the narrator in his apostrophe before
Pharsalus, with Rome itself as the sublime object. Here, it is established as a central factor in his presentation of Pompey, Rome's
Republican champion.

[56] Cf. Caesar's felling of the Massilian grove (3.399–452, esp. *caesis truncis*, 413); see
Rosner-Siegel (1983/2010) 198–9.
[57] Pompey's *truncus* in turn looks back to that of Priam's in the *Aeneid*: *iacet ingens litore
truncus, / avolsumque umeris caput et sine nomine corpus* (*Aen.* 2.558–9). See Narducci
(1973) 322; Bowie (1990), Hinds (1998) 8–10.

212

These sublime dimensions are emphasised by the Pompeian oak's location within, and reworking of, an inter- and intra-textual nexus of sublime Virgilian–Lucretian imagery, recently plotted by Hardie.[58] Mighty in his resolve to quit Carthage and unswayed by Dido's pleas, Aeneas is likened by Virgil to an Alpine oak that is buffeted by the wind but cannot be uprooted (*Aen.* 4.441–9), an image that recalls the earlier description of the towering, anthropomorphic mountain Atlas, sublimely impervious to the storms that beat around him (*Aen.* 4.246–51). Both are part of a sequence of sublime objects, rich in Lucretian echoes, that spins out from the soaring, infinitely expanding figure of *Fama* and includes the cosmically powerful Jupiter as well as Mercury who flies *sublimis*, swift as a gale (*Aen.* 4.173–278). In opposition to *Fama*'s evocation of Lucretian *Religio* and its terrors (Lucr. 1.62ff.), however, the *apatheia* of the Aenean oak and of Atlas calls to mind the sublime *ataraxia* of the Epicurean vision at Lucr. 3.1–30 (in particular the description of the gods' dwellings, *quas neque concutiunt venti*, 'which no winds ever shake', at 3.19–22, almost a translation of Homer's description of Olympus at *Od.* 6.43–5).[59] On the other hand, the Aenean oak also alludes to the oak at *Georgics* 2.290–7, which in turn recalls Lucretius' description of a long-lived giant such as the Epicurean view of the world proves to be impossible (Lucr. 1.199–204) but an example of which Virgil gives us in the shape of Atlas. Even as the Aenean oak evokes Lucretian sublimity, then, it questions the Epicurean truths on which that sublimity is based. Reading the oak as a symbol for Rome's might and endurance, Hardie suggests that this intertextual thread shows not merely Virgil's 'reaction against [the] demystification of the natural world'[60] by the Lucretian sublime but, further, 'Virgil's assertion of the sublime *thauma* of Roman history against a Lucretian world-view in which political and military achievement means nothing'.[61]

The Pompeian oak both maintains and complicates this historicisation of Lucretius' natural sublime. As was noted in Chapter 3, Lucan's presentation of Caesar relocates the sublime progress of

---

[58] Hardie (2009a) 126–9. See also Hardie (1986) 278, 280–2, 372–5.
[59] Hardie (2009b) 169.   [60] Gale (2000) 219–20.   [61] Hardie (2009a) 128.

Epicurus within the sphere of Roman history; in its emphasis on the violence and self-aggrandisement of the Caesarian *cursus*, it also explores the full implications of how a sublimity like that of Epicurus 'tramples' all beneath it. The Pompeian oak, conversely, represents a form of resistance, and hence an alternative sublimity, to Caesar's sublime onslaught. But this is not the sublimity of its immovable Aenean predecessor. Whereas the Aenean oak withstands the blasts of *Fama*, a monstrous goddess allusively likened to a thunderbolt (*Aen.* 4.174–5, cf. Lucr. 6.177, 340–2)[62] and now the driving force behind Dido's entreaties, its Pompeian relative totters and creaks, about to fall (*nutet casura*); destined to be struck down by Caesar's lightning, it offers a prefiguration of Rome's response to Caesarian *fama* (1.466–504). Looking forward to more recent history, Hardie points out how Aeneas' Alpine fixity, echoing that of Atlas, prefigures the way Rome will ultimately 'weather the storm'[63] unleashed by Hannibal, Dido's fellow Carthaginian, when he crosses the Alps. Caesar, by contrast, not only crosses the natural barrier of the Alps (1.83) but goes on to conquer Pompey and Rome itself. Yet, for all that, the Pompeian oak is described as *sublimis*. It attests a sensibility wherein the ruined speaks louder than (and indeed becomes) the monumental, collapse prompting the realisation of immensity. The resistance offered to *Fama* by the Aenean oak is present, solid, tangible. That offered by its Pompeian counterpart against Caesar remains intangible and evanescent; a *magni nominis umbra*, it makes present only what has already been lost. And in thus reworking the Virgilian simile, Lucan brings its Lucretian allusions into contact with the sublime sensibility modelled by Longinus and Ankersmit: like the objects, and subjective states, that Longinus fetishises, the Pompeian oak is 'a body in disintegration';[64] the *umbra* of Pompey's *magnum nomen* conveys something of Walter Benjamin's concept of aura, the idea that, 'paradoxically, something's essence is to be situated only in what it possesses *no longer*'.[65]

---

[62] Hardie (2009a) 71.   [63] Hardie (2009a) 129.   [64] Porter (forthcoming).

[65] Ankersmit (2005) 183. On the affinities between the historical sublime and Benjaminian aura, see further Ankersmit (2005) 180–9; see Benjamin (1999) 215–16, 223. Cf. Hertz (1978/1985) 14.

In his recent study of the relation between sublimity and scepticism, David Sedley identifies a sixteenth-century reworking of Lucan's Pompeian oak that strengthens our appreciation of its sublimity. Discussing the development from the Renaissance concept of wonder, *admiratio*, which equated grandeur with coherence and successful cognition, to that of sublimity, which found grandeur in ruin, fragmentation and cognition's collapse, Sedley quotes Sonnet 28 from Joachim Du Bellay's *Antiquitez de Rome* (1558):

> He that hath seen a great oak dry and dead,
> Yet clad with reliques of some trophies old,
> Lifting to heaven her aged hoary head,
> Whose foot in ground hath left but feeble hold;
> But half disbowel'd lies above the ground,
> Showing her wreathed roots, and naked arms,
> And on her trunk all rotten and unsound
> Only supports herself for meat of worms;
> And though she owe her fall to the first wind,
> Yet of the devout people is adored,
> And many young plants spring out of her rind;
> Who such an oak hath seen, let him record
> That such this city's honour was of yore,
> And 'mongst all cities flourished much more.[66]

As Sedley points out, Lucan's oak tree forms 'the classical basis' of the sonnet; the resemblance between the two texts in fact encourages a specific reading of the sonnet as an adaptation of the Lucanian passage. Du Bellay's use of the 'great oak dry and dead' as a direct image for Rome brings to the surface the Lucanian image's allusions to the descriptions of Rome's ruins in *Bellum civile* 1 and 7. Du Bellay also endeavours to magnify his model's sublimity. 'Like Lucan,' Sedley observes, 'Du Bellay organises his description around a paradox that challenges the opposition between grandeur and ruin.'[67] Where the sensibility of *admiratio* saw classical ruins as a starting point from which to reconstruct the splendours of antiquity, Du Bellay here suggests that the splendour lies in the ruins themselves. Sedley shows how this sublime

---

[66] The translation is Edmund Spenser's (1591), cited by Sedley (2005) 38 with modernised spelling.
[67] Sedley (2005) 39.

paradox is enacted in the sonnet's very structure. In the French the words signifying the tree's disintegration ('panché... esbranché', 'torte... supporte') are also those that anchor the rhyme scheme and so hold the poem together: 'like the oak it describes, sonnet 28 coheres by virtue of its decrepitude'.[68] We remember how in Longinus' Sapphic fragment it is through the speaker's bodily dissolution that the poem achieves wholeness. Turning back to the Lucanian passage, we may notice a similar if less obvious effect: successive phrases denoting the oak's decay (*nec iam validis... nudosque... non frondibus... nutet*, 138–41) appear not at the end of lines but in their centre, visually replicating the gnarled curvature of the trunk.

One of Ankersmit's examples offers another instructive comparison with Lucan's *quercus sublimis*. He quotes a passage from Hölderlin's novel *Hyperion* (1797–9), describing the eponymous protagonist's response on first sighting Athens:

Like an immense shipwreck, when the gales have been hushed and the sailors have fled and the corpse of the shattered fleet lies on the sandbank unrecognisable, so before us lay Athens, and the forsaken pillars stood before us like bare tree trunks of a wood that at evening was still green and, the same night, went up in flames.[69]

As Ankersmit comments, Athens is here, for Hyperion, an irretrievably lost world. Yet the metaphors of the fleet destroyed by a storm and of the fire-ravaged forest are both strangely 'suggestive of seeing a previous state in a later one':

You see the dilapidated fleet or the forest that was burned down, and then you see the original fleet or forest in it. And in both cases the image of the previous state is stronger and more powerful than the later one... There is decrepitude only in order to remind us all the more forcefully of primeval perfection. The metaphors thus invite a way of seeing the world oddly combining the dissolution of an original state with its reconstitution.[70]

In the context of the present discussion, we might add that Hyperion's likening of Athens' 'forsaken pillars' to 'bare tree trunks' recalls, as Du Bellay's sonnet does, the Pompeian *truncus*' evocation of Rome's own ruins, uniting the Republic and its beleaguered

[68] Ibid.   [69] Hölderlin (1990) 70.   [70] Ankersmit (2005) 386.

champion as *sublimis*. At the same time, Hyperion's tranquil vision of shipwreck reminds us of the Epicurean raptures of Lucr. 2.1–4, discussed in Chapter 3, and of the associated image of shipwreck at Lucr. 2.552–9. Not only, in other words, does Hyperion's initial response to Athens evoke the sublimity of the Lucanian narrator's first image of Pompey, it also, like the Lucanian simile's Virgilian precursor, helps us see the relation between this sublimity and that of the Lucretian spectator. Both combine a subjective experience of destitution, of estrangement (what Ankersmit calls disassociation), with a simultaneous sense of recuperation and enlargement.

After Pharsalus (7.647–727)

The sublimity signalled by Pompey's *quercus sublimis* is developed in two subsequent apostrophes. I turn first to the narrator's picture of Pompey following Pharsalus.

Bellum civile 7 shows the Republican leader to be, like the narrator, acutely aware of the world-changing rupture that Pharsalus represents. Before battle, addressing his men, he warns repeatedly of the severity of the situation. His words foreshadow those of the narrator's own lament later in the book. This is, he says, a crisis point (*mundi discrimen*, 7.108–9, cf. 7.617), a day that will bring untold evils upon the world: *quantum scelerum quantumque malorum / in populos lux ista feret!* (7.114–15, cf. 7.407–8). But, if it is battle that his men demand, he is resigned to the ruin that will inevitably follow: *involat populos una fortuna ruina / sitque hominum magnae lux ista novissima parti* (7.89–90, cf. 7.389ff., 630ff.). He knows, moreover, that this ruin will involve him too. At the beginning of the book the narrator observes that the night before the battle marks a dividing line in Pompey's life (*felicis Magno pars ultima vitae*, 7.7, cf. *lux . . . novissima*, 7.90); he is now at the *fine bonorum* (7.19). So before Pharsalus, whether destined to emerge victorious or defeated, Pompey knows his former self is finished: *aut populis invisum hac clade peracta / aut hodie Pompeius erit miserabile nomen* (7.120–1). This day will replace one order of existence with another. As it turns the Latin *nomen* into a *fabula* (7.391–2), so it will change forever what the *nomen* 'Pompey' signifies.

After the battle is over Pompey's prediction is confirmed as, sur-
veying the bloody field, he is himself compelled to condemn the
fortuna that had seen his name raised so high (*tota vix clade coac-
tus / fortunam damnare suam*, 7.648–9). '*Magnus*' has become
infelix (7.647–8, cf. 7.7, 674): already the *magni nominis umbra*
when we first meet him (1.135), Pompey now labours under a
nomen that has acquired the very opposite of its former sense. So
radical, in fact, is this shift that the general's previous self, the old
'Pompey', appears to him as that of someone else: *tot telis sua fata
peti, tot corpora fusa / ac se tam multo pereuntem sanguine vidit*
(7.652–3). As Rome earlier witnessed its own collapse (*ruenti*,
7.418), so Pompey, in a sudden strange moment of derealisation,
here sees himself dying (*pereuntem*). And as earlier the narrator
had addressed Rome directly, pointing how it was amid this collapse that Rome's greatness manifested itself (*quam magna cadas*,
7.419), so here he turns to Pompey to declare that the general's
past self can now, in defeat, be truly known:

> iam pondere fati
> deposito securus abis; nunc tempora laeta
> respexisse vacat, spes numquam inplenda recessit;
> quid fueris nunc scire licet.

> Now you have put aside the weight
> of destiny, and you depart, free from care; now you have leisure to look back
> on happy times; hope has vanished, never to be fulfilled;
> now you may understand what you were.   7.686–9

'What Pompey was' (*quid fueris*) has been severed by Pharsalus
from his present self.[71] His former life is lost forever, all hope (of
victory and, consequently, of a return to the past) vanished. Pompey has become *infelix*; his *tempora laeta* are no longer a state of
being, but have instead become, as Ankersmit puts it, 'an object of
knowledge'[72] (*scire*, 689). This rupture is counterbalanced, however, by a sense of tranquillity. The weight of destiny has been
lifted. In his lion simile at the Rubicon (1.212), and subsequently
at Troy (9.975), Caesar is described as *securus*; the adjective now
attaches to Pompey (687). And, amid this tranquillity, the achievements of the past shine brightly: *aspice securus voltu non supplice*

---

[71] Cf. Feeney (1986/2010) 348.   [72] Ankersmit (2005) 327.

reges, / aspice possessas urbes donataque regna (7.709–10). So earlier, in his mind's eye, the narrator saw the peoples and lands possessed by Rome (*possedit*, 7.420). Once again, the greatness of the Republican past is sensed at the very moment of its loss. Other details in the description of the fleeing Pompey augment this recuperative movement. He remains unbroken (*nec fractum adversa*, 684); the inhabitants of Larisa witness his ruin but not his defeat (*vidit prima tuae testis Larisa ruinae / nobile nec victum fatis caput*, 712–13) and run out to greet him as though he were victorious (*ceu laeto*, 715; cf. 687). Despite Pompey's predictions and the subsequent merging of the epithets *magnus* and *infelix* (7.120–1, 647–9), the narrator now assures him that his *nomen* still carries power (*scilicet inmenso superest ex nomine multum*, 717; cf. *salvaque verendus / maiestate dolor*, 680–1); the dissociation of identity that Pharsalus has caused highlights and hence, according to the logic of the sublime, perpetuates his previous greatness. Pompey is now inferior only to his former self (*teque minor solo*, 718).

The end (8.692–711, 793–872)

At the conclusion of Book 8, Pompey's defeat and flight culminates in his death and burial. It is in the narrator's response to these events that the sublime sensibility we have been tracing finds its fullest expression. As with the discrepancies between Pompey's words and actions and the narrator's perception of them, so here it is in the apostrophe's famous inconsistency that we can detect the signs of its sublimity.[73]

The narrator begins by lamenting the indignity and ingloriousness of Pompey's end:

> ultima Lageae stirpis perituraque proles,
> degener incestae sceptris cessure sorori,
> cum tibi sacrato Macedon servetur in antro
> et regum cineres extructo monte quiescant,   695

---

[73] Cf. Mayer (1981) 185: 'at one moment Pompey's tomb is a disgrace, at the next a glory; now an object of pilgrimage, now lost to sight'; 'it is as if the poet's words were the exact reflection of his uncontrolled thoughts'; see also Feeney (1986/2010) 351.

cum Ptolemaeorum manes seriemque pudendam
pyramides claudant indignaque Mausolea,
litora Pompeium feriunt, truncusque vadosis
huc illuc iactatur aquis. adeone molesta
totum cura fuit socero servare cadaver?   700
hac Fortuna fide Magni tam prospera fata
pertulit, hac illum summo de culmine rerum
morte petit cladesque omnis exegit in uno
saeva die quibus inmunes tot praestitit annos,
Pompeiusque fuit qui numquam mixta videret   705
laeta malis, felix nullo turbante deorum
et nullo parcente miser; semel inpulit illum
dilata Fortuna manu. pulsatur harenis,
carpitur in scopulis hausto per volnera fluctu,
ludibrium pelagi, nullaque manente figura   710
una nota est Magno capitis iactura revolsi.

Last offspring, soon to perish, of the stock of Lagus,
degenerate and soon to yield the sceptre to your impure sister,
though you preserve the Macedonian in consecrated cave,
and the ashes of the kings find rest beneath a piled-up mountain,
though shades of Ptolemies and their disgraceful line
are enclosed in Pyramids and Mausoleums too good for them,
the shores strike Pompey, and his headless corpse is tossed
this way and that by shallow waters. Was it such a nuisance
to keep his body whole for his father-in-law?
With this good faith Fortune to the end maintained the destiny
so prosperous of Magnus, with this she summoned him in death
from the highest peak, and brutally in a single day she made him pay
for all the disasters from which she gave him so many years of freedom;
and Pompey was a man who never saw joy and hardship
mixed: when fortunate he was disturbed by none of the gods,
when miserable spared by none; at one go Fortune knocked him down
with the hand she had so long restrained. He is battered on the sands,
torn to pieces on the rocks while drinking in the water through his wounds,
the plaything of the sea, and when no distinctive shape remains
the single mark of Magnus is the absence of the torn-off head.   8.692–711

The measure of Pompey's ruin is vertical. Mountainous monuments cover the ashes of the Pharaohs, pyramids and mausoleums
enclose the shades of the Ptolemies, but Pompey's headless corpse
has been left for the sea to batter (694–9), a *ludibrium pelagi* (710).
Reflecting on the vagaries of *Fortuna*, the narrator's words again
recall his response to Pharsalus: as *Fortuna* undid Rome's long

years of prosperity (*prospera fata*, 7.420) in a single day (*retro tua fata tulit par omnibus annis / Emathiae funesta dies*, 7.426–7), so she has now shattered Pompey's *prospera fata* (701), pulling him abruptly (*in uno / saeva die*, 703–4, cf. *semel*, 707) down from the highest peak of success (*summo de culmine rerum*, 702). The makeshift tomb that Pompey's companion Cordus subsequently erects only serves to accentuate how far the general has fallen:

> surgit miserabile bustum
> non ullis plenum titulis, non ordine tanto
> fastorum; solitumque legi super alta deorum
> culmina et extructos spoliis hostilibus arcus
> haud procul est ima Pompei nomen harena   820
> depressum tumulo, quod non legat advena rectus,
> quod nisi monstratum Romanus transeat hospes.

> A pitiable tomb arises,
> not full of any honours or the sequence of his annals
> so immense; and Pompey's name, which people were accustomed to read
> above the lofty roof-tops of the gods and arches built
> with enemy's plunder, is not far from the lowest sand, placed so low
> upon the grave that stranger may not read it standing upright,
> that Roman visitor would pass it by if it were not pointed out.   8.816–22

surgit miserabile bustum (816): verb and adjective are juxtaposed in bitter irony. Pompey's *nomen*, formerly in full view high up on the gods' temples (*super alta deorum / culmina*, 818–19) and victory arches (*extructos ... arcus*, 819; cf. *extructo monte*, 695), is now barely visible at the bottom of a humble headstone (*depressum tumulo*, 821), so near the 'lowest sand' (*ima ... harena*, 820), in fact, that were it not pointed out, and if he failed to stoop and peer, the casual tourist would miss it (821–2). Pompey earlier feared that his name would become *miserabile* or *invisum* (7.120–1) but something even worse has happened: his *nomen* is now practically invisible.

Within the terms of this contrast, however, there are indications of a response that sees more than a great leader brought permanently low. Egypt's pyramids, like mountains, were notably sublime things for Kant. Lucan's narrator introduces them in opposition to Pompey's *truncus* (698) but this opposition also recalls

Pompey's opening simile and its allusions to Aeneas as an Atlas-like Alpine oak. There, it was precisely the ruined status of the Pompeian *truncus* that made it something sublime and, the verbal echo leads us to infer, for all the ostensible, lofty magnificence of the graves of Egypt's rulers, it is Pompey's headless corpse that is here the genuinely potent object. The narrator's meditation upon *Fortuna*'s changeability strengthens this paradox. Pharsalus showed *Fortuna* ultimately to have wrought Rome's collapse but it was also because of *Fortuna*'s machinations that Rome's greatness became ultimately apparent: *munera longi / explicat eripiens aevi* (7.416–17). *Fortuna*'s hand swoops down on Pompey to similar effect: *semel inpulit illum / dilata Fortuna manu* (8.707–8); the contrast between *inpulit* and *dilata*, like that between *explicat* and *eripiens*, makes former greatness negatively palpable. As after Pharsalus (*quid fueris nunc scire licet*, 7.689), what Pompey was becomes clear: *Pompeiusque fuit qui numquam mixta videret / laeta malis* (8.705–6). Greatness makes its presence felt, even grows greater, through its sudden, startling absence. Pompey's precipitous fall allows us to see the full scale of the heights he previously attained.

This realisation has a striking effect on the narrator's perception of the grave that Cordus makes for his leader. Any monument marking the place of Pompey's burial, he says, should display all Pompey's mighty achievements:

> quod si tam sacro dignaris nomine saxum
> adde actus tantos monimentaque maxuma rerum,
> adde trucis Lepidi motus Alpinaque bella
> armaque Sertori revocato consule victa
> et currus quos egit eques, commercia tuta   810
> gentibus et pavidos Cilicas maris, adde subactam
> barbariem gentesque vagas et quidquid in Euro
> regnorum Boreaque iacet. dic semper ab armis
> civilem repetisse togam, ter curribus actis
> contentum multos patriae donasse triumphos.   815

> But if you think the rock is worthy of such a sacred name,
> then list his exploits so immense, memorials of his mightiest deeds,
> fierce Lepidus' upheavals and the Alpine war,
> the conquered army of Sertorius when the consul was recalled,
> the chariots he drove while still a knight, trade secure

for the nations and Cilicians frightened of the sea; the conquest
of the barbarian world and nomad races and all the realms
which lie in the east and in the north. Say that always after warfare
he returned to the toga of the citizen, that, content with driving chariots
three times, he waived his claim to many triumphs for his fatherland.

8.806–15

The urgent repeated imperatives (*adde, adde, adde, dic*) underscore how strongly the magnificence of these achievements now
presses upon the narrator. He wants a monument on a grand scale –
something like Egypt's pyramids. Yet, after cataloguing Pompey's
exploits for nine lines, he abruptly asks, 'What grave can hold all
this?' (*quis capit haec tumulus?* 816). Pompey's greatness turns out
to exceed the memorialising capacity of even the grandest tomb.
In attempting adequately to re-present Pompey's greatness, any
such edifice succeeds only in imposing limits upon it and, hence,
diminishing it. Enabling us to touch something whose essence lies
in its intangibility, the great monument paradoxically flattens the
greatness it would commemorate. This places the humble grave
constructed by Cordus in a new light. Far from being just a dusty
stone, unnoticed by the passing traveller (821–2), it will attract
visitors from far and wide: *quem non tumuli venerabile saxum /
et cinis in summis forsan turbatus harenis / avertet*[*?*] (855–7).
More than this, the narrator tells Pompey, 'in no way will that
grave impair your fame: if you were buried in temples and in
gold you would be a less precious shade' (*nil ista nocebunt /
famae busta tuae: templis auroque sepultus / vilior umbra fores*,
858–60). 'Temples and gold' glances back at the comparison of
Pompey's *truncus* with the tombs of Egypt's rulers (695–7) but
here the effect of the comparison is reversed. Instead of testifying
to Pompey's ruin, this lowly grave allows Pompey's grandeur to
become fully manifest. This grandeur asserts itself even against
that of his victorious enemy: *augustius aris / victoris Libyco pulsatur in aequore saxum* (861–2); Pompey's humble headstone will
be beaten by the waves, like his *truncus* (*pulsatur*, 708), yet it will
rise higher than Caesar's altars (*augustius* perhaps putting us in
mind of the name taken by Caesar's successor). The *saxum* erected
by Cordus will thus succeed in doing what the grand *saxum* of the
narrator's imaginary monument (806) could never have achieved.

223

quis capit haec tumulus? surgit miserabile bustum ('What grave can hold all this? A pitiable tomb arises', 816): in retrospect the three words following the narrator's question seem less ironic than a genuine expression of the grave's power. Pompey's pitiable tomb, it transpires, is the very thing that is uniquely able to encompass his greatness. As such, it is a monument that truly 'surges'.[74]

Pompey's tomb is thus presented by the narrator as being miserable, shameful, a marker of despair and loss, and at the same time something magnificent, demanding adoration, something that soars above both the great tombs of Egypt and Caesar's own altars. Ruin becomes grandeur, the unnoticed grave a pilgrimage site, the low high. This dialectic is expressed most powerfully and succinctly in the very words that Cordus carves on Pompey's headstone: *hic situs est Magnus* (793).[75] The sound of the sentence suggests weight and fixity: the rhythmic alternation of monosyllable and disyllable, the nominatives' consonance and rhyming assonance. As Martha Malamud has pointed out, however, the epitaph's meaning is not so easy to hold down.[76] The most obvious rendering would be, simply, 'Here lies Magnus.' But, reading *situs* as a noun ('dust', 'decay' or 'a wasting away') rather than a past participle, and *Magnus* as a common adjective rather than as a metonym for Pompey, we might also notice in the words a bitter acknowledgement of the paltry, squalid nature of Pompey's burial: 'Here is great decay.' And a further interpretation presents itself too, based on the other primary sense of *situs* as a noun ('position', 'structure'), an interpretation paradoxically gesturing towards grandeur: 'Here is a mighty tomb.' Besides naming the grave, Pompey's bald, laconic epitaph thus manages to mark it in

---

[74] Cf. Thomas (2007) 199–200 and Porter (2010) 516 on the tomb of the Flavii at Cillium in Tunisia (*c.* 150 AD), a monument with aspirations such as those fleetingly entertained by the Lucanian narrator at 8.806–15: *aetherias surgunt monimenta per auras*, and so, the Flavii's inscription proclaims, 'honour stands sublime' (*stat sublimis*); Lucan's account of Pompey's burial is based upon an altogether less concrete, and more powerful, version of sublimity. On the relations between the *Peri hupsous* and Roman architecture of the second century AD, see further Thomas (2007) 219, 238–40.

[75] Deguy (1993) 10: 'There is always . . . a relation between the sublime and the testamentary. Sublime words are words of the end.'

[76] Malamud (1995) 178.

opposite ways simultaneously.[77] The presence of the one construction within the other, the combination of collapse and exaltation, of hasty burial and cultic splendour, is what I have been describing in this chapter as the sublime and is what drives the narrator's eventual recognition that, paradoxically, the grandeur of Pompey's grave cannot be separated from its ruinous state.

And more: the epitaph also reminds us that this sublimity underpins Pompey's *nomen*. That his status as *magnus* is in a crucial sense predicated upon his fall has already been suggested by the oak tree simile and in the narrator's apostrophe to Pompey following Pharsalus. Cordus sets this dynamic in stone. Taking *situs* as a noun, the epitaph could be read as a blunt, and startling, equation of Magnus with his tomb or, worse, with rot, putrefaction and the other processes of decay. A corpse is now all that Magnus is; the epithet itself seems to crumble under the irony. But as a verb *situs* nudges the epitaph in a subtly different direction, inviting us to understand not simply that 'Magnus lies here' but that Pompey's status as *magnus* is founded upon (*situs est*) his dead body and less than illustrious tomb: it is not that Pompey's *magnitudo* has perished but, rather, that it is here, on a forsaken stretch of the Egyptian shoreline, that it is truly situated. Pompey's name, like his grave in the narrator's final estimation, is now indeed great, *magnus*.[78] As in Book 7 Rome's greatness manifested itself most fully amid the city's collapse (*quam magna cadas*, 7.419), so it is only in death that the true stature of Pompey's sublime *nomen* emerges. Like the Roman traveller whom he imagines passing the grave and failing to notice Pompey's *nomen* (8.820–2), the narrator at first fails to read the magnitude that the epitaph proclaims (8.694ff.). It is only when he looks again, when he 'stoops down' to read more carefully, that he realises that this *situs* is truly, sublimely *magnus*, a constituent part of Magnus' sublimity.

Yet the narrator's initial response to Cordus' efforts is telling. Echoing the formula of the epitaph, his words seem designed as

---

[77] Cf. Fowler (2000) 197–8 on the double edge that the word *situ* also gives to Horace's *exegi monumentum aere perennius / regalique situ pyramidum altius* (*Carm.* 3.30.1–2).

[78] Cf. Due (1962) 111; Brisset (1964) 124; Lintott (1971/2010) 264; Feeney (1986/2010) 351; Norbrook (1999) 31.

a direct riposte: while the headstone claims *hic situs est Magnus*,
the narrator asserts:

> situs est qua terra extrema refuso
> pendet in Oceano; Romanum nomen et omne
> imperium Magno tumuli est modus.

> He is buried where furthest earth floats
> on Ocean flowing back; the name of Rome and all its empire
> is the limit of his grave for Magnus.   8.797–9

At one level, the claim that Pompey's tomb is co-extensive with the
Rome he championed serves to emphasise all the more poignantly
that both Republic and general have ceased to be: the *modus*,
the boundary, of the Republic is precisely what Caesar's revolutionary *motus* has destroyed; the Roman *nomen* is no longer
a live concept but merely a *fabula* (7.391–2). Yet the narrator's
words also construct Rome's *nomen* and *imperium* as indexes
of Pompey's continuing greatness. The dead Republican champion can be accommodated only by the entire Roman world:
his tomb touches the very 'furthest earth'. This *modus*, so broad
and abstract as to be paradoxically without measure, what Kant
would call 'absolute magnitude', is the only limitation Pompey's
grave will admit. In its paradoxical, *modus*-less construction, this
non-monument offers a disorienting, scale-confounding mirror-
image to the apocalypse envisioned by the narrator as a sublime correlate of civil war at the beginning of Book 1;[79] but
where the narrator's vast, all-encompassing vision of the destruction of *modus* (1.82) pointed towards the annihilation of the
Republic, here Pompey's exiguous resting place, as it rises above
the constraints of *modus*, counterfactually denies the Republic's
obliteration.

In structural terms, the double vision of 8.797–9 is not dissimilar from that of Pompey's epitaph. Reaching for the sublime, both
Cordus and the narrator wrench majesty from abjection. But where
Cordus' inscription fixes Pompey's remains in one specific location
(*hic*, 793), the narrator's point is that the Republic's dead champion

---

[79] See Chapter 2. Cf. the limitless extent of Phemonoe's knowledge: *non modus Oceani, numerus non derat harenae* (5.182).

cannot be so easily contained. 'Reckless hand, why do you thrust
a grave on Magnus and confine his roaming shade?' (*temeraria
dextra, / cur obicis Magno tumulum manesque vagantis/ includis?*
(795–7). The physical attempt to mark and hence contain (*obicis*,
includis) Pompey's greatness is bound only to defuse it. This is the
problem with the grand monument briefly desired by the narrator.
In attempting, and failing, to capture (*capit*, 816) what Pompey
was, it would end up limiting his greatness and precluding sublimity. The grave made by Cordus, on the other hand, *is* eventually
recognised as a fitting conduit of the sublime. Pompey is *inclusum*
(864), precisely what the narrator objects to at 797 (*includis*), but
still he rises higher than Caesar's altars (and it is Caesar who at the
poem's end finds himself stuck inside the Egyptian palace, under
siege and unable to move, 10.542–3, cf. 10.445).[80]

Yet the narrator cannot entirely shake the impulse behind his first
response and the fantasy of non-burial returns, insistent, in the final
lines of the book. As it stands, Pompey's grave 'does nothing to
damage' his fame (*nil ista nocebunt*, 858) but its makeshift nature
will prove an even bigger boon in time to come:

proderit hoc olim, quod non mansura futuris   865
ardua marmoreo surrexit pondere moles.
pulveris exigui sparget non longa vetustas
congeriem, bustumque cadet, mortisque peribunt
argumenta tuae. veniet felicior aetas
qua sit nulla fides saxum monstrantibus illud;   870
atque erit Aegyptus populis fortasse nepotum
tam mendax Magni tumulo quam Creta Tonantis.

One day this will be to your advantage, that no lofty pile
with marble mass arose, to last into the future.
No lengthy time will scatter the heap of tiny
dust, the tomb will fall, and of your death
the evidence will vanish. A happier age will come,
when the people pointing out that rock will not be believed;
and Egypt in the eyes of the crowds of our descendants will be perhaps
as false about the grave of Magnus as Crete about the Thunderer's.

8.865–72

[80] See Chapter 3.

227

The idea that Pompey's grave is in fact an abstract entity, something intangible that pervades the ether, commensurate only with Rome's incomparable *imperium* and *nomen*, is restated here as a prediction that the physical tomb constructed by Cordus will soon vanish, leaving men pointing to empty space. This is the ultimate vision of sublime restitution, Pompey's true grandeur arising from his final negation.

Speculating upon the Longinian feeling for the sublime, as evidenced for instance in Pausanias but also, much further back, in the Homeric epics, Porter writes:

> Nowhere are the sites of memory more compelling than where they are least visibly supported, as in the example of empty sepulchres, which are literal monuments to memory, or else in those unmistakable signs of absence, mere gaping holes. At the furthest remove are the ultimate kinds of remains, those that are denoted not by missing objects but by their absence – that is, by pure loss – and that thus designate *the very loss of loss*. Remains like these, overwhelmingly oppressive in their felt material presence, are the most resistant to the project of description and therefore the sublimest sites of all.[81]

Porter later connects this sublimity with the *Bellum civile*'s vision of Troy's remains: *etiam periere ruinae* (9.969).[82] These vanished ruins, we have seen, are not merely what Troy has become; in Lucan's poem they point also towards Caesar's annihilation of Rome and the Republic, a ghost-land in which 'Gabii, Veii, Cora hardly will be indicated by their dust-covered ruins' (*Gabios Veiosque Coramque / pulvere vix tectae poterunt monstrare ruinae*, 7.392–3); they point, that is, towards the malign effects of the future dictator's sublimity. Lucan's paradoxical description of Pompey's burial both anticipates the vanished ruins of Troy-Rome and allows us to experience their annihilation differently. 'The single mark of Magnus is the absence of the turn-off head' (*una nota*

---

[81] Porter (2001) 74, cf. Porter (2010) 478; see Paus. 10.33.8 ('no ruins of Parapotamii remained in my time, *and the very spot on which the city stood is forgotten*', Porter's translation); Hom. *Il.* 2.811–14. Porter (2010) 515–16 identifies comparable sentiments at Thuc. 6.54.7, Enn. *Ann.* 404–6 Skutsch, Catul. 68.89–94, Ov. *Met.* 1.260–415, 15.424, Plin. *Ep.* 6.10.3–5, Juv. 10.146, Aus. *Epigr.* 37, *Anth. Pal.* 7.478, 7.479; see further Davis (1958); Scodel (1992) 66–7; Woolf (1996) 25–6.

[82] Porter (2010) 516. Cf. Martindale (1999) 247, in relation to Freud's comparison between the city of Rome and the human mind (Freud 2002: 7–9), on Rome's paradigmatic status as 'at once the site of historical change and the *urbs aeterna*'.

est Magno capitis iactura revolsi, 711), observes the narrator. In its designation of identity as a function loss, its construction of absence as an indication of presence, this aperçu perfectly conjures a sublimity that is at once the reflection and the antithesis of the sublimity generated by Caesar. *nota est... iactura* ('the mark is... absence'). In *Bellum civile* 2 the nameless old man saw himself plunged again into the nightmare of the Marian–Sullan war, searching fearfully amid the piles of decapitated corpses for his brother's severed head (*memini... perque omnis truncos, cum qua cervice recisum / conveniat, quaesisse caput*, 2.169–73):[83] the bodies have all lost their features (*iam tabe fluunt confusaque tempore multo / amisere notas*, 2.166–7); we are not told whether he found what he was looking for. With Pompey's headless body, wherein *iactura* itself becomes a *nota*, this loss is redeemed: the loss of the Republic is itself lost and so becomes sublime; dismemberment and remembrance, rupture and recuperation merge one into the other.[84] We remember the *umbra* of Pompey's *magnum nomen* (1.135): 'paradoxically, something's essence is to be situated in what it possesses *no longer*'.[85]

There is one last aspect to this vision of Pompey as an absent presence that reinforces its sublimity. In the previous chapter I argued that Caesar's antagonistic attitude towards, and encroachment upon the position of, the gods forms an important element in his construction as sublime superman. At the end of Book 8 it is Pompey who comes to attain divine status. We saw previously

---

[83] He is not alone: others too *pavido subducit cognita furto* (2.168); cf. Cordus' fearful and hasty execution of Pompey's burial rites (*e latebris pavidus decurrit*, 8.715; *ille ordine rupto / funeris attonitus latebras in litore quaerit*, 8.779–80; *semusta rapit resolutaque nondum / ossa satis nervis*, 8.786).

[84] For a much later version of this topos, see Sedley (2005) 28–9, 40–2 on Montaigne's response in his *Journal de Voyage* (1580–1) to Rome's ruins (Montaigne 1957: 79–80). Attempting to destroy the city, Rome's enemies 'shattered all the parts of [its] wonderful body'; but, though mutilated, Rome still exerted its power and so its enemies buried its very ruins, leaving only a 'sepulchre' visible – hardly even that, for 'the sepulchre itself was for the most part buried'. Yet even this sepulchre exerts a force. This force is the sublime: it surpasses the effects of physical coherence or visibility; indeed, it is a function of 'the shortcomings of all references to the grandeur that paradoxically constitutes the subject of a discourse unable to refer to it' (Sedley 2005: 42). It is a function not of knowledge but of uncertainty. Hence, too, the Lucanian narrator's prayer for a time when there will be *nulla fides* (8.870) in the site of Pompey's 'sepulchre' and its sublimity will truly shine forth.

[85] Ankersmit (2005) 183.

how Longinus describes Demosthenes' sublime invocation of the dead of Marathon as an act of 'deification' (ἀποθεώσας, *De sub.* 16.2). As Porter notes, 'capturing thematic moments of near death and resurrection . . . the sublime passes over into the realm of the numinous, the supernatural and the divine'.[86] That the narrator's presentation of Pompey can be assimilated within this discourse of sublimity is initially suggested by the oak to which the Republican leader is likened in Book 1. The tree is described both as *sublimis* (1.136) and as an object of cult: it bears generals' *sacrata . . . dona* (1.137–8) and is worshipped (*colitur*, 1.143) by the people. As the oak's *truncus* looks forward to Pompey's own transformation into a headless *truncus*, rolling on the shore of Egypt, so this sanctity is stressed again at Pompey's death: amid his murderers' blows, we are told, 'the majestic beauty of his sacred features lasted' (*permansisse decus sacrae venerabile formae*, 8.664); as the assassin Septimius prepares to sever Pompey's head, our gaze is repeatedly drawn to Pompey's *sacros . . . voltus* (8.669), his *sacrum caput* (8.677), his *verenda / . . . coma* (8.679–80). The sanctity of the Pompeian oak was derived in large measure from its decrepit status: unlike stronger surrounding trees, it totters, about to fall beneath the blasts of the wind, yet still is honoured. So in Book 8 it is at the moment of decapitation that the sanctity of Pompey's head glows brightest.

The numinous effects of a structure of feeling that derives presence from absence also permeate the narrator's enraptured response to Pompey's grave. Its paltriness prompts him to equate the Republican champion with 'the highest deity': *nunc est pro numine summo / hoc tumulo Fortuna iacens* (8.860–1). Indeed, the narrator predicts, the grave will become a pilgrimage site, its *venerabile saxum* (8.855) taking precedence over the shrine of Casian Jupiter (858). Earlier, however, the narrator had argued that Pompey's divinity was what prevented him from being contained by a single stone: *si tota est Herculis Oete / et iuga tota vacant Bromio Nyseia, quare / unus in Aegypto Magni lapis?* (8.800–2). Like the preceding equation of Pompey's grave with the unboundedness

---

[86] Porter (forthcoming).

of Rome itself, this comparison works to highlight incomparability: elevated alongside the supra-mortal majesty of Hercules and Bacchus, Pompey's greatness exceeds localised commemoration or material inscription. The idea is reiterated in the book's final couplet as the narrator foretells a time when people will not believe Egypt to be the site of Pompey's tomb any more than Crete to be that of Jupiter. Pompey could no more have a place of burial than the immortal king of the gods. Divine existence is confined by neither time nor place.

Through these intimations of divinity, moreover, Pompey's sublimity is brought, again, into direct opposition with that of Caesar. Divinity was precisely the status that Caesar aspired towards, but Pompey in his humble grave now rises higher than his enemy's altars (8.861–2). Even more striking is the following reference to the thunderbolt: *Tarpeis qui saepe deis sua tura negarunt / inclusum Tusco venerantur caespite fulmen* (863–4). The *fulmen*, the subject of Caesar's introductory simile and a central motif of the Caesarian sublime, is here associated with Pompey: as an object of worship, lodged in the Tuscan soil and contrasting with the established divinities of the Tarpeian rock, it is framed as a correlative to Pompey himself and his unmonumental burial in Egyptian sand. Here, already dead and soon to disappear from the poem completely, Pompey finally separates Caesar from sole possession of one of sublimity's most enduring symbols.

The last word of Book 8 is Jupiter's characteristic epithet, *Tonantis* (872), associating the lightning-wielder *par excellence* (*pace* Caesar's aspirations) with the dead Pompey. Still sounding in our ears, the epithet recurs in the description of Pompey's katasterism at the beginning of Book 9, where it is repeated in the same case and position at the end of the line. The association between Pompeian sublimity and divinity here reaches its apogee:[87]

> at non in Pharia manes iacuere favilla
> nec cinis exiguus tantam conpescuit umbram;
> prosiluit busto semustaque membra relinquens
> degeneremque rogum sequitur convexa Tonantis.

---

[87] Cheney (2009) 128 considers this passage 'Lucan's most memorable representation of the sublime'.

qua niger astriferis conectitur axibus aer   5
quodque patet terras inter lunaeque meatus,
semidei manes habitant, quos ignea virtus
innocuos vita patientes aetheris imi
fecit et aeternos animam collegit in orbes:
non illuc auro positi nec ture sepulti   10
perveniunt.

But his shade did not lie in Pharian embers
nor did the scanty ash imprison such a mighty ghost;
it leapt up from the tomb and, leaving half-burnt limbs
and the ignoble pyre, it heads for the Thunderer's dome.
Where dark air – all that space opening out between the earth
and paths of the moon – is linked to starry skies,
live the half-divine shades, who, innocent in life,
are enabled by their fiery excellence to bear the lower
ether, their spirit gathered into the eternal spheres:
somewhere people laid in gold or buried with incense
do not reach.   9.1–11

Abandoning his earthly self, Pompey is transfigured heavenward.
The narrator's previous assertion that Pompey's greatness cannot
be encompassed by any grave is finally confirmed. Although dead
he is not gone. Transferred to the breasts of Brutus and Cato
(9.17–18), Pompey's absent presence will enable the Republic to
live on.

Pompey's katasterism, then, can properly be conceived as carrying into Book 9 and extending the current of sublimity that has
been building throughout the final section of Book 8. And we
have seen this effect before, near the poem's beginning, when the
rapture of the Bacchic *matrona* and her prophetic vision swept
over from the closing lines of Book 1 into the narrator's mutant
prophecy at the start of Book 2. There, the jump in the text served
to underscore the metapoetic ἔκστασις of the *matrona*. Similarly
here, as it compels the reader to hover momentarily between
books and to recognise the connection between them, the physical
gap in the text itself mimics and generates the sublimity that the
account of Pompey's katasterism describes. This time, moreover,
our reading follows the upward arc of Pompey's aerial progress:

it is on the *far* side of the book break that his katasterism takes place.[88]

This replay of the end of Book 1 encourages us to look once again at the *matrona*'s flight. The death and burial of Pompey appear among the other major events of the civil war encompassed by her vision: *hunc ego, fluminea deformis truncus harena / qui iacet, agnosco* (1.685–6). How is the sublimity of this *truncus* as the narrator himself sees it in Book 8, and the corresponding sublimity of Pompey's comparison to the *truncus* of an oak, related to that of the *matrona*? We saw in Chapter 2 how the *matrona* offers a metapoetic image for the sublimity of the experience of composing the *Bellum civile* and, consequently, for the proclaimed sublimity of our own response to the poem. This experience, I have argued, pivots partly around the loss of the Republican past, symbolised most potently in Pompey's murder. The *matrona*'s recognition of Pompey's decapitated corpse makes the same point. Her flight not only anticipates that of Pompey's katasterised soul[89] but also enacts the sublime affect generated by his *truncus*. As such, it offers a compelling image for the sublime progress that I have endeavoured to trace in this chapter.

---

[88] I owe the development of the thoughts in this paragraph to a conversation with Hector Reyes at the conference on 'Ancient Aesthetics and Social Class' held at the Institute of Classical Studies, London, on 5 July 2011.

[89] So Cheney (2009) 49.

EPILOGUE

Switch back to the beginnning of the poem and forward nearly sixteen hundred years, from the world of Neronian Rome to that of seventeenth-century England, when the outbreak of another civil war saw Lucan achieve new political prominence: at the beginning of the conflict in July 1642 Bulstrode Whitelocke, speaking as a leading Parliamentarian in the House of Commons, quoted the opening three lines of the *Bellum civile*, urging his hearers' support for the Republican cause.[1] And Whitelocke was by no means alone in his use of Lucan at this time: the *Bellum civile* functioned as a source of inspiration and quotation for many writers during the civil war, among their number the soldier William Waller, the polymath Samuel Hartlib and the theologian Joshua Sprigge.[2] As Norbrook has observed, 'for Lucan's admirers, the battles of the Roman civil war were still being fought'.[3]

But it did not need the English civil war for Lucan to be read, and read with intensity. Thomas May's translation of the *Bellum civile*, for instance, published in 1627, prompted an encomium from Ben Jonson. Prefiguring Marvell's response to *Paradise Lost*,[4] with which this book began, Jonson hymns the affinity with Lucan displayed by May in terms that reveal an awareness of both poets' participation in the sublime, which in turn inspires Jonson with sublimity:

> When Rome, I read thee in thy mighty pair,
> And see both climbing up the slippery stair
> Of Fortune's wheel, by Lucan driv'n about,
> And the world in it, I begin to doubt,
> At every line some pin thereof should slack   5

---

[1] Norbrook (1999) 23–4, 214.   [2] See Norbrook (1999) 24–5, 186.

[3] Norbrook (1999) 48. It is, I suggest, no coincidence that the first English translation of Longinus, composed by John Hall in 1652, was dedicated to Whitelocke.

[4] See Shifflett (1996).

At least, if not the general engine crack.
But when again I view the parts so pays'd ...
. . .
It makes me, ravish'd with just wonder, cry
What Muse, or rather God of harmony,
Taught Lucan these true modes!   15
. . .
But who hath them interpreted, and brought
Lucan's whole frame unto us, and so wrought,   20
As not the smallest joint, or gentlest word
In the great mass, or machine there is stirr'd?
The self same Genius! so the work will say.[5]

Anxiety that Lucan, and so May, will fail in the dizzying task upon which they have embarked, expressed in language evocative of Lucan's own description of Rome's *discors machina* ('the general engine crack'), gives way to 'ravishment' and 'wonder' at the success of both poets' endeavours, a success that, following the Longinian ideal of intersubjectivity, has caused May practically to become one with Lucan ('the self same Genius'), thus allowing him to bring 'Lucan's whole frame unto us', conjuring the long-dead poet back to life.[6]

May's achievement is not necessarily as singular as Jonson would have us believe. Jonson's estimation of May's translation might equally apply to Du Bellay's powerful response in the previous century to the Lucanian comparison of Pompey to an oak tree (discussed in Chapter 4), a reading that moved Spenser to translate Du Bellay's sonnet in turn. Overshadowing both May and Du Bellay, perhaps, is Marlowe's translation, *Lucan's First Book*, whose 'massive sublimity', revealed in Marlowe's rendering of Caesar's lightning simile and throughout, renders it, in the view of one recent critic, the 'first and finest ever Englishing of Lucan'.[7]

We explored in Chapter 2 how Lucan constructs the *Bellum civile* as something sublime: sublimity underpins its theme of civil war, its representation of its own composition, and the effect it will have on its readers. Jonson's appraisal of May's translation, like those of Marlowe and Du Bellay, reveals this effect in action.

[5] Jonson, 'To my Chosen Friend, the Learned Translator of Lucan, Thomas May, Esquire'.
[6] Sedley (2005) 130.   [7] Hooley (2008) 253. Cf. Cheney (2009) 42–9.

In giving renewed life to the poem through the intensity – the sublimity – of his own response to it, each poet voices a cognitive and emotional connection with Lucan whereby he is able to make present (again) the *Bellum civile*'s unpresentable subject. As Pompey's ultimate disappearance awaits the future for full realisation (8.865–72), so Lucan claims, 'future ages will read me and you; our Pharsalia shall live' (*venturi me teque legent; Pharsalia nostra / vivet*, 9.985–6). In their different ways, May, Du Bellay and Marlowe – through the responses of their own readers and admirers – prove these assertions true.[8]

This book has explored the ways in which the *Bellum civile* generates and models such sublimity. The division between a Caesarian sublime, associated with the natural world and with tyranny, and a Pompeian sublime, associated with history and with freedom, is necessarily schematic. This division, however, has I hope kept in focus my objectives: to highlight the connections between, and the value in reading together, Longinian and post-classical theorisations of the sublime; to demonstrate the politically and ethically Janus-faced quality of these theorisations, considered both individually and collectively; to reveal the precise contours of the *Bellum civile*'s sublimity and, in so doing, to establish its position within the Western tradition as a foundational text of the sublime.

This deliberate separation of the ideological components of Lucan's sublime should not, however, blind us to the way in which, despite their position as conductors for the *Bellum civile*'s antithetical political positions, Pompey and Caesar at the level of the aesthetic are endowed with a strange unity. *par quod semper habemus, / libertas et Caesar* (7.695–6): ideologically, the civil war has for Lucan established 'freedom and Caesar' – (the dead) Pompey and tyranny – in perpetual opposition; aesthetically, in their effulgent sublimity, this extraordinary pair exert over the poet's soul an inextricable attraction, at once informing and superseding his politics. As Jean-Luc Nancy observes, borrowing the phrasing of Georges Bataille, the art of the sublime is 'indissociably "art expressive of anguish" and "that expressive of joy"'.[9] It is not simply that the sublimes of Caesar and of Pompey contribute in equal

---

[8] Cf. Henderson (1987/2010) 452.   [9] Nancy (1993b) 52.

measure to the sublimity of the *Bellum civile*; these contributions
are twin sides of the same aesthetic phenomenon.

I have on several occasions mentioned in passing the paintings
of Barnett Newman. I would like to end by referring to him once
more. Newman's vast, abstract canvases of the 1950s and 1960s,
divided by thin, lightning-like lines or 'zips', bearing titles such
as *Now*, *Here* and *Vir Heroicus Sublimis*, provide Lyotard with
a paradigmatic example of the presentation of the unpresentable,
instantiating the difference between being and non-existence.[10]
Without the flash of the zip, 'there would be nothing, or there
would be chaos. The flash (like the instant) is always there and
never there.'[11] This epiphany, I suggest, offers a visual metaphor
for the sublimity of the *Bellum civile*. 'Like a flash of lightning in
the darkness',[12] the zip is a thing of majesty and awe, a proclamation and a command: 'Being announces itself in the imperative.'[13]
It is, we might venture, something Caesarian. But as the fine,
bare line dividing what happens from what does not, and hence
what has happened from what will no longer, this flash is also
and simultaneously a thing of infinite fragility, pointing to the
ever-present imminence of loss. As Lyotard observes, referring to
Burke's interest in terror and privation, 'the sublime is kindled by
the threat of nothing further happening'.[14] It is this threat that the
Lucanian response to Pompey (who ultimately wrests control of
the lightning bolt and its symbolism from Caesar) is built upon and
confronts. And yet, as Newman reminds us, this threat is one and
the same as the thunderbolt's command. As the sublime reaches
for what lies beyond presentation, it hovers forever between transcendence and annihilation.

Newman's declaration that 'the sublime is now' was made in
1948.[15] It continues to resonate today. But I hope that I have
shown that the 'now-ness' of the sublime was also 'then' – not

---

[10] Lyotard (1991) 78–88, 89–107.

[11] Lyotard (1991) 82. Cf. Porter (2010) 11–12 on Pliny's anecdote of the line-drawing
contest between the painters Apelles and Protogenes in the fourth century BC (*Nat.*
35.81–3) as a celebration of material immediacy, of 'the sheer ability to produce a finely
traced line, a singular and inimitable specimen of its kind, blazoned forth in its own
material presence'.

[12] Lyotard (1991) 82.   [13] Lyotard (1991) 88.

[14] Lyotard (1991) 99; cf. ibid. 84.   [15] Newman (1948/1992).

just, as is widely recognised, in the eighteenth century and for the Romantics, or in seventeenth-century England, or for Longinus' first translators, but in first-century AD Rome, for Lucan and his contemporaries:[16] 'One may be tempted to imagine that our epoch is rediscovering the *sublime*, its name, concept, or questions. But clearly, this is by no means the case, for one never returns to any prior moment in history. The sublime is not so much what we're going back to as where we're coming from.'[17] Through pointing to the footsteps we have forgotten, and through the work it requires of us to see them, the sublime – that event, at once immediate and indeterminate, ever inimicable to habituation's dead weight – makes its silence heard.

[16] Work remains to be done on the sublime in Petronius and Seneca. Conte (1996) 37–72 argues for Petronius' Encolpius as a model of the failed sublime; cf. Hardie (2009c) 225–8 on Eumolpus' *Bellum civile*. So far unnoticed is the way in which the *Satyricon*'s radical melding of textual genres and registers, in destabilising (a Longinian conception of) the classical canon, constructs a new form of liberating sublimity. Schiesaro (2003) 128–32 considers the role of Caesarian-style sublimity in Seneca's *Thyestes*, especially as demonstrated by Atreus. The alternative sublimities explored in Seneca's *Troades* and in his prose await investigation.

[17] Nancy (1993a) 1; cf. Nancy (1993b) 25: the sublime is a 'fashion' that has 'the supplementary privilege of being extremely old'.

BIBLIOGRAPHY

Journals are cited using the abbreviations in *L'Année Philologique*.

Adorno, T. W., ed. G. Adorno and R. Tiedmann, trans. C. Lenhart (1984) *Aesthetic Theory* (London).

Ahl, F. (1976) *Lucan: An Introduction* (Ithaca).

Alston, R. and Spentzou, E. (2011) *Reflections of Romanity: Discourses of Subjectivity in Imperial Rome* (Columbus).

Ankersmit, F. (1989) *The Reality Effect in the Writing of History* (Amsterdam).
(1994) *History and Tropology: The Rise and Fall of Metaphor* (Berkeley).
(2005) *Sublime Historical Experience* (Stanford).

Arensberg, M., ed. (1986) *The American sublime* (Albany).

Armisen-Marchetti, M. (1990) 'Pline le Jeune et le sublime', *REL* 68: 88–98.

Armstrong, I. (2000) *The Radical Aesthetic* (Oxford).

Ashfield, A. and de Bolla, P., eds. (1996) *The Sublime: A Reader in British Eighteenth-Century Aesthetic Theory* (Cambridge).

Aymard, J. (1951) *Quelques series de comparaisons chez Lucain* (Montpellier).

Ball, K. (2008) *Disciplining the Holocaust* (Albany).

Banville, J. (2000) *Eclipse* (London).

Barchiesi, A. (2009) 'Phaethon and the Monsters', in P. Hardie, ed. (2009) *Paradox and the Marvellous in Augustan Literature and Culture* (Oxford) 163–88.

Barratt, P. (1979) *M. Annaei Lucani Belli civilis liber v: A Commentary* (Amsterdam).

Barthes, R. (1990) *The Pleasure of the Text* (Oxford).

Bartsch, S. (1997) *Ideology in Cold Blood: A Reading of Lucan's Civil War* (Cambridge, MA).

Battersby, C. (1989) *Gender and Genius: Towards a Feminist Aesthetics* (London).
(2007) *The Sublime, Terror and Human Difference* (London).

Benjamin, W. (1999) *Illuminations* (London).

Bernstein, C. L. (1991) *The Celebration of Scandal: Towards the Sublime in Victorian Urban Fiction* (University Park, PA).

Berti, E. (2000) *M. Annaei Lucani Bellum civile liber x* (Firenze).

Blix, G. (2008) *From Paris to Pompeii: French Romanticism and the Cultural Politics of Archaeology* (Philadelphia).

Bloom, H. (1973) *The Anxiety of Influence* (Oxford).

(1982/1994) 'Freud and the Sublime: A Catastrophe Theory of Creativity', in M. Ellman, ed. (1994) *Psychoanalytic Literary Criticism* (London) 173–95.

Bohnenkamp, K. E. (1979) 'Zu Lucan 1.674–95', *Gymnasium* 86: 171–7.

Bonner, S. (1966/2010) 'Lucan and the Declamation Schools', in Tesoriero (2010) 69–106.

Borges, J. L., ed. D. A. Yates and J. E. Irby (2000) *Labyrinths* (London).

Bourdieu, P. (1984) *Distinction: A Social Critique of the Judgement of Taste* (London).

Bowie, A. M. (1990) 'The Death of Priam: Allegory and History in the *Aeneid*', *CQ* 40: 470–81.

Braund, S. H., trans. (1992) *Lucan: Civil War* (Oxford).
   (2010) 'Introduction', in Tesoriero (2010) 1–13.

Brisset, J. (1964) *Les Idées politiques de Lucain* (Paris).

Brody, J. (1958) *Boileau and Longinus* (Geneva).

Brooks, L. M. (1995) *The Menace of the Sublime to the Individual Self: Kant, Schiller, Coleridge and the Disintegration of Romantic Identity* (Lewiston).

Buchheit, V. (1969/2007) 'Epicurus' Triumph of the Mind (Lucr. 1.62–79)', in M. R. Gale, ed. (2007) *Oxford Readings in Classical Studies: Lucretius* (Oxford) 104–31.

Burke, E., ed. A. Phillips (1990) *A Philosophical Enquiry into the Origin of our Ideas of the Sublime and Beautiful* (Oxford).

Cheetham, M. (2001) *Kant, Art and Art History: Moments of Discipline* (Cambridge).

Cheney, P. (2009) *Marlowe's Republican Authorship: Lucan, Liberty and the Sublime* (Basingstoke).

Cohen, T. and Guyer, P., eds. (1982) *Essays in Kant's Aesthetics* (Chicago).

Conte, G. B. (1966/2010) 'The Proem of the *Pharsalia*', in Tesoriero (2010) 46–58.
   (1994) 'Instructions for a Sublime Reader: Form of the Text and Form of the Addressee in Lucretius' *De rerum natura*', in G. B. Conte (1994) *Genres and Readers: Lucretius, Love Elegy, Pliny's Encyclopedia* (Baltimore).
   (1996) *The Hidden Author: An Interpretation of Petronius' Satyricon* (Berkeley).
   (2007) 'Anatomy of a Style: Enallage and the New Sublime', in G. B. Conte (2007) *The Poetry of Pathos: Studies in Virgilian Epic* (Oxford) 58–122.

Cronk, N. (2003) *The Classical Sublime: French Neoclassicism and the Language of Literature* (Charlottesville).

Crosset, J. M. and Arieti, J. A. (1975) *The Dating of Longinus* (University Park, PA).

Crowther, P. (1989) *The Kantian Sublime: From Morality to Art* (Oxford).
   (2004) 'Preface', in C. McMahon (2004) *Reframing the Theory of the Sublime: Pillars and Modes* (Lewiston).

D'Alessandro Behr, F. (2007) *Feeling History: Lucan, Stoicism and the Poetics of Passion* (Columbus).

Danto, A. (1983) *The Transfiguration of the Commonplace* (Cambridge, MA).

Davis, H. H. (1958) 'Epitaphs and Memory', *CJ* 53: 169–76.

de Bolla, P. (1989) *The Discourse of the Sublime: Readings in History, Aesthetics and the Subject* (Oxford).

De Lacy, P. (1964/2007) 'Distant Views: The Imagery of Lucretius 2', in M. R. Gale, ed. (2007) *Oxford Readings in Classical Studies: Lucretius* (Oxford) 146–57.

Deguy, M., trans. J. S. Librett (1993) 'The Discourse of Exaltation (Μεγαλη-γορεῖν): Contribution to a Rereading of Pseudo-Longinus', in Librett (1993) 5–24.

DeJean, J. (1989) *Fictions of Sappho: 1546–1937* (Chicago).

DeLillo, D. (1997) *Underworld* (London).

Derrida, J. (1987) *The Truth in Painting* (Chicago).

Dewar, M. (1994) 'Laying It on with a Trowel: The Proem to Lucan and Related Texts', *CQ* 44: 199–211.

Dewey, J. (1934/1989) 'Art as Experience', in J. A. Boydston and H. F. Simon, eds. (1989) *John Dewey: The Later Works, 1925–1953* (Carbondale) x: 1934.

Dick, B. F. (1963) 'The Technique of Prophecy in Lucan', *TAPhA* 94: 37–49.

(1965) 'The Role of the Oracle in Lucan's *De bello civili*', *Hermes* 93: 460–6.

Dilke, O. A. W. (1960) *Lucan: De bello civili* VII (Cambridge).

Dinter, M. (2005) 'Lucan's Epic Body', in C. Walde, ed. (2005) *Lucan im 21. Jahrhundert* (Munich) 295–312.

Due, O. S. (1962) 'An Essay on Lucan', *C & M* 23: 68–132.

Eagleton, T. (1990) *The Ideology of the Aesthetic* (Oxford).

Edwards, C. (1996) *Writing Rome: Textual Approaches to the City* (Cambridge).

Eigler, U. (2005) 'Caesar in Troja: Lucan und der lange Schatten Vergils', in C. Walde, ed. (2005) *Lucan im 21. Jahrhundert* (Munich) 186–201.

Eldred, K. O. (2002) 'This Ship of Fools: Vision in Lucan's Vulteius Episode', in D. Frederick, ed. (2002) *The Roman Gaze: Vision, Power and the Body* (Baltimore) 57–85.

Else, G. F. (1930) 'Lucretius and the Aesthetic Attitude', *HSCP* 41: 149–82.

Ende, S. A. (1976) *Keats and the Sublime* (New Haven).

Fantham, E. (1978) 'Imitation and Decline', *CPh* 73: 102–16.

(1992) *Lucan: De bello civili, Book 2* (Cambridge).

Feeney, D. (1986/2010) '*Stat magni nominis umbra*: Lucan on the Greatness of Pompeius Magnus', in Tesoriero (2010) 346–54.

(1991) *The Gods in Epic: Poets and Critics of the Classical Tradition* (Oxford).

(1995/2006) 'Criticism Ancient and Modern', in A. Laird, ed. (2006) *Oxford Readings in Classical Studies: Ancient Literary Criticism* (Oxford) 440–54.

Feldherr, A. (2009) 'Delusions of Grandeur: Lucretian "Passages" in Livy', in P. Hardie, ed. (2009) *Paradox and the Marvellous in Augustan Literature and Culture* (Oxford) 310–29.

Ferguson, F. (1992) *Solitude and the Sublime* (New York).

Ford, A. (1992) *Homer: The Poetry of the Past* (Ithaca).

(2002) *The Origins of Criticism: Literary Culture and Poetic Theory in Classical Greece* (Princeton).

Foster, H. (2011) 'The Last Column', *London Review of Books* 33.17: 17.

Fowler, D. (2000) 'The Ruin of Time: Monuments and Survival at Rome', in D. Fowler (2000) *Roman Constructions: Readings in Postmodern Latin* (Oxford) 193–217.

(2002) *Lucretius on Atomic Motion: A commentary on De rerum natura 2.1–332* (Oxford).

Frederiksen, M., ed. N. Purcell (1984) *Campania* (London).

Freeman, B. C. (1995) *The Feminine Sublime: Gender and Excess in Women's Fiction* (Berkeley).

Freud, S., ed. A. Phillips, trans. D. McLintock (2002) *Civilization and its Discontents* (London).

ed. A. Phillips, trans. D. McLintock (2003) *The Uncanny* (London).

Fry, P. (1983) *The Reach of Criticism: Method and Perception in Literary Theory* (New Haven).

Furniss, T. (1993). *Edmund Burke's Aesthetic Ideology: Language, Gender and Political Economy in Revolution* (Cambridge).

Gale, M. R. (2000) *Virgil on the Nature of Things: The Georgics, Lucretius and the Didactic Tradition* (Cambridge).

George, D. B. (1991) 'Lucan's Cato and Stoic Attitudes to the Republic', *ClAnt* 10: 237–58.

Getty, R. J. (1940) *M. Annaei Lucani De bello civili liber I* (Cambridge).

Gibbons, L. (2003) *Edmund Burke and Ireland: Aesthetics, Politics and the Colonial Sublime* (Cambridge).

Gilby, E. (2006) *Sublime Worlds: Early Modern French Literature* (London).

Goebel, G. H. (1981) 'Rhetorical and Poetical Thinking in Lucan's Harangues', *TAPhA* 111: 79–94.

Goldhill, S., ed. (2001) *Being Greek under Rome: Cultural Identity, the Second Sophistic and the Development of Empire* (Cambridge).

Goold, G. P. (1961) 'A Greek Professorial Circle at Rome', *TAPhA* 92: 168–92.

Gowers, E. (2007) 'The *cor* of Ennius', in W. Fitzgerald and E. Gowers, eds. (2007) *Ennius perennis: The Annals and Beyond* (Cambridge) 17–37.

Gowing, A. (2005) *Empire and Memory: The Representation of the Roman Republic in Imperial Culture* (Cambridge).

Green, C. M. C. (1991/2010) '*Stimulos dedit aemula virtus*: Lucan and Homer Reconsidered', in Tesoriero (2010) 149–83.

Greenblatt, S. (1980) *Renaissance Self-Fashioning: From More to Shakespeare* (Chicago).

(1990) *Learning to Curse: Essays in Early Modern Culture* (New York).

Grimal, P. (1960/2010) 'Is the Eulogy of Nero at the Beginning of the *Pharsalia* Ironic?', in Tesoriero (2010) 59–68.

(1970) 'Le Poète et l'histoire', in M. Durry, ed. (1970) *Lucain. Entretiens de la Fondation Hardt* 15 (Geneva) 51–117.

Guerlac, S. (1985) 'Longinus and the Subject of the Sublime', *New Literary History* 16.2: 275–87.

(1990) *The Impersonal Sublime: Hugo, Baudelaire, Lautréamont* (Stanford).

Guyer, P. (1993) *Kant and the Experience of Freedom* (Cambridge).

Habinek, T. (1998) *The Politics of Latin Literature: Writing, Identity and Empire in Ancient Rome* (Princeton).

Hardie, P. R. (1986) *Virgil's Aeneid: Cosmos and Imperium* (Oxford).

(1993) *The Epic Successors of Virgil: A Study in the Dynamics of a Tradition* (Cambridge).

(2009a) 'Virgil's *Fama* and the Sublime', in P. Hardie (2009) *Lucretian Receptions: History, the Sublime, Knowledge* (Cambridge) 67–135.

(2009b) 'Lucretian Visions in Virgil', in P. Hardie (2009) *Lucretian Receptions: History, the Sublime, Knowledge* (Cambridge) 153–79.

(2009c) 'Horace's Sublime Yearnings: Lucretian Ironies', in P. Hardie (2009) *Lucretian Receptions: History, the Sublime, Knowledge* (Cambridge) 180–228.

Haywood, I. (2006) *Bloody Romanticism: Spectacular Violence and the Politics of Representation 1776–1832* (Basingstoke).

Heath, M. (1999) 'Longinus, *On Sublimity*', *PCPhS* 45: 43–74.

Helzle, M. (1994/2010) '*Indocilis privata loqui*: The Characterisation of Lucan's Caesar', in Tesoriero (2010) 355–68.

Henderson, J. (1987/2010) 'Lucan: The Word at War', in Tesoriero (2010) 433–91.

Hertz, N. (1978/1985) 'A Reading of Longinus', in N. Hertz (1985) *The End of the Line: Essays on Psychoanalysis and the Sublime* (New York) 1–19.

Hill, T. (2004) *Ambitiosa mors: Suicide and Self in Roman Thought and Literature* (London).

Hinds, S. E. (1988) 'Generalizing about Ovid', in A. J. Boyle, ed. (1988) *The Imperial Muse: Ramus Essays on Roman Literature of the Empire I: To Juvenal through Ovid* (Berwick) 4–31.

(1998) *Allusion and Intertext: Dynamics of Appropriation in Roman Poetry* (Cambridge).

Hitchcock, L. A. (2008) *Theory for Classics: A Student's Guide* (London).

Hölderlin, F., ed. and trans. E. L. Santner (1990) *Hyperion and Selected Poems* (New York).

Hooley, D. (2008) 'Raising the Dead: Marlowe's Lucan', in A. Lianeri and V. Zajko, eds. (2008) *Translation and the Classic: Identity as Change in the History of Culture* (Oxford).

Housman, A. E., ed. (1927) *M. Annaei Lucani Belli civilis libri decem* (Oxford).

Hunink, V. (1992) *M. Annaeus Lucanus: Bellum civile, Book 3* (Amsterdam).

Hunter, R. (2009) *Critical Moments in Classical Literature: Studies in the Ancient View of Literature and its Uses* (Cambridge).

Hutchinson, G. O. (2011) 'Politics and the Sublime in the *Panegyricus*', in P. Roche, ed. (2011) *Pliny's Praise: The Panegyricus in the Roman World* (Cambridge) 125–41.

Innes, D. C. (1979) 'Gigantomachy and Natural Philosophy', *CQ* NS 29: 165–71.

  (1985) 'Longinus and Others', in P. E. Easterling and B. M. W. Knox, eds. *The Cambridge History of Classical Literature i: Greek Literature* (Cambridge) 646–9.

  (1995a) 'Longinus, Sublimity and the Low Emotions', in D. C. Innes, H. Hine and C. Pelling, eds. (1995) *Ethics and Rhetoric: Classical Essays for Donald Russell on his Seventy-Fifth Birthday* (Oxford) 323–33.

  ed. (1995b) *Demetrius: On Style* (Cambridge, MA).

  (1995c/2006) 'Longinus: Structure and Unity', in A. Laird, ed. (2006) *Oxford Readings in Classical Studies: Ancient Literary Criticism* (Oxford) 300–12.

  (2002) 'Longinus and Caecilius: Models of the Sublime', *Mnemosyne* 55: 259–84.

Ireland, C. (2004) *The Subaltern Appeal to Experience: Self-Identity, Late Modernity and the Politics of Immediacy* (Montreal).

Jay, M. (2005) *Songs of Experience: Modern American and European Variations on a Universal Theme* (Berkeley).

Jenkinson, J. R. (1974) 'Sarcasm in Lucan 1.33–66', *CR* 24: 8–9.

Johnson, W. R. (1987) *Momentary Monsters: Lucan and his Heroes* (Ithaca).

Kant, I., ed. P. Guyer, trans. P. Guyer and E. Matthews (2003) *Critique of the Power of Judgment* (Cambridge).

Kellner, H. (2005) 'Longinus, *On the Sublime*', in M. Ballif and M. G. Moran, eds. (2005) *Classical Rhetorics and Rhetoricians* (Westport) 245–9.

Kennedy, D. F. (1993) *The Arts of Love: Five Studies in the Discourse of Roman Love Elegy* (Cambridge).

Kirwan, J. (2005) *Sublimity* (New York).

Kristeva, J. (1982) *Powers of Horror: An Essay in Abjection* (New York).

LaCapra, D. (1994) *Representing the Holocaust: History, Theory, Trauma* (Ithaca).

Lacoue-Labarthe, P., trans. J. S. Librett (1993) 'Sublime Truth', in Librett (1993) 71–108.

Laird, A. (2006) 'The Value of Ancient Literary Criticism', in A. Laird, ed. (2006) *Oxford Readings in Classical Studies: Ancient Literary Criticism* (Oxford) 1–36.

Lapidge, M. (1979/2010) 'Lucan's Imagery of Cosmic Dissolution', in Tesoriero (2010) (Oxford) 289–323.

Lausberg, M. (1985) 'Lucan und Homer', in *ANRW* ii 32.3: 1565–1622.

Le Bonniec, H. (1970) 'Lucain et la religion', in M. Durry, ed. (1970) *Lucain. Entretiens de la Fondation Hardt* 15 (Geneva) 159–200.

Leigh, M. (1997) *Lucan: Spectacle and Engagement* (Oxford).

(1999) 'Lucan's Caesar and the Sacred Grove: Deforestation and Enlightenment in Antiquity', in P. Esposito and L. Nicastri, eds. (1999) *Interpretare Lucano: Miscellanea di studi* (Naples) 167–205.

(2006) 'Statius and the Sublimity of Capaneus', in M. J. Clarke, B. G. F. Currie and R. O. A. M. Lyne, eds. (2006) *Epic Interactions: Perspectives on Homer, Virgil and the Epic Tradition Presented to Jasper Griffin by Former Pupils* (Oxford) 217–41.

Librett, J. S., ed. and trans. (1993) *Of the Sublime: Presence in Question* (Albany).

Lintott, A. W. (1971/2010) 'Lucan and the History of the Civil War', in Tesoriero (2010) 239–68.

Lounsbury, R. (1975) 'The Death of Domitius in the *Pharsalia*', *TAPhA* 105: 209–12.

Luck, G. (1967) 'Die Schrift vom Erhabenen und ihr Verfasser', *Arctos* 5: 97–113.

Lyotard, J.-F., trans. G. Bennington and B. Massumi (1984) *The Postmodern Condition: A Report on Knowledge* (Minneapolis).

trans. G. Bennington and R. Bowlby (1991) *The Inhuman: Reflections on Time* (Cambridge).

trans. J. S. Librett (1993) 'The Interest of the Sublime', in Librett (1993) 109–32.

trans. E. Rottenberg (1994) *Lessons on the Analytic of the Sublime* (Stanford).

Macfarlane, R. (2004) *Mountains of the Mind: A History of a Fascination* (London).

Maes, Y. (2005) 'Starting Something Huge: *Pharsalia* 1.83–193 and the Virgilian Intertext', in C. Walde, ed. *Lucan im 21. Jahrhundert* (Munich) 1–25.

Malamud, M. A. (1995) 'Happy Birthday, Dead Lucan: (P)raising the Dead in *Silvae* 2.7', in A. J. Boyle, ed. (1995) *Roman Literature and Ideology: Ramus Essays for J. P. Sullivan* (Bendigo) 169–98.

Marti, B. (1945) 'The Meaning of the *Pharsalia*', *AJPh* 66: 352–76.

(1975) 'Lucan's Narrative Techniques', *La Parola del Passato* 30: 74–90.

Martindale, C. (1976) 'Paradox, Hyperbole and Literary Novelty in Lucan's *De bello civile*', *BICS* 23: 45–54.

(1980) 'Lucan's Nekuia', in C. Deroux, ed. (1980) *Studies in Latin Literature II: Collection Latomus 168* (Brussels) 367–77.

(1984/2010) 'The Politician Lucan', in Tesoriero (2010) 269–88.

(1993) *Redeeming the Text: Latin Poetry and the Hermeneutics of Reception* (Cambridge).

(1999) 'Ruins of Rome: T. S. Eliot and the Presence of the Past', in C. Edwards, ed. (1999) *Roman Presences: Receptions of Rome in European Culture 1789–1945* (Cambridge) 236–55.

(2005) *Latin Literature and the Judgement of Taste: An Essay in Aesthetics* (Oxford).

Masters, J. (1992) *Poetry and Civil War in Lucan's Bellum civile* (Cambridge).

(1994) 'Deceiving the Reader: The Political Mission of Lucan's *Bellum civile*', in J. Elsner and J. Masters, eds. (1994) *Reflections of Nero: Culture, History and Representation* (Chapel Hill) 151–77.

Matthews, M. (2008) *Caesar and the Storm: A Commentary on Lucan De bello civili*, Book 5 lines 476–721 (Bern).

Maxwell, C. (2001) *The Female Sublime from Milton to Swinburne: Bearing Blindness* (Basingstoke).

Mayer, R. (1981) *Lucan: Civil War* VIII (Warminster).

McMahon, C. (2004) *Reframing the Theory of the Sublime: Pillars and Modes* (Lewiston).

Michel, A. (1969) 'Rhétorique, tragédie, philosophie: Sénèque et le sublime', *Giornale Italiano di Filologia* 21: 245–57.

(1976) 'Rhétorique et poétique: la théorie du sublime de Platon aux modernes', *REL* 54: 278–307.

Miller, P. A. (2004) *Subjecting Verses: Latin Love Elegy and the Emergence of the Real* (Princeton).

Milton, J., ed. A. Fowler (2007) *Paradise Lost* (Harlow).

Mishra, V. (1994) *The Gothic Sublime* (Albany).

Monk, S. H. (1935/1960) *The Sublime: A Study in Critical Theories in 18th Century England* (New York).

Montaigne, M., trans. D. M. Frame (1957) *The Complete Works of Montaigne* (Stanford).

Moore, L. E. (1990) *Beautiful Sublime: The Making of Paradise Lost, 1701–1734* (Stanford).

Morford, M. P. O. (1967) *The Poet Lucan: Studies in Rhetorical Epic* (Oxford).

Mosco, V. (2004) *The Digital Sublime: Myth, Power and Cyberspace* (Cambridge, MA).

Most, G. W. (1992) 'The Rhetoric of Dismemberment in Neronian Poetry', in R. Hexter and D. Selden, eds. (1992) *Innovations of Antiquity* (New Haven) 391–419.

(2003) 'Il sublime oggi?', *Aevum Antiquum* 3: 41–62.

Murray, P. (2000) 'Introduction', in T. S. Dorsch and P. Murray, eds. and trans. (2000) *Classical Literary Criticism* (London) vii–li.

Nancy, J.-L., trans. J. S. Librett (1993a) 'Preface to the French Edition', in Librett (1993) 1–3.

trans. J. S. Librett (1993b) 'The Sublime Offering', in Librett (1993) 25–53.

Narducci, E. (1973) 'Il tronco di Pompeo (Troia e Roma nella *Pharsalia*)', *Maia* 25: 317–25.

(1979) *La providenza crudele: Lucano e la distruzione dei miti augustei* (Pisa).

Newman, B. (1948/1992) 'The Sublime is Now', in C. Harrison and P. Wood, eds. (1992) *Art in Theory 1900–1990: An Anthology of Changing Ideas* (Oxford) 572–4.

Ngai, S. (2005) *Ugly Feelings* (Cambridge, MA).

246

Nicolson, M. H. (1959) *Mountain Gloom and Mountain Glory: The Development of the Aesthetics of the Infinite* (Ithaca).

Nock, A. D. (1959) 'Posidonius', *JRS* 49: 1–15.

Norbrook, D. (1999) *Writing the English Republic: Poetry, Rhetoric and Politics, 1627–1660* (Cambridge).

Nye, D. E. (1994) *American Techological Sublime* (Cambridge, MA).

O'Hara, J. J. (2007) *Inconsistency in Roman Epic* (Cambridge).

O'Higgins, D. (1988) 'Lucan as *vates*', *CA* 7: 208–26.

Ormand, K. (1994/2010) 'Lucan's *auctor vix fidelis*', in Tesoriero (2010) 324–45.

Paulson, R. (1980) 'Burke's Sublime and the Representation of Revolution', in P. Zagorin, ed. (1980) *Culture and Politics from Puritanism to the Enlightenment* (Berkeley) 241–70.

(1983) *Representations of Revolution: 1789–1820* (New Haven).

Phillips, A. (1990) 'Introduction', in Burke (1990) ix–xxiii.

Porter, J. I. (2001) 'Ideals and Ruins: Pausanias, Longinus and the Second Sophistic', in S. E. Alcock, J. F. Cherry and J. Elsner, eds. (2001) *Pausanias: Travel and Memory in Roman Greece* (Oxford) 63–92.

(2006a) 'What is "Classical" about Classical Antiquity?', in J. I. Porter, ed. (2006) *Classical Pasts: The Classical Traditions of Greece and Rome* (Princeton) 1–65.

(2006b) 'Feeling Classical: Classicism and Ancient Literary Criticism', in J. I. Porter, ed. (2006) *Classical Pasts: The Classical Traditions of Greece and Rome* (Princeton) 301–52.

(2007) 'Lucretius and the Sublime', in S. Gillespie and P. Hardie, eds. (2007) *The Cambridge Companion to Lucretius* (Cambridge) 167–84.

(2010) *The Origins of Aesthetic Thought in Ancient Greece: Matter, Sensation, Experience* (Cambridge).

(forthcoming) *The Material Sublime* (Cambridge).

Quint, D. (1993) *Epic and Empire: Politics and Generic Form from Virgil to Milton* (Princeton).

Ram, H. (2003) *The Imperial Sublime: A Russian Poetics of Empire* (Madison).

Rancière, J. (2004) *The Politics of Aesthetics: The Distribution of the Sensible* (London).

Ray, G. (2005) *Terror and the Sublime in Art and Critical Theory: From Auschwitz to Hiroshima to September 11* (New York).

Roche, P. (2009) *Lucan: De bello civili, Book 1* (Oxford).

Roller, M. B. (2001) *Constructing Autocracy: Aristocrats and Emperors in Julio-Claudian Rome* (Princeton).

Rosner-Siegel, J. (1983/2010) 'The Oak and the Lightning: Lucan, *Bellum civile* 1.135–157', in Tesoriero (2010) 184–200.

Rossi, A. (2001) 'Remapping the Past: Caesar's Tale of Troy', *Phoenix* 55: 313–26.

(2005) '*Sine fine*: Caesar's Journey to Egypt and the End of Lucan's *Bellum civile*', in C. Walde, ed. (2005) *Lucan im 21. Jahrhundert* (Munich) 237–60.

Roth (1995) *The Ironist's Cage: Memory, Trauma and the Construction of History* (New York).

Rouse, W. H. D., trans., M. F. Smith, rev. (1992) *Lucretius: On the Nature of Things* (Cambridge, MA).

Russell, D. A., ed. (1964) *Longinus: On the Sublime* (Oxford).

    (1965) 'Introduction', in D. A. Russell, trans. (1965) *'Longinus' On Sublimity* (Oxford) i–xx.

    (1979) *'De imitatione'*, in D. West and T. Woodman, eds. (1979) *Creative Imitation and Latin Literature* (Cambridge) 1–16.

    (1981a) *Criticism in Antiquity* (London).

    (1981b) 'Longinus Revisited', *Mnemosyne* 34: 72–86.

    (1995) 'Introduction', in W. H. Fyfe, ed. and trans., D. Russell, rev. (1995) *Longinus, On the Sublime* (Cambridge, MA) 145–58.

    ed. and trans. (2001) *Quintilian: The Orator's Education, Books 11–12* (Cambridge, MA).

Saylor, C. F. (1978) *'Belli spes improba*: The Theme of Walls in Lucan, *Pharsalia* VI', *TAPhA* 108: 243–57.

    (1990) *'Lux extrema*: Lucan *Pharsalia* 4.402–581', *TAPhA* 120: 291–300.

Scarry, E. (1999) *On Beauty and Being Just* (Princeton).

Schiesaro, A. (2003) *The Passions in Play: Thyestes and the Dynamics of Senecan Drama* (Cambridge).

Schrijvers, P. H. (2006) 'Silius Italicus and the Roman Sublime', in R. Nauta, ed. (2006) *Flavian Poetry* (Leiden) 97–112.

Scodel, R. (1992) 'Inscription, Absence and Memory: Epic and Early Epitaph', *Studi Italiani di Filologia Classica* 10: 57–76.

Sedley, D. L. (2005) *Sublimity and Skepticism in Montaigne and Milton* (Ann Arbor).

Sedley, D. N. (1998/2007) 'The Empedoclean Opening', in M. R. Gale, ed. (2007) *Oxford Readings in Classical Studies: Lucretius* (Oxford) 48–87.

Segal, C. P. (1959) 'ΥΨΟΣ and the Problem of Cultural Decline in the *De sublimitate*', *HSCP* 64: 121–46.

    (1987) 'Writer as Hero: The Heroic Ethos in Longinus, *On the Sublime*', in J. Servais, ed. (1987) *Stemmata: mélanges offerts à Jules Labarbe* (Liège) 207–17.

Selb, H. (1957) 'Probleme der Schrift *Peri hupsous*', diss. Heidelberg.

Sharpe, M. (2002) 'The Sociopolitical Limits of Fantasy: September 11 and Slavoj Žižek's Theory of Ideology', in *Cultural Logic* 5, available at: http://clogic.eserver.org/2002/sharpe.html, last accessed 23/9/2012.

Shaw, P. (2006) *The Sublime* (London).

Shifflett, A. (1996) '"By Lucan Driv'n About": A Jonsonian Marvell's Lucanic Milton', *Renaissance Quarterly* 49: 803–23.

Silverman, H. J. and Aylesworth, G. E., eds. (1990) *The Textual Sublime: Deconstruction and its Differences* (Albany).

Sklenár, R. (2003) *The Taste for Nothingness: A Study of virtus and Related Themes in Lucan's Bellum civile* (Ann Arbor).

Stewart, S. (1984) *On Longing: Narratives of the Miniature, the Gigantic, the Souvenir, the Collection* (Baltimore).

Tatum, W. J. (1984/2007) 'The Presocratics in Book 1 of Lucretius', in M. R. Gale, ed. (2007) *Oxford Readings in Classical Studies: Lucretius* (Oxford) 132–45.

Tesoriero, C. (2005) 'Trampling over Troy: Caesar, Virgil, Lucan', in C. Walde, ed. (2005) *Lucan im 21. Jahrhundert* (Munich) 202–15.

  ed. (2010) *Oxford Readings in Classical Studies: Lucan* (Oxford).

Thomas, E. (2007) *Monumentality and the Roman Empire: Architecture in the Antonine Age* (Oxford).

Thompson, L. (1964) 'Lucan's Apotheosis of Nero', *CPh* 59: 147–53.

Thompson, L. and Bruère, R. T. (1968/2010) 'Lucan's Use of Virgilian Reminiscence', in Tesoriero (2010) 107–48.

Too, Y. L. (1998) *The Idea of Ancient Literary Criticism* (Oxford).

Tsang, L.-C. (1998) *The Sublime: Groundwork towards a Theory* (Rochester, NY).

Varsamopoulou, E. (2002) *The Poetics of the Künstlerinroman and the Aesthetics of the Sublime* (Aldershot).

Walker, J. (2000) *Rhetoric and Poetics in Antiquity* (Oxford).

Walsh, G. B. (1988) 'Sublime Method: Longinus on Language and Imitation', *ClAnt* 7: 252–69.

Wang, B. (1997) *The Sublime Figure of History: Aesthetics and Politics in Twentieth-Century China* (Stanford).

Warren, R. (1989) 'Sappho: Translation as Elegy', in R. Warren, ed. (1989) *The Art of Translation: Voices from the Field* (Boston) 199–216.

Wehrli, F. (1946) 'Der erhabene und der schlichte Stil in der poetisch-rhetorischen Theorie der Antike', in F. Wehrli (1946) *Phyllobolia für Peter Von der Mühll* (Basel) 9–34.

Weigel, M. (2001) 'Terrorism and the Sublime, or Why We Keep Watching', available at: www.margaretweigel.com/oldsitecomment/portSublime.pdf, last accessed 23/9/2012.

Weiskel, T. (1976) *The Romantic Sublime* (Baltimore).

West, D. A. (1969) *The Imagery and Poetry of Lucretius* (Edinburgh).

West, M. (1995) '"Longinus" and the Grandeur of God', in D. Innes, H. Hine and C. Pelling, eds. (1995) *Ethics and Rhetoric: Classical Essays for Donald Russell on his Seventy-Fifth Birthday* (Oxford) 335–42.

Whitmarsh, T. (2001) *Greek Literature and the Roman Empire: The Politics of Imitation* (Oxford).

  (2011) *Narrative and Identity in the Ancient Greek Novel: Returning Romance* (Cambridge).

Williams, G. W. (1978) *Change and Decline: Roman Literature in the Early Empire* (Berkeley).

Wilson, R. (1991) *American Sublime: The Genealogy of a Poetic Genre* (Madison)

Wlecke, A. O. (1973/2010) 'A Poem about Interiors', in H. Bloom and B. Hobby, eds. (2010) *The Sublime* (New York) 157–85.

Woolf, G. (1996) 'Monumental Writing and the Expansion of Roman Society in the Early Empire', *JRS* 86: 22–39.

Yaeger, P. (1989) 'Toward a Female Sublime', in L. Kauffman, ed. (1989) *Gender and Theory: Dialogues on Feminist Criticism* (Oxford) 191–212.

Yardley, J. C., trans. (2006) *Livy: Hannibal's War (Books 21–30)* (Oxford).

Zammito, J. H. (1992) *The Genesis of Kant's Critique of Judgement* (Chicago).

Žižek, S. (1989) *The Sublime Object of Ideology* (London).

(2000) *The Art of the Ridiculous Sublime: On Lynch's Lost Highway* (Seattle).

(2002) *Welcome to the Desert of the Real: Five Essays on September 11 and Related Dates* (London).

Zwierlein, O. (1986/2010) 'Lucan's Caesar at Troy', in Tesoriero (2010) 411–32.

INDEX LOCORUM

255

INDEX RERUM ET NOMINUM

257

Bellum civile (cont.)
  suicide, 189–90, 191–6, 197
  Sulla. *See Bellum Civile*: Cornelius
    Sulla Felix, L.
  violence, 17, 28, 79–82, 83–4, 86, 101,
    111, 190–1, 207–9
  virtus, 194–6
  Vulteius, 89, 193–4, 195–6, 197
Bloom, Harold, 57–8
  'anxiety of influence', 57–8
Boileau-Despréaux, Nicolas, 11, 14, 36,
  48
Bourdieu, Pierre, 24
Burke, Edmund, 14, 27, 48–52, 54, 55, 62,
    68, 69, 90, 97, 110, 112, 117, 126,
    127, 129, 138, 141, 149, 160, 176,
    182
  delight, 49–50, 51, 133, 134–5, 145
  language, 50, 51, 78–9
  obscurity, 49, 78–9, 121, 133, 136–7,
    162
  pain and pleasure, 49, 53, 54, 181
  terror, 16, 48, 49–50, 51, 53, 67, 68,
    70–1, 78, 121–2, 137, 182, 188,
    189, 237
Burnet, Thomas, 5, 10

Caecilius of Caleacte, 63
Caesar. *See* Julius Caesar, C.
Catullus, 18
Cicero, 108
Conte, Gian Biagio, 42, 85, 126, 175
Criticism, literary
  aesthetic, 18–19, 20–1, 22, 23, 24–5, 26,
    27, 105
  hermeneutic, 19–23, 105
  ideological, 24–5, 26–7

Danto, Arthur, 187
De rerum natura. See Lucretius
DeLillo, Don
  Underworld, 8–10
    Einstein, Albert, 48
Demetrius
  On Style, 33–4
Demosthenes, 16, 31, 35, 38, 41, 49, 61,
    67–8, 84, 85, 88–9, 101, 108,
    203–4, 206, 229–30
Derrida, Jacques, 14, 19, 20

Discordia. *See Bellum civile: discordia
  and* Ennius: *Discordia. See also*
    Homer: Eris
Du Bellay, Joachim, 215–16, 235, 236

Earthquakes, 4, 43, 46, 47, 69–70, 82, 134,
    135, 148, 149, 206, 210
Ennius, 119
  Discordia, 79, 81–2
Epicurus. *See* Lucretius: Epicurus
Experience, 104
  aesthetic, 20–4, 26, 236–7
  historical, 21, 27, 179, 181
  sublime, 2, 3–4, 5, 13, 15, 17, 26, 28,
    30, 31, 42, 47, 49, 53, 54, 55, 56,
    58, 70, 72, 90, 93, 97, 98, 100, 102,
    104, 116, 147, 152, 156, 165, 179,
    186–7, 189, 207

Fama. See Virgil: *Fama*
French Revolution, 68, 184, 189
Freud, Sigmund, 55–8, 62–3
  agon, 55, 63
  the Uncanny, 55, 57–8
Fry, Paul, 63

Gadamer, Hans-Georg, 20, 22, 23
Genesis. *See* Longinus: Genesis
Gibbons, Luke, 70
Gilby, Emma, 38, 87
Grand style. *See* Demetrius: *On Style*

Hardie, Philip, 79, 81–2, 106, 118, 132,
    154–5, 213, 214
Hegel, Georg W. F., 36, 66
Henderson, John, 82
Hertz, Neil, 56–7, 62, 152, 206
Hiroshima, 8, 68, 69
Hölderlin, Friedrich
  Hyperion, 216–17
Holocaust, the, 8, 68, 70
Homer, 31, 33, 41, 109, 146, 228
  Eris, 76, 77, 78, 79, 96, 97, 101
  Iliad, 18, 34, 49, 56–7, 59–61, 76–9,
    119–20, 125, 141, 144, 172,
    175
  Odyssey, 32, 146, 171, 213
Horace, 18, 95, 96
Hyperides, 49

261